ISLE OF MAN TT

Phil Wain

Published by Collins
An imprint of HarperCollins Publishers
1 Robroyston Gate
Glasgow G33 1JN
www.collins.co.uk

HarperCollins Publishers
Macken House
39/40 Mayor Street Upper
Dublin 1, D01 C9W8, Ireland

First published 2026

© HarperCollins Publishers 2026
Text © Phil Wain 2026
Photographs © see credits page 255

Collins® is a registered trademark of HarperCollins Publishers Ltd

All rights reserved. No part of this publication may be reproduced, stored in a retrieval system, or transmitted, in any form or by any means, electronic, mechanical, photocopying, recording or otherwise without the prior permission in writing of the publisher and copyright owners.

Without limiting the exclusive rights of any author, contributor or the publisher of this publication, any unauthorised use of this publication to train generative artificial intelligence (AI) technologies is expressly prohibited. HarperCollins also exercise their rights under Article 4(3) of the Digital Single Market Directive 2019/790 and expressly reserve this publication from the text and data mining exception.

HarperCollins does not warrant that any website mentioned in this title will be provided uninterrupted, that any website will be error free, that defects will be corrected, or that the website or the server that makes it available are free of viruses or bugs. For full terms and conditions please refer to the site terms provided on the website.

A catalogue record for this book is available from the British Library

ISBN 978 0 00 878383 9

10 9 8 7 6 5 4 3 2 1

Printed in India by Multivista Global Pvt. Ltd.

If you would like to comment on any aspect of this book, please contact us at the above address or online.
email: collins.reference@harpercollins.co.uk

Contents

Foreword   4
Introduction   6

Chapter One 1907–1914   8

Chapter Two 1920–1939   28

Chapter Three 1947–1976   64

Chapter Four 1977–2000   120

Chapter Five 2000–2025   178

Index of Riders and Teams   252
Acknowledgements   255

Foreword

I am delighted to have been asked to contribute to Phil Wain's book which excellently documents the history of the Isle of Man TT. I've known Phil for almost thirty years, with our racing journeys overlapping, and he is as passionate as I am about the TT. Thousands of people from all four corners of the globe feel the same and once you've experienced the TT on any level, not just as a rider, you get hooked on it. It never gets to the point where you're not impressed.

The pages that follow will show just why the Mountain Course is so unique. To understand just how special it really is though, you have to see it for yourself as it's like nothing else you'll ever experience. The likes of HRH the Prince of Wales and Valentino Rossi will confirm that.

As riders, or even spectators and organisers, it's easy to overlook the history of the TT and that's something we should never ignore. If it wasn't for what took place in 1907, we wouldn't be doing what we do today, and I'd love to have been a fly on the wall when the idea was first conceived – and even more so when the decision was made to move it from the 15-mile St John's Course to the present-day 37.73-mile Mountain Course! I can only begin to imagine what it must have been like in 1911...

My first TT was in 1982, and I remember vividly standing behind a rope at the bottom of Bray Hill, watching the likes of Joey Dunlop and Mick Grant flash by. I was fascinated by it all and couldn't believe what I was seeing. I'd grown up with bikes in the family, but it was only when I'd seen the TT with my own eyes that it became such a huge part of my life. I obviously never thought I'd win one race let alone 23 but whether you're a rider or a spectator, everyone's been on their own journey to get there. Sacrifices will have been made, and everyone has their own story to tell.

There are so many special things about the TT. The surface may have changed, gates and trees may have been removed, and speeds have increased but the Mountain Course is practically the same today as what it was back in 1911. Look at some of the black and white photos in the book from the 1920s or 30s, for example, and you'll recognise where it is on the course straightaway.

There's no denying the TT is dangerous, and it can be a brutal place. It's a much bigger challenge than people realise and, arguably, it's the most extreme sport in the world bar none. But we all know that. We accept it and deal with it as best we can, and the organisers have to be commended for constantly improving course safety. No stone is left unturned when it comes to preparation both on and off track.

As riders, we know what we're undertaking when we enter and contest the TT, and I have to bite my tongue when I hear critics saying we're lunatics. If that was the case, you wouldn't last more than thirty seconds at the TT. They're being disrespectful to competitors who are at the very top of their profession and who are sacrificing everything to reach the pinnacle of their sport. Every competitor is dedicated to what they do, and they all spend days learning, practising and improving to be the best we possibly can. That dedication results

▲ John McGuinness, Honda and Bray Hill – an iconic Isle of Man TT combination.

in military precision and being inch-perfect on each lap. Dedication which exists in every other sport.

It's not just the racing that makes the TT unique though. There's camaraderie like nowhere else and everyone looks out for each other, whether it's the riders, fans or the Manx population. It's as genuine and authentic as it gets and the fact that everything is so accessible makes the TT stand out from other sporting events. Whether it's the people who were there in the 1950s, or the new generation, stories are shared and everyone's there to enjoy themselves and celebrate the event.

Other events have come and gone but not the TT. It's survived two world wars, seaman's strikes, foot-and-mouth and the Covid pandemic, but it's always bounced back. Its appeal now is as strong as it's ever been simply because it's without doubt, the greatest event on the motorcycle racing calendar. And long may that continue.

Enjoy the book.

John McGuinness MBE

Introduction

The Isle of Man TT is one of sport's most iconic institutions and the last of the great motorcycle tests in the world today. At almost 120 years old, the races show no signs of slowing down, and instead of creaking and rocking, the event is right back at the top of not just the motorcycle tree but the motorsport tree, revered and known all around the world.

With history, triumph, passion, tragedy and exhilaration that knows no bounds, the TT runs deep in the veins of all those who are part of it, and the legendary 37.73-mile Snaefell Mountain Course that plays host to it is like no other. With almost 300 corners and speeds in excess of 200mph on roads lined with brick walls, lamp posts and hedgerows, it remains the greatest test of man and machine. For two weeks in June, the little island nestled in the Irish Sea is the place where all motorsport eyes are focused.

The event started in 1907, and when those early pioneers pushed, pedalled and rode their machines around the original 15-mile St John's Course they would have had no idea of the legacy they were creating, or what historical significance they would be a part of. They probably wouldn't have believed it would be still in existence all these years later.

▼ With a current total of 33 victories, Michael Dunlop is the most successful rider in the history of the Isle of Man TT Races.

If someone had the idea now it would never get to turn a wheel amid the increasingly restrictive rules and regulations of today. But the TT stands firm and resolute. It will always have its critics, but the magnetic attraction for riders, manufacturers and motorsport fans alike will always pull more strongly than any form of bureaucracy telling them the opposite.

The TT has continually grown and evolved, frequently dealing with adversity and developing into a brand that is known across the globe. Its worldwide identity is second to none, a proud and unique achievement that has done more than stand the test of time – it's gone from strength to strength.

The TT has, quite literally, seen it all, and whatever has been thrown at it, it has responded positively, playing host to some of the most illustrious names in motorcycle sport. Woods, Guthrie, Simpson, Duke, McIntyre, Surtees, Hailwood, Ubbiali, Agostini, Redman and Read all hail from the halcyon days when motorbike riders were household names.

When the TT lost its World Championship status in the 1970s, many thought it was the beginning of the end, but instead it became a haven for road race specialists who were keen to pit their wits against the Mountain Course, the most challenging and demanding in the world. They did so not for fame or fortune, but simply to achieve their personal ambitions and conquer the motorcycling equivalent of Mount Everest.

Names like Grant, Williams, Rutter, Hislop, Fogarty, McCallen, Molyneux, Jefferies, McGuinness and Birchall all came to the fore, but for the past 50 years one name has stood out: Dunlop. First there was Joey, who did it in his own unique way and for whom no challenge was too big, and no rival too great. Many still regard him as the greatest, but nephew Michael followed him, surpassing his uncle's legendary achievements to become the most successful TT racer of all time.

The second century of the Isle of Man TT Races is fully up and running, and its importance on the motorsport calendar is as high as it's ever been. The level of professionalism mirrors that of a World Championship event, and with TV coverage, event sponsorship, investment and promotion at new highs, the event is being showcased to its biggest-ever audience.

The TT continues to look forward while maintaining the tradition and values of those pioneering individuals from 1907, but the fact that it remains the pinnacle of two-wheel motorsport is testament to the islanders. They pride themselves on the event's heritage but also ensure it moves with the times too, to keep it in its rightful place.

The Manx government and population continue to embrace the TT with warm hearts and open arms, welcoming all those who make the trip to their island each and every year to pay homage not only to the races but to the island itself.

The two- and three-wheeled action undoubtedly remains the main focal point of the event, but the Isle of Man itself has its own special attraction. It remains a unique, magical and traditional place, bringing people together from all walks of life, where they're all welcomed and where they all feel at home.

Welcome to the Isle of Man TT Races, the greatest motorcycle road race in the world.

CHAPTER ONE

1907–1914

At 10am on Tuesday 28 May 1907, the first two riders pushed off to start the inaugural Isle of Man Tourist Trophy motorcycle race, with little thought as to the history they were making. No1 Frank Hulbert and No2 Jack Marshall were the two riders in question. Starting in pairs at one-minute intervals, 23 more intrepid riders awaited their turn.

Conditions were cool and cloudy for the ten laps of the 15.85-mile St John's Short Course. Fuel rationing meant that carburation of the various motorcycles was set as lean as possible and the attached pedals would need to come into play at various times.

▲▲ A busy start line sees riders assemble ahead of the 1914 Junior TT.
▼ Competing on the original St John's Course, Charlie Collier speeds to victory on his Matchless.

There was a compulsory ten-minute refuelling stop at the halfway point of the race, when refreshments were also available! Riders competed with spare inner tubes draped around them and their jackets full of spark plugs – the bikes were at the cutting edge of the era's technology.

Hulbert, Marshall and the Matchless pairing of Harry and Charlie Collier were expected to dominate the single-cylinder class, and it was Harry Collier who set the fastest lap of 41.81mph before retiring. Marshall lost time after a spill that allowed Charlie Collier to pull clear, and he eventually came home more than 11 and a half minutes clear of Marshall. He completed the ten laps in a time of 4hrs 8min 8s.

The concurrently run twin-cylinder event was won by Birmingham's Rem Fowler riding a Norton with a 700cc Peugeot engine. Both he and Billy Wells had to constantly repair punctures, change tyres, change plugs and mend broken belts, but Fowler was encouraged to continue and finished half an hour in front of Wells. Fowler set the fastest lap overall in a time of 22min 6s, at 42.91mph. Twelve of the initial 25 riders completed the race.

With no serious injuries, the first TT was deemed a success by the organising Auto Cycle Club (soon to become the Auto-Cycle Union, or ACU) although the event was moved to late September the following year and ran alongside the car TT, with the race format remaining the same.

The previous year's controversy surrounding the use of pedals, a clear advantage for some, was solved by simply banning them. The entry was again dominated by bikes using single gearing and direct belt drive, and both reliability and performance had improved considerably.

A total of 36 entries were received, 15 singles and 21 twins, with all the leading UK riders lining up once again, along with riders from Germany and Switzerland. First away on this occasion were 1907 winners Collier (Matchless single) and Fowler (Norton twin), with the latter the first to complete the lap.

◄ Winner of the inaugural twin-cylinder race, Rem Fowler stands alongside his Norton which produced just 5bhp.
▼ A resplendent Robert Arbuthnot with his Triumph; the combination would finish third in the 1908 single-cylinder race.

▲ Racing through the streets of Peel on the St John's Course.

Collier and Marshall again did battle in the single-cylinder class and, despite losing time due to a crash and having to replace a broken exhaust valve, Marshall was the quicker rider in the second half of the race and defeated Collier by two minutes. Fowler retired in the twin class, allowing Harry Reed and his Peugeot-engined DOT to claim victory.

Mudguards and saddles were still the order of the day in 1909, but fuel rationing was done away with (petrol was cheap) as were strict exhaust silencer rules. But the biggest change was to run the singles and twins in a straight race together, with singles limited to 500cc and the twins 750cc. Entries jumped up to 54, but they weren't the only thing on the rise – lap speeds were now more than 50mph and it was estimated 70mph was being reached on the fastest stretches.

The increased speeds came with a cost though – reliability. By half-race distance, 20 riders had already been forced to retire, including 1907 winner Charlie Collier, who was forced to park his Matchless twin with a broken belt fastener.

Collier's brother Harry took over the lead after the mid-race refuelling stop, and although Marshall, who'd started at number one, moved into second he was another high-profile name to retire, this time with valve problems.

After that, Harry Collier had an untroubled ride to victory with his race-winning speed some 9mph up on Marshall's from the year before. He also set a new lap record of 52.27mph, the first 50mph and sub-20-minute lap, which was more than four minutes quicker than the previous mark.

The Beginning

In 1904, Tynwald, the Manx parliament, passed a Road Closure Act to allow the Automobile Club of Great Britain (now the RAC) to carry out speed trials ahead of the Gordon Bennett Cup international car races in France. The reason the Isle of Man was chosen was simple – British roads had a speed limit of 20mph. For the Manx government, the potential to attract tourists and publicity was the main appeal. The following year, the four-wheel contingent competing for the Tourist Trophy were joined by their two-wheel counterparts when the Auto Cycle Club (ACC), the forerunner of the Auto Cycle Union, hosted their own trials for the International Cup races.

However, both the Gordon Bennett and International Cup were abandoned after several arguments and disagreements. In their place, the Auto Cycle Club pursued the possibility of running an event similar to the car TT. The Marquis de Mouzilly St Mars provided a magnificent trophy, which is still presented today to the winner of the Senior TT, and at their annual dinner in January, the ACC announced that a Tourist Trophy race would be held on the Isle of Man on 28th May 1907.

The next step was to determine a suitable course. The ACC briefly considered using the same 40-mile course used by the cars, but this idea was quickly dismissed due to its arduous, punishing nature. The 24-mile Douglas-Castletown-Ballacraine course, used for the International Cup trials, was also discussed but it was agreed this would only be suitable if a large entry was assembled. Instead, it was decided that a shorter course would be devised, and the Manx authorities agreed to close and marshal a 15.85-mile route starting at St John's, near Tynwald Hill.

The triangular course ran anti-clockwise and headed to Ballacraine where it turned left and joined the Glen Helen section of today's Snaefell Mountain Course as far as the village of Kirk Michael. The course then took a sharp left turn southwards along the coast road to the streets of Peel, which included negotiating the famous Devil's Elbow. Passing through the small town, the course then headed back to St John's. Marquees, tents and spectator accommodation was set up at Tynwald Hill, with the paddock based beside the old stone wall of Tynwald Inn.

The race was set at ten laps (158 miles), with pairs of riders starting at one-minute intervals. Regulations were simple: there was to be no engine capacity or weight limit, but effective silencers were required, along with a proper saddle, mudguards and two-inch diameter tyres. Pedalling was allowed to assist on the hills, which would be invaluable on the climb out of Glen Helen up Creg Willy's Hill. Spare belts, inner tubes and a tool kit were essential.

The course was untarred the whole way round, and riders had to negotiate clouds of dust in the dry and pools of mud in the wet. Early morning practice sessions were even held with regular traffic still using the roads – a far cry from today's controlled environment.

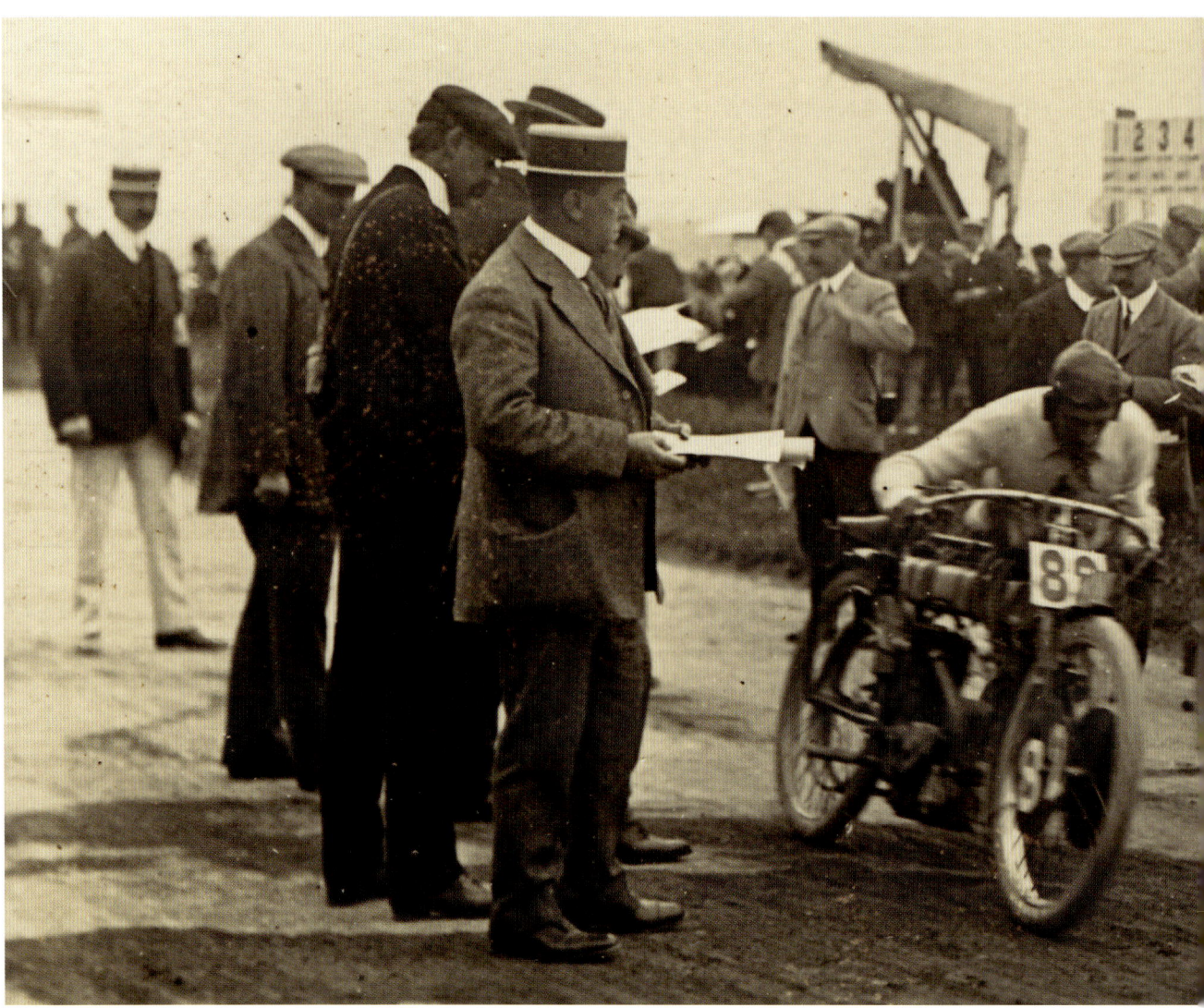

Lee Evans, riding an Indian, finished second, with Billy Newsome and his Triumph the best of the singles in third. Only 19 of the 54 starters were able to complete the ten laps.

In 1910, the TT moved to the end of May, where it has remained ever since, although the death of King Edward VII earlier in the month meant practice was suspended for a day of national mourning. The road surface was improved and a wooden banking added to cover the jagged wall on the exit of Ballacraine.

The capacity for twin-cylinder machines was reduced from 750cc to 670cc with half of the field, which now boasted an impressive 83 entries, entered on twins. Both Indian and Humber were using aero-type cylinders turned from solid steel, with steel pistons on their machines, while the Indians also had all-chain drive. Number plates were now fitted to the machines.

Two interesting entries came in the form of James Norton, on his new single-cylinder side-valve machine, and Walter Bentley, who later founded the car

▲ Duggie Brown and Sam Wright get their 1910 race underway on their Humber machines. Both riders would be forced to retire.

company of the same name. The latter suffered a puncture and crashed out, collecting a policeman on his way, and the same fate befell the Indians too, their punctures blamed on semi-perished inner tubes.

Castrol R became a familiar smell around the paddock and spectators lined the entire course as the BAT twins of Harry Bashall and Harry Bowen set the early pace. Bashall went out when his bike caught fire at the refuelling stop and Bowen crashed out at the new-look Ballacraine.

That allowed the Matchless twins of the Collier brothers to take over, and it was Charlie who got the win from Harry by five minutes. The best single again finished third and was again a Triumph, this time in the hands of Billy Creyton, and lap records for both classes were also set.

The ACU now realised the status of the event they'd created and announced a bold move for 1911: the TT would switch to the 37.5-mile Snaefell Mountain

The Anatomy of a Classic TT Bike

While spectators can see some of these bikes at the Classic TT in a celebration of the past, it can sometimes be easy to forget that, in their day, these were at the cutting edge of two-wheel sport. Back then, riders faced the same hazards as modern riders, and while it might have been slower, they did so with fewer technological advancements. There was no traction control, advanced suspension or modern braking systems, and tyres were narrow and offered unpredictable grip, which makes their achievements all the more special.

The Classic Classes

Over the decades, various classes have come and gone, but some of the most iconic remain etched in TT folklore. The Senior TT first ran in 1911 and has remained the pinnacle race of the event. The first year was open to 500cc single-cylinder and 585cc twin-cylinder motorcycles, but 1912 saw it limited to 500cc machines, and it remained so until 1985.

The Junior TT also began in 1911, and has always been aimed at those machines with a smaller capacity and more agile performance. The Lightweight and Ultra-Lightweight classes saw 250cc and 125cc machines take to the TT course, while the Production TT was the predecessor to the Superstock class and ran in various forms between the late 1960s and early 2000s.

1. Engine

Classic TT bikes were typically powered by air-cooled single-, twin- or early four-cylinder engines. Power outputs ranged from around 30 to 70bhp, but these machines still reached incredible speeds thanks to their lightweight design. The key to a successful TT engine was one that was mechanically simple, incredibly durable and easy to repair.

2. Frame and Chassis

Frames and chassis geometry were far less refined than those of today's machines, with designers having to strike a balance between strength and sufficient flexibility to manage uneven surfaces.

3. Suspension

Early TT bikes featured rudimentary suspension up front and either rigid rear-ends or basic twin-shock setups at the rear. Damping was minimal or non-existent, and most of the shock absorption came through the tyres and the rider's body.

As the course developed and speeds increased, more advanced twin-shock systems were introduced; however, even then the bikes could still be extremely unsettled by bumps, jumps and uneven surfaces.

4. Brakes

Classic TT bikes used drum brakes, either in single or twin leading-shoe designs, which offered very limited stopping power compared to modern disc systems. Wet-weather performance was also particularly poor, with brake fade and overheating being very common issues for riders.

5. Tyres

Classic tyres were often narrow, providing far less grip and predictability compared to their modern counterparts. The compounds used were far harder as well, ensuring they could endure the long races, but they offered very little grip at lean.

6. Aerodynamics and Bodywork

Early TT bikes were completely naked, but by the 1950s fairings started to appear, and fans will likely remember the distinctive 'dustbin' designs. These were aimed at improving top speed, but the large front fairings were eventually banned due to stability concerns in crosswinds.

Unlike modern Superbike development, where bikes spend hours in wind tunnels, back then much of the aerodynamic design came down to trial and error.

7. Electronics

Nowadays, electronics can make or break a TT week, but for a long time classic bikes featured nothing of the sort. There were no ECUs, sensors or traction-control systems, and ignition systems were mechanical. Riders monitored their bike by ear, feel and smell, and although rev counters were sometimes fitted, there were no warning lights or telemetry.

8. Fuel Tank

Classic TT bikes were often fitted with large, hand-formed aluminium fuel tanks to allow for longer stints without refuelling. Capacities varied depending on class and expected distance, and fuelling was managed by gravity-fed petcocks with manual reserve settings. Being without today's quick-fill systems, pit stops required mechanics to manually pour in fuel using large jugs and funnels.

9. Dashboard and Switchgear

Classic bikes had minimal instrumentation, and the most advanced bikes would perhaps feature a rev counter and an oil pressure gauge. Gear changes were often made with a right-side lever or, in earlier bikes, by hand. Clutches were cable-operated and throttle operation was direct, without any form of assistance.

◀ Double 350cc World Champion and two-time TT winner Bill Lomas pictured in 1955 on his 500cc Moto Guzzi.

Course pioneered by the cars. The course was a quarter of a mile shorter than the modern-day course as it turned right at Cronk-ny-Mona and came out at the top of Bray Hill via Willaston.

A new set of regulations was required, and manufacturers were already starting to think about gearing development that would be a necessity for the climb out of Ramsey. Single-gear machines simply wouldn't cut it, and only a third of the field stuck with this methodology. Triumph opted for a three-speed Sturmey-Archer hub gear, similar to modern-day bicycles, Matchless devised a six-speed belt and AJS designed a three-speed gearbox. The Indian manufacturer in the US devised two-speed gears driven by chain drive to the rear wheel.

At more than double the length of the St John's Course and with a peak elevation of nearly 1,400 feet, the Mountain Course quite clearly presented a formidable challenge to both riders and manufacturers, with fatigue and stamina undoubtedly factors. Only the seven-mile stretch from Douglas to Ballacraine was tarred and the mountain 'road' was nothing more than a cart track with cattle, sheep and gateways to negotiate.

The start line was between Bray Hill and Quarter Bridge, and refuelling depots were stationed at Braddan and Ramsey. Two races were taking place: the Junior TT for 300cc singles and 340cc twins, held over four laps; and the Senior TT for 500cc singles and 585cc twins. The Senior was five laps with the winner receiving the original Marquis de Mouzilly St Mars trophy.

▼ 1911 saw the Races switch to the formidable Mountain Course, with Duggie Brown seen here rounding Ramsey Hairpin.

▲ HV Colver's Royal Enfield undergoes a technical inspection ahead of the 1911 Junior race.

Entries passed 100 for the first time, two-thirds of them in the Senior, but the Junior was first to tackle the Mountain Course, with 16 different manufacturers in the line-up. It soon became a battle between the Colliers on their new Matchless singles and the Humber of Percy Evans. It was Evans who prevailed, aided by the fastest lap of 53m 24s, at 42mph. Despite the severity of the Mountain Course, 25 of the 34 starters finished.

Two days later it was the turn of the Senior TT, although the Rudge team were non-starters after 19-year-old Victor Surridge crashed in practice at Glen Helen. Sadly, Surridge was the first TT fatality.

As with the previous year, it was predominantly a Matchless versus Indian contest, with flamboyant American Jake DeRosier leading initially for the latter.

Norton
1907–2019
43 wins

Few names are as synonymous with the Isle of Man TT as Norton; the British marque's legacy on the Mountain Course stretches back longer than any other manufacturer. Lining up on the grid at the very first TT in 1907, the brand has enjoyed incredible success since that moment and left an indelible mark on the event.

Norton's first victory came in that inaugural year, with Rem Fowler triumphing in the inaugural twin-cylinder race, setting the stage for more than a century of success. Through the inter-war years, Norton was the dominant force, with riders such as Alec Bennett, Stanley Woods and Jimmie Guthrie cementing the brand's place at the forefront of road racing.

By the early 1930s, when it was led by young designer Arthur Carroll and Joe Craig, who went on to a managerial role, Norton had established itself as the manufacturer to beat, amassing a remarkable string of victories that set new standards for performance and reliability. It wasn't unusual for the Birmingham-based manufacturer to have a clean sweep of the Junior and Senior race podiums.

▲ A determined Ray Amm jumps Ballaugh Bridge on his way to winning the 1954 Senior TT. The Rhodesian won three TT races for Norton in 1953–54.

Norton returned to competition in style following the Second World War, and from the late 1940s into the 1950s, the works Norton team and its iconic Manx 'Featherbed' model became the machine of choice. The marque remained at the forefront of TT racing for years.

Riders including Geoff Duke, Reg Armstrong, Ray Amm and Harold Daniell all claimed victories around the Island during this period, but subsequent decades saw Norton fall down the pecking order as the Italian and Japanese manufacturers took over.

Norton's success returned for a short spell in the late 1980s and early 1990s with the rotary Wankel-engined machines – Steve Hislop's Senior victory in 1992 is still talked about to this day – but the brand faced substantial financial issues and its presence on the island halted.

However, Norton returned in 2009, and while it was unable to replicate the success of its glory years, Josh Brookes took the brand's best result in the modern era with fifth place and a fastest lap of 131.745mph in the 2018 Senior.

However, he crashed second time around and it became a direct battle between Charlie Collier on his Matchless and the Indian of Oliver Godfrey.

Fuel stops for Collier handed Godfrey the lead and he went on to win, making Indian the first foreign manufacturer to come out on top. Collier was later disqualified from second due to taking on fuel away from the designated depots, and Indian celebrated further with a clean sweep of the podium places.

The inaugural TT on the Mountain Course was deemed a success but it did have its critics, none more so than the substantial number of residents who had their previously peaceful lives disrupted by the riders speeding by their property.

Spectators were accused of improper behaviour and, to make matters worse for the 1912 event, most of the British manufacturers boycotted it due to the difficulty of the Mountain Course. Riders were also unhappy with having to practise with vehicles and animals on the course and talk began to surface about the TT being moved elsewhere.

Thankfully, a crisis was averted as diplomacy prevailed, so the Mountain Course was once again available for use. But entries fell by a third, with the majority being private owners who'd managed to secure works machinery from

▼ Wet roads at Ballig Bridge greet Percy Evans (Humber) during the 1911 Junior race.

the year before. The race format remained the same, with practice taking place on no less than 14 mornings. The Junior's maximum capacity was 350cc and the Senior's 500cc.

The Junior race saw wet conditions for the first time which was advantageous for the countershaft gearing of the Douglas machines, as opposed to those that were belt driven, and Harry Bashall and Eddie Kickham took a 1–2 for the British manufacturer. Meanwhile, Frank Applebee won the Senior on one of the fancied Scotts; it was technically ahead of its time and the first victory for a two-stroke, and for a water-cooled machine.

The dip in the TT's popularity was thankfully brief and entries soared to 147 in 1913. The manufacturers were back with a vengeance, with 16 different makes in the Junior and an incredible 32 in the Senior. That resulted in organisers introducing a special Manufacturer's Team Award and, for the one and only time,

▼ A rider exits Braddan Bridge to start the high-speed run to Ballacraine in 1913.

▲ The original start line was between Bray Hill and Quarter Bridge, with the full line-up of machinery assembled here in 1913.

each race was spread over two days – the Juniors did two laps on their first day and the Seniors three, before the remainder was completed the following day.

Douglas, with 13 of their reliable flat twins, were well placed to repeat their Junior win of the year before, but instead it was the NUT of Hugh Mason that came out on top in a race that was now held over six laps. Mason had been hospitalised after a practice crash but checked himself out and defeated Billy Newsome's Douglas by just 46s.

Rudge, Triumph, Indian, Ariel, Brough, Rover and Scott were just some of the manufacturers represented in the seven-lap Senior, and Tim Wood (Scott) led Frederick Bateman (Rudge) after the first day. Bateman took the lead the following day, but a puncture caused him to crash on the drop down from Keppel Gate and, tragically, he died later from his injuries. Wood won the race by the slender margin of 5s from the Rudge of Ray Abbott, with Rover taking the Manufacturer's Award.

As war clouds gathered, Bateman's accident led to mandatory hard helmets being worn in the 1914 races (but not, strangely, in practice) and the two-day format for each race was dropped, the Junior now taking place over a straight

five laps and the Senior six. The start and finish were moved to the top of Bray Hill, where the pits were located, and this was the only location for refuelling.

The Junior race was once again held in wet and misty conditions, which led to several accidents, and it quickly became a tussle between AJS, Royal Enfield and Douglas. The lead continually changed hands, but it ended with a 1–2 for AJS with Eric Williams and Cyril Williams (no relation) finishing first and second. This was AJS's first Junior success for a single-cylinder machine.

Almost 100 starters, evenly split between singles and twins, lined up for the Senior, and 35 different manufacturers were represented, including Sunbeam for the first time. But it was Tim Wood on the latest Scott who blazed a trail at the start of the race, with a new lap record of 53.50mph.

However, Wood went out with a burnt magneto shortly afterwards and the Collier brothers, in their final TT, also fell by the wayside: Charlie had hub gear problems and Harry crashed out at 70mph. The new leader was Cyril Pullin (Rudge), who went on to win ahead of the 1911 winner Oliver Godfrey (Indian) and Howard Davies (Sunbeam), the two riders tying for second place after being given identical times.

It was another six years before the races would take place again, as Europe was plunged into the First World War, thus halting the early momentum of the TT.

◀ Oliver Godfrey pushes his 500cc Indian machine at the start of the 1914 Senior; Godfrey would finish joint second.

▼ The original scoreboard seen in 1914.

CHAPTER TWO

1920–1939

After four years of war it took a while to adjust back to normal life, but the ACU was keen for the TT to resume at the earliest opportunity. They proposed a meeting for 1920, provided that 30 entries were received for each class. This was duly achieved, with, promisingly, half of the entries being newcomers.

The biggest change was to the Mountain Course itself when the final section from Cronk-ny-Mona was altered to include Signpost Corner, Bedstead, the Nook and the famous Governor's Bridge dip. This brought the course onto Glencrutchery Road, which also provided a safe and suitable place for the start and finish.

Little had been done to the course during the war, and when the races resumed in 1920 the only tarred sections were from Douglas to Ballacraine and a short stretch in Ramsey. From Ballacraine onwards, the surface was plain macadam of rolled earth and stones, which produced either clouds of dust or slippery mud.

Beyond Ramsey, the mountain section was little more than a moorland track occasionally used by farm carts, with stones and wandering sheep adding to the hazards faced by competitors.

A double scoreboard, pits and a wooden grandstand were erected, with the grandstand linked to every part of the course and also acting as the communications centre. Although primitive by today's standards, when decked with flags and full of spectators it still provided plenty of atmosphere.

▲▲ Jimmie Guthrie approaches Quarter Bridge in 1937.
▼ Racing resumed in 1920 but the road surface in many areas was simply macadam of rolled earth and stones.
▶ Doug Prentice starts the mountain climb on his 350cc New Imperial in the 1921 Junior.

The first race saw 19 Junior machines and four Lightweight machines take part, with the former including no less than six works AJSs – the manufacturer was eager to replicate their success of 1914.

Riders Eric Williams, Howard Davies and HF Harris took an early lead, but one by one they retired, allowing another AJS rider, Cyril Williams, to build a 20-minute lead. He encountered transmission trouble at Keppel Gate but managed to freewheel and then push through the new final section of the course.

The weary Williams still managed to win by nine minutes from the Blackburne of Jack Watson-Bourne. RO Clark crashed his 250 Levis machine near Keppel but finished fourth overall and won the inaugural Lightweight class.

Four factory teams – AJS, Sunbeam, Indian and Norton – entered the Senior, with Norton maintaining their record of contesting every TT to date. Sunbeam's George Dance took an early lead, and the newcomer set a new lap record of 55.62mph before retiring. That allowed the Norton of Manxman Duggie Brown to inherit the lead, but he was overhauled by Tommy de la Hay, who gave Sunbeam their first TT victory.

The TT got truly back into its stride in 1921, when the number of entries shot up to 133 and many of the works teams returned, including no fewer than 12 in the Senior race. The race days followed the same pattern, although a coal strike affected the Steam Packet ships ferrying the spectators to the island.

The Junior had 65 entries, including 21 in the Lightweight, where two-stroke Velocettes and four-stroke New Imperials joined the Levis. AJS introduced a new, more reliable three-speed model for the Junior, and they dominated proceedings, with Eric Williams, Howard Davies and Tom Sheard taking a 1–2–3. Davies set a new lap record of 55.15mph as he battled his way back from a puncture. Doug Prentice and his New Imperial were the clear winners of the Lightweight.

For the Senior, Freddie Dixon was in the Triumph team and Irish-Canadian newcomer Alec Bennett was part of Sunbeam's challenge, and Davies entered on his 350cc AJS. The new scoreboard came into its own as each of the six laps produced a new leader.

Davies ran in second for much of the race, but he moved into the lead after the fifth lap and, sensationally, the 350cc AJS beat all the 500cc machines. Davies came home two and a half minutes clear of Bennett as Freddy Edmond upped the lap record to 56.40mph.

> Davies came home two and a half minutes clear of Bennett as Freddy Edmond upped the lap record to 56.40mph

With the first 60mph lap not far away, concerns were raised about the speed and safety of the machines, but the only change in 1922 was the Lightweight class becoming a five-lap race. However, the course did change slightly in Ramsey, with the road connecting Parliament Square and May Hill being used instead of the town's streets.

In 1922 entries matched those achieved pre-war, and three riders who were to have long and illustrious TT careers made their first appearance: Wal Handley, Jimmy Simpson and Stanley Woods.

▲▲ Eric Williams, pictured at the Waterworks with the pier on the Queen's Promenade in the background, won the 1921 Junior race.
▲ The versatile Freddie Dixon with his 500cc Indian ahead of the 1922 Senior.

Bert le Vack's JAP-engined New Imperial set the early pace in the Junior, followed by a gaggle of AJS riders, but when his engine failed Sheard took over to give the Isle of Man its first home-grown TT victory. Woods finished fifth despite his machine catching fire at a fuel stop.

The Lightweight race saw Handley set a new lap record of exactly 51mph before breaking down, allowing racer and journalist Geoff Davison – who would go on to produce the first TT Special newspaper in 1927 – to become the first name on the Lightweight TT trophy.

In the Senior, Bennett and his Sunbeam were the favourites, and they led from start to finish, the first time the feat had been achieved. He overcame the challenge of Dixon and fell just one second shy of the first 60mph lap. Triumph's Walter Brandish took second.

The TT was beginning to catch the attention of many, and it was now being viewed as a serious commercial enterprise. As development costs grew, the manufacturers sought financial gain through sales, and riders now wanted something more than the honour of a works ride and a trophy.

The costs of promoting the TT strained relations between the Manx government and the ACU, who were seriously contemplating an invitation from Belgium to host the TT. The Manx, who provided the majority of the personnel

▼ Freddie Dixon and passenger Walter Perry won the inaugural Sidecar race in 1923 with their Douglas outfit.

▲ Tom Sheard won the 1923 Senior on his 500cc Douglas and remains the only Manxman to have won the prestigious race.

required to stage the races, responded by saying they had enough expertise to organise the TT themselves.

Diplomacy ruled the day, though, and in 1923 a record 177 entries were received, and a new Sidecar class was introduced. This decision wasn't popular, as manufacturers believed it would lead to negative publicity for their machines. But fears about safety were unfounded, and Freddie Dixon, whose passenger used a lever to bank the Douglas outfit around corners, won the race with an impressive fastest lap of 54.69mph.

Silver replica trophies were introduced for the first time, and all solo races now covered six laps of the Mountain Course. Sulby Bridge was widened, and the corner above Hillberry was named after Walter Brandish, who broke his leg after crashing there during practice,

Bennett and Simpson switched to Douglas and AJS machinery for the Junior race with a new name – Jimmie Guthrie – riding for Matchless, who returned to the TT after a long absence. However, it was Woods and his Cotton who emerged victorious, while Simpson set the first of several fastest laps.

The Lightweight race, now dominated by the faster and more reliable four-strokes, went the way of Scottish rider Jock Porter and his New Gerrard after Handley retired at the halfway stage, and for the first time since 1912 wet conditions were the order of the day in the Senior.

AJS fielded their 350s in the Senior race again, while Douglas was back in earnest with a redesigned flat twin and new braking system, and it was one

Jimmie Guthrie

▲ Jimmie Guthrie (seated) shakes hands with Stanley Woods after winning the 1937 Junior race, his sixth and final TT victory.

From	Hawick, Scotland
Years Active	1923–1937
Wins	6
Podiums	12
Fastest Lap	86.9mph
Manufacturers	Norton, AJS, Matchless, New Hudson, OK-Supreme

Jimmie Guthrie made his TT debut in 1923, but success on the Mountain Course wasn't immediate, and after retiring from that year's Junior he didn't return until 1927.

After his tentative debut Guthrie was very much a dark horse, but he impressed everyone on his New Hudson and, after taking second to Alec Bennett in the Senior, he returned every year until 1937, riding for Norton initially, then AJS and then back with Norton.

His first victory came on an AJS in the 1930 Lightweight race, when he worked his way through the field from sixth on the opening lap, but Guthrie is most closely associated with Norton. After more second-place finishes in the 1931 Junior and Senior and 1932 Junior races, he excelled in 1934 with victory in the Junior and Senior races, making him just the third rider to win two races in a week.

The following year saw Guthrie involved in a thrilling Senior race, where he battled throughout with Stanley Woods riding for Moto Guzzi. He had a final lap lead of 26s and was hailed as the winner when he completed the race, but Woods was flying and a new lap record gave him the win by just four seconds.

Guthrie got his revenge in the 1936 Senior, and his sixth victory came in the 1937 Junior. He retired in the Senior race at The Cutting above the Gooseneck and it proved to be his last TT, as he died at the German Grand Prix two months later. A stone monolith was erected at The Cutting, which was renamed the Guthrie Memorial; it's a permanent reminder of one of the sport's early greats.

▲ The Sidecar class remained on the schedule in 1924 but proved unpopular with the manufacturers.

of their riders, Sheard, who won. He used his local knowledge to maximum effect in the rain and mist, adding his name to the trophy. He remains the only Manxman to have won the Senior TT.

In 1924, the ACU introduced an Ultra-Lightweight race for 175cc machines and, to the horror of many, there was a massed start. Luckily, all 17 starters made it down Bray Hill unscathed, but it was some time before such a scene was repeated. Jock Porter won the race to take his second TT victory.

The Junior had already got race week underway, and history was made when Simpson and his AJS set the first 60mph lap of the Mountain Course. His quickest lap proved to be 64.54mph, but he retired, along with Handley and Len Horton, leaving Kenneth Twemlow on the New Imperial to take the win.

George Tucker won the Sidecar race after long-time leader Dixon retired, and on the final race day organisers opted to run the Lightweight and Senior concurrently, with a gap of only five minutes separating the classes. Confusion reigned as the faster Senior machines soon caught the smaller Lightweights and had to queue up to get by!

Handley again set the pace in the Lightweight only to retire once more, and Porter took over the lead before crashing on the last lap. That allowed Eddie Twemlow, brother of Junior race winner Kenneth, to take another win for New Imperial.

In the Senior race, a determined Dixon led for the first four laps, but his pace slowed and he dropped back to an eventual third. Bennett, now riding for Norton, took the win ahead of Harry Langman and Dixon.

▲ Alec Bennett (500cc Norton) makes a pit stop during his race-winning ride in the 1924 Senior.

The programme remained the same in 1925, the only exception being the Ultra-Lightweight race was now run over four laps. History was made when Handley became the first rider to win two races in a week.

Luck had been in short supply since Handley made his debut, but that all changed when he opened race week with a trouble-free run in the Junior. Riding a Rex-Acme, Handley led from start to finish and won at a speed 8mph faster than the previous year's race. Howard Davies on his own-manufactured HRD took second ahead of Simpson's AJS.

Handley then had limited opposition in the Ultra-Lightweight race, where there were only seven starters, and it was another start-to-finish victory for the Birmingham rider as he again set new lap and race records. It could have been

Wal Handley's Double
1925

Born in Birmingham in 1902, Wal Handley made his TT debut in 1922 – the same year as Stanley Woods and Jimmie Guthrie – but he was immediately ridiculed when he set off in the wrong direction of the course in practice. He showed he was a quick learner, though, by setting the fastest lap of the Lightweight race before retiring from the lead on the second lap.

More retirements from the lead followed in subsequent years, but his luck finally changed in 1925, when he had the distinction of becoming the first rider to win two TT races in a week.

His first victory came after a trouble-free run on the 350cc Rex-Acme in the Junior, setting new race and lap records, the former being a whopping 35 minutes faster than the previous year's winner. Handley was almost four minutes clear of second-placed Howard Davies, with Jimmy Simpson more than six minutes further back in third.

The Ultra-Lightweight was even easier, as there were only seven starters, and he once again set lap and race records, his winning margin on this occasion more than six minutes. It could have been three wins in a week too, as he was leading the Lightweight race after two laps until a puncture caused him to crash out at Signpost Corner, another lap record being his only consolation.

Handley won again in the 1927 Lightweight and completed the full set of race victories in 1930, when he defeated Graham Walker (father of Murray) by more than three minutes in the rain-soaked Senior.

A brilliant rider, Handley's last TT came in 1934; he then retired from two wheels with four TT wins and nine podiums to his name, and the honour of being the first rider to lap the Mountain Course under 30 minutes. He died in November 1941 while serving as a pilot with the Air Transport Auxiliary during the Second World War.

Handley has a corner on the Mountain Course named after him – Handley's Corner – a high-speed 'S' bend between the eleventh and twelfth milestones, where he had a high-speed spill during the 1932 Senior. A memorial seat can also be found at the top of Alexander Drive in Douglas.

◄ Wal Handley (350cc Rex-Acme) rounds Governor's Bridge on his way to victory in the 1925 Junior.

▲▲ A year after finishing second, FG Morgan (Cotton), seen here at Parliament Square, retired from the 1925 Ultra-Lightweight race.
▲ Future BBC broadcaster Graham Walker and his Sunbeam exit Governor's Dip during the 1925 Sidecar race.

▲ With Ramsey Town Hall in the background, JE Wade negotiates Parliament Square in the 1926 Senior race.

three in a week, too, as Handley led the Lightweight race in the early stages. However, a crash at Signpost left him with a flat rear tyre, and Eddie Twemlow came through to take the win from Paddy Johnston.

Davies won the Senior from Frank Longman and Bennett, and although 11 manufacturers were represented in the Sidecar race, the fact that only 18 entries had been received meant it was another disappointing race, with Len Parker taking the win.

Unsurprisingly, the lack of support for the Ultra-Lightweight and Sidecar races meant both were scrapped for 1926, and the three-race programme of the Junior (Monday), Lightweight (Wednesday) and Senior (Friday) remained in place until 1939.

All races were now seven laps, and the ACU had a firm grip of the technical regulations – methanol was now banned – while the Manx authorities, pleased with the ever-increasing number of spectators and publicity, continued to spend considerable sums of money on course improvements; tarmac was now laid around the entire Mountain Course.

1926 was notable for the first appearance of Italian manufacturers Garelli, Bianchi and Moto Guzzi, which gave an indication of what was to come, particularly the performances of the Guzzis.

Practice had shown the capabilities of Pietro Ghersi, the Moto Guzzi rider, and he led six of the seven laps in the Lightweight. However, Johnston was always within touching distance, and when Ghersi stopped to refuel on the

Moto Guzzi
1926–2002
11 wins

▲ A smiling Maurice Cann won the 1948 Lightweight TT on a Moto Guzzi.

One of Italy's most famous marques, Moto Guzzi has carved out a unique and celebrated chapter in Isle of Man TT history. Primarily active between the 1920s and 1950s, the manufacturer combined striking innovation with consistent success, securing 11 victories on the Mountain Course and establishing itself as a formidable force in international road racing.

Established in 1921 by two aircraft pilots and their mechanic who served in the Italian Air Corp – Giorgio Parodi, Giovanni Ravelli and Carlo Guzzi – the brand made its TT debut just five years later in 1926. Their rider Pietro Ghersi finished second in the Lightweight race and set the fastest lap, only to be excluded for a technical infringement.

Moto Guzzi's first podium came the following year, when Luigi Archangeli finished runner-up in the Lightweight race, but they had to wait until 1935 to taste the winner's champagne, when the signing of Stanley Woods signalled their intent. The Dubliner doubled up with victory in the Senior and Lightweight TTs, and two years later Omobono Tenni became the first foreign rider to win a TT with victory in the Lightweight event.

The post-war period saw Moto Guzzi become a true powerhouse, and through the 1940s and 1950s the Italian marque dominated the Lightweight class, with Manliff Barrington, Maurice Cann, Tommy Wood and Fergus Anderson all opting for Guzzi power on their way to victory. Bill Lomas and Ken Kavanagh also claimed Junior TT wins, with Kavanagh becoming the first Australian winner in 1956.

Success in the 500cc class was harder to come by, but Dickie Dale did take the mighty V8 to fourth in the 1957 Senior race. Kavanagh's victory would be Moto Guzzi's last around the Mountain Course as they withdrew from racing, along with Mondial and Gilera, at the end of the 1957 season due to rising costs and falling motorcycle sales. Privateer machines continued to appear at the TT, but Moto Guzzi's presence on the TT grid slowly disappeared, although their impact during the 1930s–1950s cannot be underestimated.

last lap, Johnston took the lead to win by 20s. Ghersi was then excluded from second place when post-race scrutineering revealed he'd used a different spark plug than the one specified.

The Junior went the way of Bennett and his new four-stroke Velocette, making him the first three-time TT winner, with Simpson and Handley joining him on the podium, while the Senior saw a terrific duel between Handley and Stanley Woods.

Handley and the twin-cylinder Rex-Acme made the early running, but he lost seven minutes on lap two when he changed a rear cylinder plug. Try as he might, he couldn't close the gap and Woods, riding for Norton, won by four minutes. Simpson and his AJS recorded the first 70mph lap of the Mountain Course.

To minimise the disruption for the locals, early morning practice continued to take place on open roads with riders taking their own precautions. Understandably, this led to several near misses, and in 1927 Archie Birkin was killed when trying to avoid a van making its early morning deliveries.

As a memorial, the fast corner just after Kirk Michael village was named Birkin's Bend, while the Manx Parliament amended the Road Closure Act to include practice sessions as well as the races.

Handley's up-and-down relationship with the TT continued as he dominated the first six laps of the Junior race on the latest Blackburne-engined Rex-Acme, only to retire halfway round the last lap, with Freddie Dixon and the HRD taking the win. Two days later, fortune smiled on Handley as he won the Lightweight race, while Moto Guzzi officially appeared in the results with Luigi Archangeli in second.

▼ Wal Handley takes a tumble in 1927.

▲ Double TT winner Eddie Twemlow speeds away from Ballaugh Bridge during the 1928 meeting.
▶ TL Hatch and his 500cc Scott finished thirteenth in the 1929 Senior race. Hatch had finished third the year before.

The Senior, meanwhile, saw the new overhead camshaft, single-cylinder Norton ridden by Woods, Bennett and Joe Craig. Practice times made Woods the favourite, and he led the first four laps after setting a new lap record of 70.90mph. However, a slipping clutch led to his retirement, and Bennett claimed his fourth TT win ahead of an impressive Jimmie Guthrie on a New Hudson.

In 1928 blazing sun meant melting tar was an added issue for the riders, but Bennett and his Velocette had no problems in the Junior, with new lap and race records giving him a comfortable fifth TT win over teammate Harold Willis.

The Lightweight was held in similar conditions, with Frank Longman (OK-Supreme) and Handley (Rex-Acme) doing battle for the first five laps before Handley again retired. Longman went on to win by more than 17 minutes, a record margin.

The sun then gave way to torrential rain, which meant seven miserable laps in the Senior, and most of the expected front-runners disappeared in the early stages. After Simpson retired Charlie Dodson (Sunbeam) took the lead, and although Graham Walker (Rudge) – father of Murray – nosed ahead at Ramsey on the final lap, it was Dodson who was first to emerge from the gloom of Governor's Bridge to take the win.

The rain stayed away in 1929, and Velocette again ruled the roost in the Junior race with Bennett and Freddie Hicks, although Handley, now AJS-mounted, pushed them hard. There was little to choose between them, but it was Hicks who sprung a surprise to win, with Handley in second splitting the two Velocette riders.

Ghersi, on a Moto Guzzi, returned to lead the first five laps of the Lightweight race before retiring, his only consolation taking the fastest lap, and Syd Crabtree was the eventual winner on his Excelsior.

▲ The local constabulary and a volunteer marshal ensure spectators remain behind the barrier in 1929.

The sun continued to shine for the Senior, in complete contrast to the conditions of the year before. HG Tyrell-Smith led on his Rudge, who were having their first serious attempt at the TT since 1914, before crashing at Glen Helen. After receiving treatment in the hotel, he eventually took third, before discovering that he'd cracked three ribs. Although Tim Hunt took over the lead on his Norton, Dodson hit the front on lap five and won the Senior for the second successive year.

By 1930, the Manx government and Douglas Corporation were playing a bigger role in promoting the TT and Tynwald voted the first cash grant of £5,000 to assist the ACU with prize money. Race winners were now awarded £200, and travel expenses encouraged more overseas riders. The result was an entry boasting 19 nations, including riders from as far as Australia, Japan and South Africa.

Course improvements had been made on the narrow Glen Helen and Kirk Michael sections, and Rudge introduced a new four-valve single-cylinder machine for the Junior, ridden by Tyrell-Smith, Ernie Nott and Walker. That was the final order after seven laps, with less than a minute separating the three riders.

In the Lightweight race Guthrie took his first TT win, and the BBC broadcast part of the Senior race for the first time. Originally entered on an FN, Handley switched to a privately entered Rudge and set a new lap record of 76.28mph, the first sub-30-minute lap of the Mountain Course. Walker, on another Rudge, finished second, with Norton's Simpson third.

British machines were now in the ascendancy, with engineers spurred on by the economic rewards of a TT win. Most were based in the industrial heartland of the Midlands, with Velocette, Norton, Sunbeam, Rudge and AJS in the west and Raleigh, Blackburne and JAP engines, which powered Rex-Acme and

▲▲ Jimmie Guthrie passes Kate's Cottage during the 1930 Junior, although machine problems meant he later retired.
▲ Ernie Nott (Rudge) enters Parliament Square in the 1931 Junior. Nott would finish third behind Tim Hunt and Jimmie Guthrie.

OK-Supreme machines, in the east. Despite the economic gloom of the Great Depression, the 1930s was a golden era for British manufacturers.

In 1931 Norton, with a strong line-up of Woods, Hunt, Guthrie and Simpson, were determined to get the better of Rudge, and race week started perfectly. Hunt won the Junior from Guthrie in a race-winning time more than eight minutes quicker than Tyrell-Smith and Rudge had managed the year before.

Nott salvaged Rudge's pride in third, and the Coventry-based manufacturer got back to winning ways in the Lightweight, with Walker claiming the honours from Tyrell-Smith. Their celebrations were short-lived, though, as Norton swept to a 1–2–3 in the Senior, a feat never achieved before, with Hunt winning from Guthrie and Woods, and Simpson setting the first 80mph lap before retiring.

Stanley Woods

▲ Stanley Woods flies down Bray Hill on his way to winning the 1935 Senior.

From	Dublin, Ireland
Years Active	1922–1939
Wins	10
Podiums	14
Fastest Lap	88.99mph
Manufacturers	Cotton, Norton, Moto Guzzi, Velocette, Husqvarna, DKW, Royal Enfield, New Imperial, Scott

Son of a toffee salesman, Woods was one of the first motorcycling superstars. Born in 1903, he is one of the youngest ever riders to win a TT, doing so in just his second year of racing on the Mountain Course, the 1923 Junior.

His debut came a year before, along with other TT greats Jimmy Simpson and Wal Handley, and after taking his first win on a Cotton he was soon signed by Norton, spending eight years with the British manufacturer. This spell brought five victories in total, including a Junior-Senior double in both 1932 and 1933.

By then he was becoming increasingly frustrated with Norton's team orders and, after a short period with Husqvarna, a move to Moto Guzzi saw Woods claim a Lightweight-Senior double in 1935. A subsequent move to Velocette yielded further wins, aided by his engineering prowess which saw a rear-sprung frame design introduced. Double overhead camshafts were also used for the first time.

During his 18-year career, Woods also rode for Royal Enfield, Douglas, Ariel, New Imperial, Scott, Husqvarna and DKW. When the Second World War broke out he'd racked up ten wins and 14 podiums at the TT, despite the stiff opposition posed by, among others, Simpson, Handley, Jimmie Guthrie, Alec Bennett and Freddie Frith.

Woods was equally successful on the Continent, and although the war effectively ended his career the Irishman remained a popular presence in the paddock. His personality and ability made him one of the sport's greatest riders and personalities, and he participated in parade laps well into his 80s.

It was another Norton v Rudge battle in 1932, and both teams fielded four riders – the best of the day – unchanged from the previous year. Simpson set the pace in practice for both the Junior and Senior, but both he and Hunt retired before half-race distance in the Junior. Handley's Rudge took over the lead, but with a new lap record of 78.62mph Woods was flying, and he won by two minutes. Tyrell-Smith completed the podium in third.

The largely unfancied Leo Davenport upset the form book in the Lightweight, the New Imperial rider defeating the Rudges of Walker and Handley, and one of the King's younger sons, Prince George, watched the Senior race from the Grandstand and Creg-ny-Baa.

It proved to be another dominant race for the Norton team, with their second successive 1–2–3; on this occasion Woods took the win from Guthrie and Simpson. Simpson had led in the early stages with a new lap record, and Handley crashed out of third on the fourth lap just beyond the eleventh milestone, the bend subsequently being named after him.

Norton were rapidly becoming the team to beat, largely due to their brilliant young designer Arthur Carroll, aided by Joe Craig, and in 1933 they were untouchable as they added a Junior 1–2–3 to the same result yet again in the Senior.

▼ A thoughtful-looking Tim Hunt with his Norton in 1933; he finished second and third in that year's Junior and Senior races.

▲ Wal Handley takes a spill at Governor's Bridge in 1933.

Woods led from start to finish in the Junior, but it was close – Hunt was only 7s adrift in second, and Guthrie completed the podium in third. The next seven places were KTT Velocettes, with not a single Rudge on the entry.

The Lightweight race was a lot more open, with six manufacturers battling for supremacy. Handley made the early running on an Excelsior, but his teammate Syd Gleaves soon overtook him to secure the victory from 1928 and 1929 Senior race winner Charlie Dodson.

Woods again emerged winner of the Senior, this time ahead of Simpson and Hunt, as Norton filled the first four places, and in fifth place Nott was the first of the three Rudges. Victory for Woods was his sixth in total, which saw him overtake Alec Bennett as the most successful TT racer.

Simpson had decided 1934 was going to be his final TT, and after several podiums and countless fastest laps he finally got a victory in a wet and misty Lightweight race. Contesting the class for the first time, the Rudge-mounted Simpson defeated the fellow Rudges of Nott and Walker.

Nott had moved to the Swedish Husqvarna team for the Junior and Senior races, where he was, surprisingly, joined by Woods, who had left the all-conquering Norton team. Norton were also without Hunt, who'd sustained a broken thigh at the Swedish Grand Prix, and so they relied on the two Jimmies, Guthrie and Simpson.

They duly delivered, with Guthrie leading Simpson home in both races, Nott taking third in the Junior, and Walter Rusk doing the same for Velocette in the Senior as Woods retired from both races. Simpson then retired from racing, but his memory lives on in the form of a bronze statuette of him, awarded each year to the rider who sets the fastest lap of the meeting.

▲▲ The instantly recognisable Creg-ny-Baa corner.
▲ Having already won the Junior race, Jimmie Guthrie takes the chequered flag at the end of the 1934 Sunior.

Velocette
1913–1984
11 wins

A true British thoroughbred, Velocette earned a proud place in Isle of Man TT history through innovation, perseverance and a run of successes spanning four decades. Entering the fray in the 1910s, the family-run Birmingham marque quickly showed its intent with the popular K series.

Velocette had to wait until 1926 for its first victory, when Alec Bennett powered to success in the Junior TT; Gus Kuhn and Fred Povey finished in the first nine to give the manufacturer the team prize.

The 1920s and 1930s saw Velocette regularly challenging at the sharp end, with Bennett, Stanley Woods and Freddie Hicks all contributing to their tally of wins. And nowhere was their reliability seen more than in the 1933 Junior race when the KTT Velocette took seven of the top ten positions.

▲ Bob Foster won the 1947 Junior when riding a 350cc Velocette. He also won the 1950 350cc World Championship for the British manufacturer.

Post-war, Velocette reaffirmed its credentials with a new generation of riders and machines. Bob Foster and Freddie Frith continued the brand's dominance in the Junior class, with both riders also winning the 350cc World Championship.

However, as the TT became part of the Grand Prix season and the island began welcoming manufacturers from across the globe, the small Velocette factory was no match for the much larger brands.

This, coupled with the business struggling in the late 1950s and early 1960s, saw the manufacturer stop their racing programme, but not before Neil Kelly and Keith Heckles made it a 1–2 in the very first Production TT race on the 500cc Velocette Thruxtons in 1967.

Although the machines haven't graced the Mountain Course for almost half a century (Classic races excepted), the Velocette name remains woven into the fabric of the Isle of Man TT and holds a soft spot in many spectators' hearts.

▲ The young crowd looks on as Stanley Woods sits astride his Moto Guzzi in 1935.

Woods was on the move again in 1935, this time lining up on 250cc and 500cc Moto Guzzis, some of the first to be equipped with rear suspension. Handley had joined Velocette, but his TT career had an ignominious end during practice when he lost part of his thumb on the Sulby Straight when trying to adjust the rear brake.

That year a general strike greeted everyone when they arrived on the island – there was no gas, electricity or public transport. For the first time, travelling marshals were stationed on the Mountain Course.

Norton had another 1–2–3 in the Junior, Guthrie leading home his teammates Rusk and 'Crasher' White, but Guzzi claimed their first TT win in the Lightweight race, and Woods set a new lap record as he defeated the Rudges of Tyrell-Smith and Nott.

The meeting again concluded with the Senior, although the race was postponed until Saturday because of mist, the first time that had ever happened.

The Guardians of the Course

While the majority of the attention around the Isle of Man TT is naturally on the gladiators riding the bikes, none of it would be possible without the unsung heroes working tirelessly behind the scenes to make it happen. It is these hundreds of people, ranging from Isle of Man government officials through to volunteers giving up their time, who ensure the races run safely, smoothly and fairly.

It is no exaggeration to say that without them the TT simply would not happen. Every practice, qualifying and race session relies on a complex hierarchy of volunteers and professionals who ensure the 37.73-mile circuit is as safe as possible.

Marshals

No bike can set off down Glencrutchery Road until the huge 'orange army' is in place. For every practice, qualifying and race session there are 580 dedicated marshals lining up around the course at 260 marshalling posts. These posts are located in 'line of sight', which means that in certain places, such as Laurel Bank, a marshal can't see the marshals at the point in front of or behind them, but the riders never leave the sight of the marshals, so as one marshal loses sight of the rear of the motorcycle, the next marshal point already has sight of the front of the bike.

Armed with a full complement of flags, and radios that give them a direct line to their sector marshal, who in turn is in contact with the organisers, marshals are responsible for everything from managing minor incidents and clearing debris to initiating emergency protocols in the event of a serious crash. TT marshals also have unique legal powers that allow them to secure the closed roads and apprehend anyone who trespasses onto the course once it's closed and locked down for practising and racing.

The work of this vast army of volunteers is coordinated and supported by the TT Marshals Association (TTMA). This organisation is responsible for the recruitment, training, registration and deployment of marshals, and before taking to the course every marshal must have completed the TTMA training.

Sector Marshals

Sector marshals are some of the most experienced marshals around the Isle of Man TT and are responsible for coordinating all of the marshals within their zone. There are twelve chief sector marshals and then more than 120 deputy sector marshals, and they act as the link between those on the ground and the officials in Race Control, located at the start and finish.

▲ Marshals in position at Signpost Corner.

It is the sector marshals' duty to maintain clear lines of communication, verify any incident reports and ensure that all safety protocols are followed precisely. Of course, the role goes far beyond logistics. A good sector marshal will be a mentor, mediator and leader to the others, requiring composure and clarity in high-pressure situations.

Travelling Marshals

One of the more unique and iconic aspects of the Isle of Man TT is the role of the travelling marshal. These marshals are ex-racers with extensive TT racing experience; they ride high-powered motorcycles and provide vital and welcome support to marshals during an incident.

Travelling marshals first became part of the TT in 1935, and there are currently eight who are stationed around the course. They report directly to the Clerk of the Course, not only about incidents but also weather conditions. Each of these eight riders is medically trained to a higher degree than the regular marshals, allowing them to take control of incidents until the medical helicopter arrives.

In addition to their safety role, travelling marshals are also responsible for leading sighting laps and supporting newcomers, as well as carrying out course inspections before and during the races. They also hold a technical officials licence, which empowers them to decide whether a rider can continue once they have been black-flagged and stopped at their location.

Medical Teams

The medical infrastructure behind the Isle of Man TT is nothing short of world class. It comprises a specialist crew of medics and paramedics stationed strategically around the course, supported by mobile response units to ensure riders are attended to as quickly as possible.

At the heart of the operation is Noble's Hospital in Douglas. Calling in more doctors, nurses, surgeons and ambulances for the fortnight, elective surgeries are put on pause to ensure coverage not only for the racers, but also the tens of thousands of fans who flock to the island to celebrate the TT.

Officials, Timekeepers and Beyond

Managing the army of marshals and keeping the show running relies on Race Control and the vast experience and knowledge of the Clerk of the Course (Gary Thompson) and the Deputy Clerks of the Course (John Barton and Lizzie Kinvig).

Working throughout the year, they are responsible for risk assessments, event safety plans, liaising with the Department of Infrastructure regarding resurfacing, and keeping Isle of Man residents informed. During the TT fortnight, it is the Clerk of the Course who makes the critical decisions on stoppages, red flags, timing, liaising with medical teams, police and everything in between.

In addition, a host of other professionals help keep the wheels turning including timekeepers, scrutineers, start-line officials, TV hosts, medical officers, paddock managers, race teams, and media. It's a collaborative effort to keep the show on the road.

▲ Jimmie Guthrie pushes his Norton away from the line at the start of the 1935 Senior.
▶ Guthrie tackles Governor's Dip but lost out on the victory by just four seconds.

It proved to be a battle royal between Guthrie and his Norton, starting at number one, and Woods and the Moto Guzzi, starting 15 minutes later at number 30.

Guthrie led throughout and held a lead of 26s going into the final lap. The Norton team expected Woods to refuel the Moto Guzzi but they went straight through, although few expected Woods to claw back the deficit. Guthrie completed the race and was initially announced the winner, but Woods's last lap was a new record of 86.53mph, and he snatched victory by just 4s.

In 1936 there was a significant change to the course when Ballig Bridge was both flattened and straightened. Moto Guzzi were absent, due to Italy's involvement in the war in Abyssinia, so Woods moved to Velocette, who were now running experimental pivot-fork rear suspension. He also rode the German water-cooled twin two-stroke DKW in the Lightweight race, one of the noisiest machines ever heard.

Norton were running spring frames with Guthrie, Crasher White and Manx GP winner Freddie Frith. Guthrie took an early lead in the Junior when Woods retired at Kirk Michael on the opening lap. Guthrie stopped to replace his chain at Hillberry on the fifth lap, and although he continued he was stopped at Ramsey, where he was told he was to be disqualified after receiving outside assistance.

Guthrie was furious and decided to continue, finishing fifth as Frith won a TT race at his first attempt. The ACU later stated they were wrong to disqualify

Guthrie and allowed him to collect second prize, although the official results listed him as a finisher only.

The Lightweight race had the highest number of entries, and Woods initially led from Bob Foster's New Imperial. Foster went ahead on lap four, and although Woods fought back to regain the lead, the DKW eventually stopped on the mountain.

After the confusing Junior race, Guthrie was out for revenge in the Senior, where he again battled with Woods. Both riders broke the lap record, but on this occasion Guthrie came out on top by 18s, with Frith joining them on the podium in third.

▼ Italian ace Omobono Tenni and his 350cc Moto Guzzi.

Tenni Becomes First International Race Winner
1937

Word soon spread about the Isle of Man TT Races, but while international manufacturer success came quickly – the American company Indian dominated the 1911 Senior with a 1–2–3 result – individual rider glory was harder to come by. Indeed, it took three decades before the first international race winner was crowned.

American Jake DeRosier had briefly challenged for the win in that race and Italian Pietro Ghersi came close, finishing second in the 1926 Lightweight, only for the Moto Guzzi rider to be disqualified when scrutineering revealed he'd used a different spark plug to the one originally specified.

Ghersi returned in 1929 and held the lead in the Lightweight for the first five laps, only to retire sixth time around, a new lap record of 66.63mph his only consolation. But eight years later, Italy did come out on top.

Two-time European motorcycle champion Omobono Tenni made his TT debut in 1935, riding as teammate to Stanley Woods for the factory Moto Guzzi team. Although this heralded the real start of the foreign 'invasion', Tenni had an inauspicious debut, crashing out of second after encountering fog on the mountain.

Two years later he wasn't to be denied. Nicknamed the 'Black Devil' for his black hair and wild riding style, Tenni and his Guzzi went head to head with German Ewald Kluge (DKW) and Woods (Excelsior), and when Woods stopped briefly on the final lap, Tenni seized control. Aided by a new lap record of 77.72mph, the 31-year-old defeated Woods by 37 seconds to become the first foreign rider to win a TT race.

▲ The delighted Moto Guzzi team look on as Omobono Tenni takes a well-earned drink after winning the 1937 Lightweight.

Tenni suffered serious injuries in events elsewhere in 1938 and 1940 but returned to the TT in 1948. Leading the Senior race after setting the fastest lap of the race, 88.06mph, he had to stop at Union Mills on the fifth lap before rejoining to finish ninth. He died just over a month later during practice at the Swiss Grand Prix and has a football stadium in Treviso, Stadio Omobono Tenni, named in his memory.

The first evening practice session was held in 1937, which was a popular move, and Moto Guzzi returned to the Lightweight class. However, it was Norton who again reigned supreme in the Junior, Guthrie leading Frith and White home for yet another clean sweep of the podium.

The Lightweight race saw Woods's Guzzi and Ewald Kluge's DKW do battle in the early stages, until Kluge retired. Woods stopped at Sulby on the final lap, which allowed his Italian teammate Omobono Tenni to take the win, the first foreign winner of a TT race.

For the third year in a row, Guthrie kept Woods at bay for much of the Senior, only to stop at the cutting above the Gooseneck on the fifth lap. Frith pulled out all the stops, though, and he was level on time with Woods going into the final lap, setting the first-ever 90mph lap, 90.27mph, to win by 15s.

A second evening practice session was added in 1938, when DKW returned with a faster engine and Norton had their new double overhead cam 350s and 500s and a new telescopic fork. The Junior was another Norton–Velocette duel, and the latter's engines were particularly fast. Indeed, Woods and his teammate Ted Mellors led throughout; Woods took the victory by four minutes and Frith finished third for Norton.

Moto Guzzi were absent from the Lightweight, which presented DKW with a golden opportunity, as Kluge was joined in the team by Siegfried Wünsche and Ernie Thomas. By lap three only Kluge was left, but he was riding superbly and pushed the class lap record beyond 80mph for the first time. He maintained his pace and won by more than 11 minutes over the Excelsiors of S 'Ginger' Wood and Tyrell-Smith.

> Once again the Senior proved to be the race of the week

Once again the Senior proved to be the race of the week, with Frith, Woods and new Norton recruit Harold Daniell separated by just 8s after four laps. The gap closed further next time around, and Daniell took the lead with the first sub-25-minute lap. He went quicker still, and with a lap of exactly 91mph he beat the Velocette of Woods by 15s, with Frith only 1.6s behind in third.

A year later, in 1939, war clouds were gathering considerably and the German government had determined that national prestige could be boosted by dominating international sporting events. The TT was no exception, and so BMW, DKW and NSU dispatched work machinery to the island, adopting a win-at-all-costs attitude.

Norton opted not to compete due to their commitment to a military contract, and although they sent their 1938 machines for Frith and Daniell to ride, they had no preparation or factory mechanics, which limited their ability to counter the overseas onslaught.

The week started well for the British, though, as Woods won the Junior for Velocette, his tenth TT victory, from Daniell's Norton. The Lightweight, held in bad weather, saw a surprise win for the Italian Benelli factory in the hands of Ted Mellors, who led home Kluge's DKW.

▶ Jock West (BMW) leads Freddie Frith (Norton) round Governor's Bridge in the 1937 Senior, a race which Frith won.

▲ A busy grid ahead of the 1938 Senior race with Freddie Frith leading the way.
◄ A smiling Georg Meier with his 500cc BMW in 1939. The German won the Senior but soon afterwards, war was declared.

That just left the Senior, and the clash of the supercharged BMW twins and the all-conquering British singles. With a top speed of 135mph, the BMWs had impressed in practice, and despite Karl Gall's death in a crash at Ballaugh the team and riders Georg Meier and Jock West decided to compete.

Meier grabbed the lead in dry conditions on the opening lap and never looked back, defeating West by two minutes. Frith and Woods took third and fourth for Norton, the latter competing in his final TT. Just three months later, all thoughts of racing were put on hold as the Second World War began.

CHAPTER THREE

1947–1976

The end of the Second World War brought with it both challenges and optimism, rebuilding lives and homes combining with brighter futures and hope. A feel-good factor spread around the UK as troops were welcomed home, and the Isle of Man was quick to capitalise.

It had been eight long years since the TT last took place, but it finally returned in 1947, although it was a low-key event compared to its huge popularity of the 1930s.

It took some time before the landscape of the world returned to normal, but for the Isle of Man government, getting the TT back up and running was a clear priority, although in fact the first races back on the Mountain Course after the war were the Manx Grand Prix in September 1946.

Nine months later, and despite severe petrol rationing and general shortages, the TT was back, with the programme following the pre-war pattern of Senior, Junior and Lightweight, each over seven laps. The Clubman races were added for standard machines complete with lights and kick starters.

Superchargers were banned, and competitors had to use low-octane 'pool' petrol, which saw a reduction in speeds, but excitement greeted the return of the TT nevertheless. Popular thought was that the international races would be poorly supported, but more than 100 riders entered across the three classes.

▲▲ Shop staff look on as Florian Camathias/Hilmar Cecco (BMW) go through the streets of Onchan in 1959, the last year the Clypse Course was used.
▼ Officials congratulate Artie Bell after his victory in the 1948 Senior as Norton team manager Joe Craig (left) looks on.

▲ The 1949 Lightweight race continued to see a mass start, Ireland's Manliffe Barrington winning for the second time.

Sadly, some of the pre-war heroes, such as Wal Handley, had died serving their country, while others, including Stanley Woods, had retired. But many were back, among them Harold Daniell, Freddie Frith and Maurice Cann, and it was Daniell and Norton who won the Senior, adding to their 1938 success. The quality of the pool petrol could be seen in a fastest lap almost 7mph down on Daniell's record lap, and Frith was ruled out after dislocating his right shoulder in a practice crash at Ballacraine.

Norton and Velocette machinery dominated the Junior entry, Bob Foster winning by more than four minutes, while the Italian Moto Guzzis were expected to dominate the Lightweight race if they kept going. Their only opposition were 20-year-old British machines, and sure enough it was a 1–2 for the Italian manufacturer, Ireland's Manliffe Barrington getting the win after Cann had to stop to fit a new valve spring at the end of the fifth lap.

Entries doubled in 1948, firmly dispelling any post-war blues, and the Jimmy Simpson Trophy was introduced for the rider who set the fastest lap of the meeting, a more than appropriate homage to someone who set so many fastest laps. The first recipient was Italian ace Omobono Tenni, who lapped at 88.06mph in the Senior before problems with his Moto Guzzi dropped him from first to ninth.

Ireland's Artie Bell, second the year before, won by almost 11 minutes from his Norton teammate Bill Doran, with Daniell retiring from second at the thirteenth milestone on the final lap. Earlier in the week, Bell had finished third in the Junior where the returning Frith was triumphant over Velocette teammate Foster.

The Lightweight race saw previous year's winner Barrington lead until he went out on lap three, which allowed Cann and his Guzzi to make up for their disappointment the year before, winning by almost ten minutes from Roland Pike on his pre-war Rudge. The race also saw the first massed start since 1924.

1949 proved to be a defining moment for the TT, when not only was it chosen to be one of five rounds of the all-new FIM World Road Race Championship, but it also had the honour of hosting the very first round. A European series had taken place throughout the 1930s when, strangely, neither the TT nor the UK hosted a round, but that now changed.

Other rounds took place at Bremgarten (Switzerland), Assen (Netherlands), Spa-Francorchamps (Belgium), Clady (Northern Ireland) and Monza (Italy), but on Monday 13 June 1949 it was the Junior TT that lit the World Championship fire. For the first time ever on the Mountain Course, riders started in pairs with a 20-second interval between them, although 1948 winner Frith had the honour of starting the very first World Championship race alone.

AJS, with Les Graham and Bill Doran, looked odds-on favourite for the win, but leader Graham retired with clutch trouble on the second lap and Doran's hopes of victory cruelly ended at the Gooseneck on the final lap with gearbox issues.

By that time, though, Frith was scorching round the course, and with the fastest lap of the race he took his fourth TT win, Velocette teammate Ernie Lyons taking second. Frith would go on to be crowned the first ever 350cc world champion.

Barrington repeated his Lightweight victory of two years before, in a race that saw long-time race leader Dickie Dale break Ewald Kluge's 11-year-old lap record. Norton, AJS, Velocette and Moto Guzzi were all in with a chance of success in the Senior, started by Prince Philip; amazingly, three riders tied for the lead after the first two laps: Graham, Foster and Ted Frend.

Frend came off at Glen Helen on lap four and then Foster went out with clutch trouble at Sulby Bridge on the penultimate lap. That meant Graham led Daniell by more than 90s going into the final lap, but it was then announced he was pushing in from Hillberry!

Graham was thought to be out of petrol, but it was the magneto shaft that had sheared, and so Daniell took his third Senior TT win in one of the most dramatic TT races witnessed, as Graham limped home tenth.

> By that time, though, Frith was scorching round the course, and with the fastest lap of the race he took his fourth TT win

The next two decades saw the World Championship flourish, both on and off the track, and the Isle of Man TT was no different. It continued to be seen as the ultimate challenge for both man and machine, and riders and manufacturers flocked to the little island in the Irish Sea, although the solo races of the 1950s were primarily disputed between Britain and Italy, both riders and manufacturers.

As well as the factory teams from the UK, teams such as Guzzi, Benelli, Mondial, Gilera and, particularly, MV Agusta were in the ascendancy for Italy, while NSU offered a threat from Germany, which was slowly being accepted back into the sporting world.

The early 1950s saw the British manufacturers continue to reign supreme, especially when Bell was joined at Norton by 27-year-old Geoff Duke. The St Helens rider had already triumphed twice on the Mountain Course, winning both the 1949 Senior Clubman TT and that year's Senior Manx Grand Prix, and he lined up alongside Bell, Daniell and Johnny Lockett for the 1950 season.

This was when Norton unveiled the 'Featherbed' machine, a revolutionary frame designed by Belfast brothers Rex and Cromie McCandless, and after Bell claimed the top spot from Duke in the Junior race, the roles were reversed in the Senior when Duke set a new lap record of 93.33mph.

Bell and Lockett finished second and third with Daniell in fifth, with only the fourth-placed AJS of Graham preventing a clean sweep for Norton. The

▼ The factory Norton mechanics preparing the machinery of riders Geoff Duke, Artie Bell, Harold Daniell and Johnny Lockett.

Geoff Duke

▲ A jubilant Geoff Duke strides towards the podium after winning the 1950 Senior TT.

From	St Helens, England
Years Active	1949–1959
Wins	6
Podiums	8
Fastest Lap	99.97mph
Manufacturers	Norton, Gilera, BMW

A dispatch rider in the army during the Second World War, Duke took up trials riding in 1947 for the BSA team, while working for the firm as an engine tuner. His attentions soon turned to road racing, though, and with his potential noticed by Artie Bell he was brought into the Norton team.

The war meant Duke was already 25 when he made his road racing debut, but after retiring in the 1948 Junior Manx Grand Prix he returned to the Mountain Course the following year to win both the Clubman Senior TT and Senior Manx Grand Prix races.

Success at the TT was instant too, as Duke took first in the Senior and second in the Junior 1950 races. The following year he won both races, as well as the 500cc and 350cc World Championships, and quickly established himself as the best motorcycle rider of his time.

Norton took another TT win in 1952, but Duke was quick to spot that they were in decline while the Italian manufacturers were heading in the opposite direction. A move to Gilera subsequently followed, but although Norton won three straight 500cc world titles from 1953 to 1955, the same period yielded just one TT win – the 1955 Senior, when he was wrongly credited with the first 100mph lap of the Mountain Course.

Further glory was halted when he was banned by the FIM for six months in 1956 after supporting a privateer's strike, and his career was effectively ended after a shoulder injury in early 1957 curtailed another campaign. Duke retired at the end of the 1959 season, aged 36, before briefly managing his own Gilera team four years later.

AJS camp had suffered a setback in practice when Doran came off near Ballig Bridge, sustaining a fractured leg, resulting in a new name on the TT Course, Doran's Bend.

Meanwhile, the Lightweight race was still taking place with a massed start, and it saw the closest finish in TT history. Italian Dario Ambrosini (Benelli) battled Cann's Moto Guzzi, and the British rider led by almost 40s at one stage. Ambrosini grabbed the lead for the first time as they descended the Mountain for the final time, though, and won by just 0.2s.

Bell suffered serious injuries at the Belgian GP less than a month later, ending his impressive career, and Daniell retired, so Duke – who missed out on the 1950 500cc World Championship to Gilera's Umberto Masetti by a single point – was Norton's number one in 1951. Lockett retained his place and was joined by Jack Brett and Australian Harry Hinton.

In 1951 the Lightweight race reverted to an interval start and was cut from seven laps to four, while the Senior and Junior riders now started singly at ten-second intervals. A 125cc race, held over two laps, was introduced for the first time.

▼ Geoff Duke and his Norton speed along Glencrutchery Road during the 1950 Senior.

Duke was untouchable as he won both the Junior and Senior races with lap and race records, and Lockett and Brett joined him on the Junior podium for a Norton 1–2–3, only Hinton's spill at Laurel Bank, where he sustained hand and knee injuries, dampening their mood slightly.

Ambrosini missed out on a second successive Lightweight win by just 8s when Tommy Wood's Moto Guzzi got the better of him, and the honour of being the first ever 125cc winner went to Mondial's Cromie McCandless. It was a clean sweep for the Italian manufacturer with teammates Carlo Ubbiali and Gianni Leoni joining McCandless on the podium.

Duke's TT success was now transferred onto the world stage, where he won both the 350cc and 500cc World Championships in 1951, and although Masetti and Gilera regained the latter the following year, the Italian manufacturer thus far resisted competing at the TT. MV Agusta were proving to be Norton's major competition on the island, having hired 1949 world champion Graham.

The 500cc MV was somewhat of a handful, but Graham claimed a good second in the 1952 Senior. It wasn't behind Duke, though, as he was forced to retire from the lead with clutch trouble at the end of lap four, Friday the thirteenth living up to its reputation as being unlucky for some.

Instead, it was teammate Reg Armstrong who took the win, and although Friday the thirteenth was unlucky for Duke, the opposite rang true for Armstrong, as his Norton's chain broke as he crossed the line. Rhodesian Ray Amm on another Norton finished third.

Duke had won the Junior race from Armstrong earlier in the week, with Italy again coming out on top in the smaller classes — Moto Guzzi and MV winning the 250cc and 125cc races with British riders Fergus Anderson and Cecil Sandford respectively. Anderson's win came after Italian teammate and race leader Bruno Ruffo, who broke the lap record on the second lap, ran into trouble on the final lap and dropped back to sixth.

> Duke and Armstrong 'defected' to Italy to ride for Gilera

There was big change in 1953 as both Duke and Armstrong 'defected' to Italy to ride for Gilera, the multi-cylinder machines now, arguably, the bike to beat in the 500cc category. Norton recruited Amm and Australian Ken Kavanagh to replace them, while Graham now had both 350cc and 500cc MV Agustas at his disposal. Germany also had an increased presence with DKW and NSU machinery, the latter being particularly strong in the smaller classes.

Graham was fastest in practice for the Junior, only to hit trouble on the opening lap with Rod Coleman leading on his AJS. A lap later the New Zealander and Amm were joint leaders, but next time around Coleman's oil tank split, and although Kavanagh briefly took over, Amm took the win by just 9.6s after seven hard-fought laps, Anderson taking third on an experimental Guzzi.

Anderson repeated his Lightweight victory of 1952, holding off the double-pronged German attack of Werner Haas (NSU) and Siegfried Wünsche (DKW), and Haas also had to settle for second in the 125cc race. Graham, who made his TT debut in 1938, took a much-deserved win with his MV Agusta teammate Sandford taking third.

MV Agusta
1951–2015
34 wins

▲ Flying high over Ballaugh Bridge – all six of John Surtees' TT victories came on MV Agusta machinery.

Few manufacturers embody the golden era of the Isle of Man TT quite like Italian brand MV Agusta. First arriving on the island in 1951, the marque combined artistry and innovation and proved dominant during the late 1950s, 1960s and 1970s, amassing a total of 34 victories around the Mountain Course.

MV Agusta's first TT triumph came in 1952, when Cecil Sandford claimed victory in the Ultra-Lightweight race. Les Graham repeated that feat the following year, and as the 1950s progressed riders such as Bill Lomas, Carlo Ubbiali and Tarquinio Provini all added their names to MV's winners list; their machines dominated the 125cc and 250cc categories.

The signing of John Surtees, who brought with him considerable engineering and design skills, helped transform MV Agusta's 350cc and 500cc fortunes, and the second half of the 1950s saw Surtees take six TT victories, with the same success in the World Championship.

Teammate John Hartle also played his part before Gary Hocking took over as team leader, and the signing of Mike Hailwood confirmed Count Agusta's intent of securing the best talent available. Hailwood was victorious in the 1962 Junior TT and 1963, 1964 and 1965 Senior TTs aboard the four-cylinder MV Agusta.

By 1966 another Italian giant, Giacomo Agostini, picked up the baton, and between 1966 and 1972 'Ago' and MV Agusta were virtually unstoppable at the TT, with the Italian maestro claiming ten victories. True, their opposition was limited, but Ago's pace and mastery of the Mountain Course was clear for all to see.

At the conclusion of the 1972 meeting, MV withdrew from TT competition, and while various riders have ridden an MV around the course since then – Martin Finnegan finished fourth in the 2007 Superstock race and Peter Hickman took eleventh in the second Supersport race of 2015 – the manufacturer has never experienced the same level of success again.

Nonetheless, while it may have been a long time since an MV rider has taken to the top step of a TT podium, the Italian brand's legacy remains unparalleled.

Just a day later Graham – who had flown Lancaster bombers during the Second World War and was awarded the Distinguished Flying Cross – was dead. The popular 41-year-old lost control of the MV Agusta on the second lap of the Senior as he took the rise just after the bottom of Bray Hill and was killed instantly.

Jammed forks were given as the reason, and the MV racing team withdrew from the rest of the year's World Championship as a mark of respect. The commemorative Graham Memorial shelter was subsequently built at Bungalow Bridge in 1955.

The race itself saw Duke get off to a cracking start and he quickly caught Amm, who'd started a minute ahead of him, on the road. Amm responded with a new lap record of 97.41mph and pressurised Duke into a rare mistake, the Brit coming to grief at Quarter Bridge on lap four.

The drama wasn't over, though, as Amm came off at Sarah's Cottage on the final lap. But any hopes Armstrong had of taking advantage were dashed when he was forced to stop at Ramsey to replace his chain. Amm remounted and

▼ New Zealander Rod Coleman won the 1954 Junior TT riding a 350cc AJS.

went on to complete the Junior-Senior double by 12s, with Brett runner-up on a second Norton and Armstrong third.

The following year's Senior was equally dramatic, with Amm and Duke and Norton and Gilera again going head to head. Hopes of the first ever 100mph lap were dashed by the weather, and Duke's opening lap was down at 88.18mph.

At the end of the second lap, Duke led Amm by 2s, and as he stopped for petrol at the end of lap three, Amm went straight through to lead by 28s with Armstong and Brett in third and fourth. The stewards then decided to stop the race at the end of lap four, so Amm took his second successive Senior win from Duke and Brett.

1954 saw several innovations, and sidecars returned to the meeting for the first time since 1925, despite objections from the manufacturers. A new course, the 10.79-mile Clypse Course, was used to accommodate them and the 125cc class, with both races taking place over ten laps.

> The Sidecar race saw Inge Stoll become the first female competitor at the TT

The Sidecar race saw Inge Stoll become the first female competitor at the TT, and she finished fifth with Jacques Drion, but it was Norton's Eric Oliver/Les Nutt who won ahead of the BMWs of Fritz Hillebrand/Manfred Grunwald, and Willi Noll/Fritz Cron.

Meanwhile, the NSU of Rupert Hollaus defeated the MVs of Ubbiali and Sandford in the 125cc race. Twenty-three-year-old Hollaus won the first four 125cc Grands Prix but was tragically killed in practice for the final round at Monza and became the first and only posthumous world champion.

At the TT, Coleman and AJS made up for retiring the year before by winning the Junior race; Amm had stopped at the thirteenth milestone on the fourth of five laps when holding a near-minute lead. The 250cc race was also reduced in length, from four laps to three, and NSU prevailed once more, the impressive Haas leading from start to finish as he beat teammates Hollaus, Armstrong and Hermann Paul Müller.

Regular British success in the Senior and Junior classes was put on hold as Norton and AJS announced the withdrawal of their factory machines, and the well-financed Italian factories took over. Amm switched to MV Agusta but the mouth-watering prospect of him battling with Duke and Gilera never materialised as he sadly died on his debut for MV at Monza in April 1955.

The popular Rhodesian's TT career was brief, spanning just eight races, but Amm won three of them, took third in another and set three lap records, so his impact cannot be underestimated.

Duke and Armstrong continued at Gilera and they duly took a 1–2 in the Senior, Duke winning by almost exactly two minutes, but the race will be remembered for a dramatic announcement after the Lancastrian was declared as having set the first ever 100mph lap of the Mountain Course. Just minutes later, it was announced that the lap was 99.97mph, although for years afterwards many felt that 'morally' Geoff had set the first ton-up lap.

Kavanagh had finished third in the Senior on his Moto Guzzi and was well-placed in the Junior, which was back up to seven laps, only to retire at Ballaugh

The Clypse Course

The year 1954 saw several innovations at the TT, including the return of the Sidecar class to the event for the first time since 1925. The Mountain Course was deemed too punishing for the three-wheelers so a new course, the Clypse Course, came into being.

The sidecars and 125cc machines were to use the new 10.79-mile course, with both races to be held over ten laps – the 250cc class was introduced to the course the following year when all races were cut to nine laps. The move came at considerable expense to the ACU thanks to the duplication of safety and maintenance tasks, and rumours circulated that at some stage all classes would switch to the Clypse Course. Thankfully, these proved untrue.

The start and finish was on Glencrutchery Road, just like the Mountain Course, but instead of going past St Ninian's crossroads and heading down Bray Hill towards Quarter Bridge, the course turned right at Parkfield Corner onto Ballanard Road.

After half a mile, it turned right again at Willaston Corner and wound its way up Johnny Watterson's Lane, including the sharp left and right Edge's Corner, named after early TT car racer Selwyn Edge, to Cronk-ny-Mona where it joined the Mountain Course.

However, it did so in reverse down towards Hillberry and up to Brandish all the way to the Creg-ny-Baa. Here, the course turned right for a two-mile narrow stretch down Ballacarrooin Hill and past the highest part of the course (856 feet above sea level) onto Ballacour Corner, where the course reached its halfway point and once again made a tight right turn, known locally as Five and a Half Mile Corner.

Another two-mile stretch, including a short climb, saw riders head towards Laxey, taking in the swooping Cronk-y-Garroo right-hander and heading past Ennemona towards Morney Corner. There followed a left-hander at Begoade before a hard right at Hall Corner, the eight-mile mark, saw the course join the Laxey to Douglas road.

Passing Ballakilmartin and plunging down White Bridge Hill, the course rose uphill again as it headed into Onchan village, where it took a sharp right at the Manx Arms public house. Through the Nursery Bends, this stretch of road took the riders to Signpost Corner, where they turned left to rejoin the Mountain Course, taking in Bedstead, the Nook and Governor's Bridge and missing out the dip, before heading back onto Glencrutchery Road.

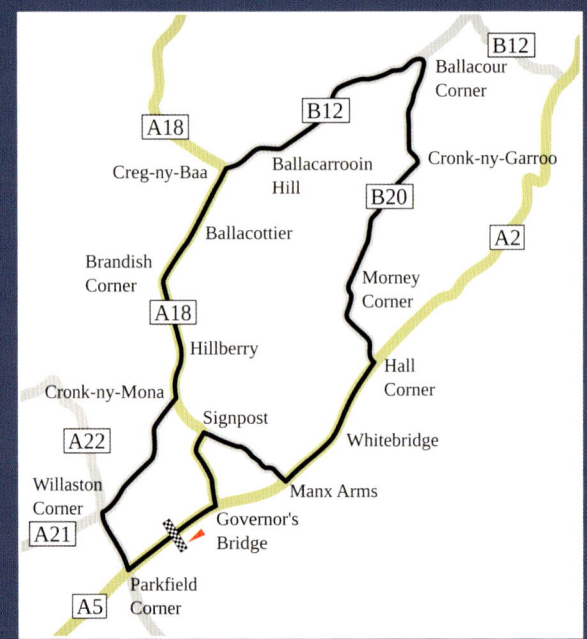

The first year of action saw Rupert Hollaus (125cc) and Eric Oliver/Les Nutt (Sidecar) victorious, with Hollaus setting the fastest lap at 9min 3.4s, 71.53mph. The lap record for 125s on the Mountain Course was 78.21mph, which highlighted the twisting nature of the Clypse Course.

In 1957, all three races had the distance increased back up to ten laps, and Tarquinio Provini set a new lap record of exactly 78mph in the 250cc

▲ Carlo Ubbiali, Tarqunio Provini, Bob Brown and Mike Hailwood battle on the Clypse Course during the 1958 Lightweight race.
▶ The twisty and technical 10.79-mile Clypse Course used some of the existing Mountain Course before heading through the streets of Onchan.

race before retiring. However, the Italian, along with fellow countryman Carlo Ubbiali, proved to be a master of the circuit and both riders took four victories, primarily for MV Agusta. Walter Schneider/Hans Strauss dominated the Sidecar class with three wins.

In 1959, Provini set what would prove to be the final lap record, his victory over Ubbiali in the 250cc race seeing him lap at 8min 0.4s, 80.22mph.

At the conclusion of the 1959 TT, it was deemed that the Clypse Course had become surplus to requirements and it was more practical to run all five races on the Mountain Course rather than just the Senior and Junior. This proved to be a popular decision with competitors and spectators alike.

The Clypse Course had served its purpose, but its bumpy and twisting nature didn't make it a rider's favourite, certainly not when compared to the fast and flowing Mountain Course, and spectators found viewing points limited on the most challenging northern section of the course. Few mourned its loss, although it certainly has its place in TT history, as it was 1959 when Honda made their debut in the 125cc race.

The Clypse Course was never used again for racing after 1959, although some parts of the course have been used for cycle racing, hill-climb events and classic car racing. The Manx Rally and Rally Isle of Man also used parts of the course, including the B12 Creg-ny-Baa 'back road' and the B20 Begoade Road. Notably, in 17 races across six years of action on the Clypse Course, there were no fatalities.

Carlo Ubbiali

▲ Italian ace Carlo Ubbiali was an undisputed master of the 125cc and 250cc machines.

From	Bergamo, Italy
Years Active	1951–1960
Wins	5
Podiums	12
Fastest Lap	95.51mph
Manufacturers	MV Agusta, Mondial

Born in 1929, Carlo Ubbiali finished fourth in the inaugural 125cc World Championship, and for the next decade he proved to be the ultimate master of the lightweight machines.

Riding for Mondial, Ubbiali took his first Grand Prix victory at the 1950 Ulster GP, and a year later he claimed his first world title with victory in the 125cc division. He made his TT debut in 1951, claiming second place in the two-lap 125cc race on the Mountain Course.

In 1953 he returned to MV Agusta, the brand he's most associated with, and over the next eight years he competed against and beat the very best, including the likes of Cecil Sandford, Werner Haas, Luigi Taveri and MV teammates Tarquinio Provini and Gary Hocking.

Ubbiali took several world titles, including 125cc-250cc doubles on three occasions, and while his World Championship success wasn't quite replicated at the TT, it wasn't far off. Five wins and 12 podiums showed his talent.

An ultimate tactician, Ubbiali was always able to extract the most from his machinery while maintaining reliability, and he took four wins in total on the Clypse Course. He also proved he could master the Mountain Course, setting two lap records in 1960 alongside victory in the 125cc race.

However, after turning down lucrative offers from Honda, Ubbiali announced his retirement at the end of the year aged just 29 and, with 39 GP wins, still very much at the peak of his powers. By then he'd accumulated nine world titles, and despite the fact that he retired more than 60 years ago that tally remains bettered by only two riders, Giacomo Agostini and Angel Nieto.

on lap four. Bob McIntyre and his Joe Potts-prepared Norton led after four laps, but Bill Lomas on a second Guzzi took over and never relinquished the lead as he beat McIntyre by exactly a minute. Sandford finished third on yet another Guzzi.

Over on the Clypse Course, Lomas was also victorious in the 250cc race, which had moved from the Mountain Course, but this time on an MV Agusta. Sandford led for much of the race, but when Lomas took over on lap seven Cecil crashed as he tried to regain the lead. He remounted but Lomas was 51.2s ahead at the chequered flag, with NSU's Müller taking another podium in third.

BMW's domination of the Sidecar class, which would last for two decades, got underway with eventual world champions Walter Schneider/Hans Strauss winning from the British outfits headed by Bill Boddice and Pip Harris, while two World Championship greats, Carlo Ubbiali and Luigi Taveri, finished first and second for MV Agusta in the 125cc race. It was Ubbiali's first TT win, and he and Taveri would rack up 69 Grand Prix wins and 157 podiums between them.

After the loss of Amm, MV Agusta signed young up-and-coming British rider John Surtees to challenge Duke and Gilera for both the 1956 350cc and 500cc World Championships, but Gilera suffered a blow when Duke had to serve a six-month ban at the start of the season for supporting a strike by privateer riders over start money at the 1955 Dutch TT.

Surtees was just 22, and he and MV had a dream start to their 500cc World Championship campaign when they won the Senior TT after leading from start to finish. Both Lomas, fastest in practice on his Moto Guzzi, and McIntyre occupied second at one stage, but McIntyre retired at Crosby and problems on the final lap saw Lomas drop back to fifth, so the Nortons of John Hartle and the consistent Jack Brett joined Surtees on the podium.

> Surtees was just 22, and he and MV had a dream start to their 500cc World Championship campaign

Lomas had also topped the practice leaderboard in the Junior class, and he led Surtees at the end of the opening lap by 23s, the gap extending to 50s on the fifth of seven laps when Ken Kavanagh moved up to third. Lap six saw Lomas retire at Guthrie's Memorial and Kavanagh closed to within three-fifths of a second of new race leader Surtees. But John retired at the Stonebreaker's Hut on the last lap, which meant Kavanagh took his, and Australia's, first TT win.

The Clypse Course continued to play host to the three other classes. Former Luftwaffe pilot Fritz Hillebrand, having finished second on his debut two years before, claimed victory with Manfred Grunwald in the Sidecar class, and Ubbiali and MV Agusta completed a 250cc-125cc double after seeing off the challenge of Sammy Miller (NSU) and teammate Roberto Colombo in the 250, and the Spanish Montesa pairing of Cama and Gonzalez in the 125.

1957 saw the TT celebrate its Golden Jubilee and it proved to be a memorable week on the island with superb weather seeing the lap records broken in every class. The only significant change to previous years came in the Senior race, which was upped from seven laps to eight. The 301-mile race remains the longest ever seen in the World Championship.

▲ Bob McIntyre (Gilera) leads John Surtees (MV Agusta) on his way to a record-breaking victory in the 1957 Senior TT.

The thousands of fans who had flocked to the island were again denied a Duke v Surtees battle after Duke crashed at Imola over the Easter weekend and was unable to compete. Gilera responded by signing Scottish ace McIntyre and Australia's Bob Brown as they looked to regain the 500cc title that Surtees and MV Agusta both won for the first time in 1956.

McIntyre and Brown got the week off to a great start for Gilera, finishing first and third in the Junior race with eventual world champion Keith Campbell (Moto Guzzi) splitting them in second. McIntyre set a new lap record of 97.42mph with Surtees finishing fourth after Campbell's teammate Dickie Dale and Norton's Hartle crashed at Quarry Bends.

The ultimate moment of McIntyre's career came in the Senior a few days later. Conditions were perfect and, starting at number 78, his first lap was 99.99mph. But expectant fans didn't have to wait long for history to be made, and lap two

John Surtees

▲ John Surtees (right) with his 500cc Norton at the 1954 TT, the year he made his debut on the Mountain Course.

From	Tatsfield, England
Years Active	1954–1960
Wins	6
Podiums	8
Fastest Lap	104.08mph
Manufacturers	MV Agusta, Norton

John Surtees, son of Jack Surtees, a successful sidecar racer, started racing on the grass before he switched to the tarmac in 1951. After initially enjoying success on a 500cc Vincent Grey Flash, he invested in a 500cc Manx Norton that saw him win countless national races in the UK.

On his Norton and 250cc NSU, Surtees won 65 of the 72 races he entered in 1954, which brought him to the attention of the factory Norton team, although in 1955 their machinery didn't match the considerable talent of Surtees.

Ambitious, determined and sometimes forthright in his opinions, Surtees could see that the British machine had fallen behind its Italian counterparts, and when he was offered a works ride in 1956 with the MV Agusta factory he needed no second invitation. His first TT win came in that year's Senior.

He was also technically gifted and an outstanding engineer, and after playing second fiddle to Bob McIntyre and Gilera at the 1957 TT, Surtees won both the Senior and Junior races in 1958, repeating the feat the following year. Gearbox trouble saw him finish second to MV teammate John Hartle in the 1960 Junior, but he responded with a new lap record and victory in the Senior.

The MVs were far superior to the opposition, but Surtees, always immaculate and measured, was almost invincible on his Norton. After six TT wins and six world titles, he quit two wheels for Formula One at the end of the 1960 season, aged just 26. Success followed him there, and he remains the only man in history to win world titles on both two and four wheels.

Golden Jubilee Meeting Sees McIntyre Set First 100mph Lap

1957

As soon as Freddie Frith set the first 90mph lap of the Mountain Course in 1937, speculation turned to when the magical 100mph barrier would be broken. However, the Second World War and the use of low-octane petrol when racing resumed in 1947 meant it would take longer than expected to reach that milestone.

The fierce rivalry between the British and Italian manufacturers in the early 1950s resulted in speeds climbing again, and Geoff Duke and Gilera thought they'd cracked the ton in 1955. Timekeepers incorrectly announced that he'd lapped at exactly 100mph on lap three of the Senior before the speed was downgraded to 99.97mph.

In 1957, the year the TT celebrated its Golden Jubilee, conditions were perfect all week. Although Duke was absent through injury, Scottish Bob McIntyre took his place on the brilliantly engineered Gileras, and with teammate Bob Brown he set to do battle with the sole MV Agusta of reigning world champion John Surtees.

To celebrate its fiftieth anniversary, the Senior race distance was increased to eight laps. Despite starting at number 78, which meant he had to encounter a lot of traffic, McIntyre – who had won the Junior earlier in the week – set a fierce pace on the opening lap with a time of 22min 38.4s, just two-fifths of a second away from the first 100mph lap.

Neither McIntyre nor the thousands of spectators had to wait long, though, as he hunted down Surtees, who had started at number 64. McIntyre put his name in the history books forever when his second lap was clocked at 101.03mph, and the crowd went wild when the speed was announced.

With his lead over Surtees more than a minute, McIntyre pushed on, and after lapping at 100.54mph on lap three, the next circuit saw him set the fastest lap of the race at 101.12mph. Another 100mph+ average was set on lap six, and after more than three hours of racing Bob eventually won the race by more than two minutes, his average speed for the eight laps 98.99mph.

▲ Pictured at the bottom of Bray Hill, Bob McIntyre set the first ever 100mph lap of the Mountain Course during the 1957 Senior race.

▲ Fred Taylor leads the pack through Parkfield Corner at the start of the 1957 Sidecar race.

saw the Scot clock a speed of 101.03mph to record the first 100mph lap of the Mountain Course and enter the history books forever.

In total, four 100mph+ laps were set by the 'Flying Scot', the best of which was 101.12mph on lap four, as he led from start to finish to defeat Surtees by over two minutes. Brown completed Gilera's celebrations in third as Dale brought the mighty V8 Moto Guzzi home in fourth.

Mondial claimed the bragging rights in the 250cc and 125cc races on the Clypse Course, with Sandford and another rapid Italian, Tarquinio Provini, emerging victorious while Hillebrand/Grunwald took their second successive Sidecar victory. Sandford's victory came when Sammy Miller crashed his NSU at Governor's Bridge in sight of the finishing line.

However, 1957 would mark the end of a golden era in motorcycle racing. The impressive variety of machinery competing during the 1950s, which included works teams from AJS, Norton, Gilera, MV Agusta, Moto Guzzi and BMW, had seen the factories compete with singles, twins and multi-cylinder machines, and it had made for some extreme competition.

The German NSU manufacturer withdrew in 1956 and the Italian firms did likewise at the end of the 1957 season, announcing that they would be pulling out of racing, with escalating costs and dwindling motorcycle sales given as the reason.

All but MV Agusta went through with their decision to quit, and with their competition gone the Italian firm dominated for the next few years – and in the 500cc class for a lot longer than that. Dominance on the world stage was mirrored at the TT, but the competition received a boost, in the smaller classes at least, with the introduction of two-strokes, a German company called MZ being the first to score points.

At the 1958 TT dustbin fairings were banned due to their instability in crosswinds, and MV's domination was clear as their multi-cylinder machines could not be matched by the British singles. With Surtees and Hartle spearheading their 350cc and 500cc attack and the Italian pairing of Ubbiali and Provini doing likewise in the 125cc and 250cc categories, MV had both the best riders and the best bikes.

Success for MV in the Junior and Senior races on the Mountain Course looked to be a foregone conclusion, and sure enough Surtees won both; Hartle was forced to retire on each occasion, his MV spectacularly catching fire and burning out on the exit of Governor's Dip in the Senior race.

The Norton privateers, which now included Duke, McIntyre and Brown, were in their own race for second, with Bob Anderson and Dave Chadwick taking the runners-up positions in the Senior and Junior respectively.

Close racing looked more likely on the Clypse Course due to its shorter length and twistier layout, but the 250cc and 125cc races still went the way of MV, for Provini and Ubbiali respectively. A new name appeared on the 125cc podium as a young Mike Hailwood finished third, with Schneider/Strauss getting back to their winning ways in the Sidecar race.

The following year saw an almost exact repeat of the results, with Surtees again taking a Senior-Junior double, the former coming despite rain lashing down in the second half of the race. This caused lap times to plummet, and riders needed treatment for hypothermia at the race's conclusion. Hartle had earlier come to grief at Glen Vine, but he did finish second to Surtees in the Junior.

> A new name appeared on the 125cc podium as a young Mike Hailwood finished third

In 1959 two new races were added to the schedule: the Formula One 500cc and 350cc for machines bought over the counter. That ruled out the Italian multis, so it was essentially an excuse for the British manufacturers to get some glory. It was held over three laps of the Mountain Course, and McIntyre and fellow Scot Alistair King took the spoils.

Another change in 1959 was that it was the last year of racing on the Clypse Course. Provini won both the 250cc and 125cc races for MV Agusta ahead of teammate Ubbiali in the 250cc race and Luigi Taveri's MZ – team owner Walter Kaaden having made a significant breakthrough in two-stroke performance – in the 125cc encounter, where Hailwood was again on the podium, this time riding a Ducati. Earlier in the week he had been third in the Formula One 350cc race on a Norton. The sidecars had the honour of competing on the course for the final time, with Schneider/Strauss taking their third win.

Luigi Taveri

▲ Popular Swiss rider Luigi Taveri enjoyed a long and distinguished career, both at the TT and in the World Championship.

From	Zurich, Switzerland
Years Active	1955–1966
Wins	3
Podiums	12
Fastest Lap	95mph approx.
Manufacturers	Honda, MV Agusta, Ducati, MZ, Kreidler

Although best known as a small-bike specialist, Luigi Taveri made his World Championship debut in the 500cc class in 1954; he also acted as passenger for Hans Haldemann in the Sidecar class. He has a permanent place in history as the only rider to have scored points in six Grand Prix classes: 50cc, 125cc, 250cc, 350cc, 500cc and Sidecar.

The Swiss rider was approached by MV Agusta for the 1955 season and won his first Grand Prix at Montjuich Park, Spain. Just over a month later he made his TT debut on the Clypse Course, where he retired from the 250cc race but finished second, by just two seconds, to teammate Carlo Ubbiali in the 125cc race.

From that moment on, Taveri was almost always on the leaderboard, and after four seasons with MV, accompanied by short spells with Ducati and MZ, he moved to Honda in 1961.

Honda is where Taveri is most fondly remembered; as well as winning the 125cc World Championship on three occasions – 1962, 1964 and 1966 – he was also a three-time winner at the TT, with victories in the 1962 and 1964 125cc races and the 50cc race in 1965. In total, Taveri stood on a TT podium on 12 occasions.

With Honda on the verge of withdrawing, Taveri decided to retire at the end of the 1966 season. Despite facing stiff opposition from the likes of Ubbiali, Tarquinio Provini, Jim Redman, Phil Read and Hugh Anderson throughout, he ended with three World Championships, 30 Grand Prix wins and 89 podiums.

Perhaps the most significant event of the 1959 TT was not who won the races, or where they took place, but the appearance of new machinery: the unknown Honda brand. Soichiro Honda had first visited the TT in 1954 and returned home with the intention of competing, and winning, at the TT.

It took Honda five years to fulfil his dream of competing at the TT, and his machines and Japanese riders were nowhere near as strong as the opposition. But they were well engineered and reliable, and with sixth, seventh and eighth they took the team prize and made the racing world take note. Honda realised plenty of work was still to be done to enable his machines to compete for the win, and he would need to employ star riders, but success would come quickly.

◀ Honda made their TT debut in 1959 with Naomi Taniguchi finishing a fine sixth in the Ultra-Lightweight 125cc race.
▼ John Hartle was a formidable teammate to John Surtees at MV Agusta and deservedly won the 1960 Junior race.

Mike Hailwood

▲ A pensive-looking Mike Hailwood ahead of the 1978 Formula One race. Hailwood won the race in a sporting comeback still talked about today.

From	Oxford, England
Years Active	1958–1979
Wins	14
Podiums	19
Fastest Lap	114.12mph
Manufacturers	Norton, MV Agusta, Honda, Ducati, Suzuki, Yamaha, Mondial, Paton, AJS, NSU, Benelli, EMC

It's almost 60 years since Mike Hailwood last won a Grand Prix and 47 years since his final victory at the Isle of Man TT, but he's still regarded by many as the greatest motorcycle rider ever to have lived.

That speaks volumes of the talent Hailwood possessed, and although he was given a helping hand at the start of his career by his millionaire father Stan, who bought him the best bikes available, it was Mike riding the bike and twisting the throttle.

Hailwood started racing in 1957 and a year later made his TT debut, competing in all four solo races. His best result that year was a brilliant third place in the 250cc race.

Equally at ease on a 125 as he was on a 500, Hailwood was competitive on whatever bike he rode, and in 1961 he became the first rider to win three TT races in a week. A move to MV Agusta followed, and he won three consecutive Senior races from 1963 to 1965.

Switching to Honda, Hailwood claimed a second hat-trick in 1967, but when the Japanese manufacturer withdrew from racing Mike retired before embarking on a successful four-wheel career.

Injury curtailed his car-racing aspirations but the lure of the TT remained, and in 1978 he returned to the Mountain Course, his victory in the Formula One race going down in sporting folklore. A further victory came in the 1979 Senior as well as a close second in the Classic.

After doing battle on some of the world's most dangerous circuits, Hailwood was killed in a car crash in April 1981, along with his nine-year-old daughter Michelle, when a lorry driver carried out an illegal U-turn on a dual carriageway.

With all classes reverting to the Mountain Course in 1960, the programme was re-jigged and the 125cc, Sidecar (both three laps) and 250cc (five laps) races all took place on a busy Monday. The Junior race moved to Wednesday and the Senior remained on Friday; both races were reduced to six laps with the riders starting in pairs at ten-second intervals in all classes.

Surtees and MV took their third successive Senior victory, two and a half minutes clear of teammate Hartle, with Hailwood taking third on his Norton. The similarly mounted Derek Minter set the first 100mph lap by a single-cylinder machine, a feat Hailwood also achieved, and Surtees upped the lap record to 104.08mph.

Hartle finally got the better of Surtees in the Junior race for his first TT win, taking the lead on the fifth lap; McIntyre ran third throughout on his AJS. MV Agusta also dominated the smaller classes, with Ubbiali adding a Mountain Course victory to those he'd already racked up on the Clypse Course, coming home almost 20s clear of his new Rhodesian teammate Gary Hocking.

Hocking was rapidly making a name for himself in racing circles, having finished joint second on an MZ in the previous year's 250cc World Championship. In just his second year at the TT he won the Lightweight race from Ubbiali, who set another lap record, and Provini, who was now riding a Morini. The Sidecar race was won by Helmut Fath/Alfred Wohlgemuth after long-time leader Florian Camathias dropped to fifth on the final lap.

At the end of the 1960 season both Surtees and Ubbiali retired from two-wheel racing, despite being in their racing prime, aged just 26 and 29 respectively, paving the way for new stars to emerge.

In 1961 the World Championship was expanded to 11 rounds, although only the 125 and 250s raced at each. MV Agusta promoted Hocking up to the 500cc class, and withdrew from the 125cc and 250cc classes, where Honda were rapidly making strides forward.

> Derek Minter set the first 100mph lap by a single-cylinder machine

As well as having a factory team, Honda also leased machinery to various importers, resulting in a glittering array of talent riding their machines at the 1961 TT, including Hailwood, McIntyre, Taveri, Jim Redman and Tom Phillis.

Indeed, not only did Soichiro Honda realise his dream of winning a TT race in 1961, but Hondas won both the 125cc and 250cc races and took all three steps of the podium in each; Hailwood won on each occasion to claim his first TT victories. The 125cc race was close, though, as Taveri was only 7.4s adrift at the chequered flag as Phillis took third.

McIntyre set a new lap record of 99.58mph in the 250cc race as he opened a lead of more than 30s over Hailwood. But luck deserted Bob on the final lap as he was forced out at Sulby with engine trouble. That gave Hailwood a comfortable lead and he won from Phillis and Redman as Honda filled the first five places.

The threat from Japanese manufacturers was growing all the time, and rapidly too. Suzuki had made their TT debut a year after Honda with a focus on the smaller classes, and in 1961 it was Yamaha's turn, Fumio Ito taking sixth

▲ Bob McIntyre, pictured at Whitegates, led the 1961 Lightweight 250cc race after setting a new lap record of 99.58mph, but retired on the final lap.

in the 250cc race for the manufacturer more readily associated with musical instruments. Another defining moment came later in the year when Phillis clinched the 125cc World Championship to give Honda its first title.

Back to the 1961 TT and Hocking and MV were clear favourites for the Junior and Senior races. A new lap record of 99.80mph saw him lead the Junior by more than a minute after the first two laps. On lap three his lead was reduced, and when he stopped for fuel he also changed a plug, which lost him more time, allowing Hailwood to take over.

Just when it looked like Hailwood would take the first ever hat-trick, a gudgeon pin broke on his AJS, forcing him to retire, but it wasn't Hocking who won. Instead, 22-year-old Phil Read, competing in his first TT after winning the 1960 Senior Manx Grand Prix, won by more than a minute from Hocking to take his maiden TT victory.

Hailwood's Hat-trick
1961

After Wal Handley became the first rider to win two TT races in a week in 1925, only a select few were able to match his achievement over the next few decades, including Tim Hunt, Stanley Woods, Jimmie Guthrie, Geoff Duke, Bob McIntyre and Ray Amm. But the wait for the first ever hat-trick continued.

Handley himself had come close to three wins in a week, retiring from the Lightweight while holding onto a comfortable lead, but the increase in races during the 1950s, as well as improved reliability, meant three wins in a week was now a more realistic proposition.

Mike Hailwood's Isle of Man TT career started in 1958, and he immediately demonstrated his versatility when he finished inside the top 15 of the Senior, Junior, Lightweight and Ultra-Lightweight races. By 1961 his star was getting brighter all the time. Still only 21, Mike had factory Hondas at his disposal for the Lightweight 250 and Ultra-Lightweight 125cc races and he made it count, winning both, the latter by just 7.4s from teammate Luigi Taveri.

Both victories were taken on the same day, and when pre-race favourite Gary Hocking ran into trouble on his MV Agusta, Mike took over the lead of the Junior. His lead over Phil Read after five laps was more than two minutes, but with just 14 miles of the race to go his AJS ground to a halt. The hat-trick would have to wait.

However, he didn't have to wait long. Luck again deserted Hocking at half-race distance, when he was forced to retire with a sticking throttle despite having a lead of almost 30 seconds. This allowed Hailwood and his Norton to take over, and he went on to win the race from Bob McIntyre and Tom Phillis in a Norton 1–2–3, duly becoming the first rider to win three TTs in a week. He repeated the feat in 1967, but it was another 18 years before it was done again, when Joey Dunlop won three races in 1985.

▲ 1961 Ultra-Lightweight 125cc race winner Hailwood celebrates with Honda teammates Tom Phillis (left) and Luigi Taveri (middle).

Hailwood didn't have to wait long for his place in the history books, as two days later he won the Senior to complete his hat-trick. Hocking again led in the early stages, and his lead was up to 30s after three laps, but he retired at the pits with a sticking throttle at the end of the fifth lap. Hailwood and his Norton took over and won comfortably from the similarly mounted McIntyre and Phillis.

The Sidecar class, which had now attracted almost 40 entries, was again dominated by BMW, with Max Deubel/Emil Horner taking a record-breaking start-to-finish victory over Fritz Scheidegger/Horst Burkhardt. Deubel and Scheidegger would do battle at both the TT and the World Championship for the next six years.

Continuing the theme of having the best riders on their bikes, MV Agusta signed Hailwood on a full-time basis alongside Hocking for the 1962 season. The slightly older Hocking – 24 to Hailwood's 22 – had won the 350cc and 500cc world titles the year before and was named team leader. The firm now focused their efforts solely on the 350cc and 500cc classes, where the horde of British single-cylinder machines would again be outgunned.

The 125cc and 250cc classes, as well as the new-for-1962 50cc race, were now the domain of the Japanese, and Honda were considered the ones to beat as Suzuki and Yamaha sought to close the gap with their more experienced rivals. Despite their distinct lack of finance, the East German MZ company continued to battle gamely.

MZ were hit hard by the defection to the West by their lead rider and engineer Ernst Degner, who took many of Walter Kaaden's secrets with him to Suzuki. This gave Suzuki a major advantage and Degner duly won the inaugural 50cc TT race ahead of Taveri and Tommy Robb's Hondas. Degner's fastest lap of 75.52mph astounded the critics and he went on to win the world title.

> Continuing the theme of having the best riders on their bikes, MV Agusta signed Hailwood for the 1962 season

Chris Vincent ended seven years of BMW domination with victory for BSA in the Sidecar race, where Max Deubel retired and Florian Camathias crashed, but Honda were still dominant in the 125cc and 250cc races, with Taveri and Derek Minter winning and sharing the podium with Robb, Redman and Phillis. Minter wasn't a member of Honda's works team but rode a machine loaned to him by the British Honda importer instead; Honda weren't overjoyed to have been beaten by essentially a privateer!

Tragedy struck in the Junior, though, when Phillis, riding a bored-out 285cc Honda in a bid to get the better of the MVs, crashed on the approach to Laurel Bank on the second lap trying to keep up, sustaining fatal injuries. Hailwood won his first race for MV just 5s ahead of Hocking.

Hocking got his revenge in the Senior, where he set a new lap record of 105.75mph as clutch trouble relegated Hailwood from second to twelfth. However, Hocking was so affected by the death of his close friend Phillis that he quit the sport mid-season, turning his back on more world titles and the riches that came with it.

Gary Hocking

▲ Gary Hocking had a short but brilliant career.

From	Bulawayo, Rhodesia (now Zimbabwe) (born: Newport, Wales)
Years Active	1959–1962
Wins	2
Podiums	5
Fastest Lap	105.75mph
Manufacturers	MV Agusta, Norton

Gary Hocking's TT career spanned just four years and eight races, but in that time he more than proved he had all the attributes to become a multiple TT winner and world champion.

Born in Newport, Wales, Hocking was just seven when he moved to Rhodesia with his family, where he honed his skills first on grass tracks and then on the road racing circuits. At the age of 20 he headed to Europe and was quickly snapped up by MZ, finishing second in the 1959 250cc World Championship.

MV Agusta recognised his obvious talent and secured his services in 1960. In his second TT race, the 125cc, Hocking finished runner-up to his vastly more experienced teammate Carlo Ubbiali. Just a few hours later he turned the tables on the Italian, winning the 250cc race for his maiden TT victory.

In 1961, MV restricted Hocking to the 350cc and 500cc classes. He was the hot favourite for Senior and Junior TT honours, but reliability issues denied him the opportunity and second in the Junior was all he had to show for his efforts. He did, however, win both world titles.

The following year saw Hocking set lap and race records on his way to winning the Senior TT and taking second place once more in the Junior. However, Hocking's close friend Tom Phillis died in the race and that, along with MV's controlling management style, led the quietly spoken rider to quit the sport immediately after the TT.

Hocking switched to car racing and was on his way to joining Formula One when, only six months after his final TT win, he was killed at the Natal Grand Prix aged just 25.

▲ The first three in the 1962 Junior TT: František Šťastný (3rd), Mike Hailwood (1st) and Gary Hocking (2nd).

The double world champion felt too many riders were losing their lives and switched to the safer confines of car racing, where he soon made his mark. Ironically, he died at the Natal Grand Prix just six months after his Senior TT victory.

MV Agusta cut back further in 1963, running just Hailwood in the 500cc and 350cc classes, but the MV was finding the going tough in the 350cc, where Honda were now in the ascendancy. Only the 500cc class was yet to be included in their impressive repertoire. Indeed, 1962 had seen Honda win the 125cc, 250cc and 350cc World Championships with Redman and Taveri.

Redman was the man to beat in the 250cc and 350cc divisions, and in 1963 he won both races at the TT, but the big story of the year was the return of Gilera managed by Geoff Duke, former hero of the Arcore factory. Hartle and Minter were recruited in their bid to topple the mighty MV, although a short circuit crash ruled Minter out of the TT and he was replaced by Phil Read.

However, with the only changes being new tyres, suspension and fairing, the six-year-old bikes were no match for the MVs or Hondas in the 350cc class, and Redman defeated Hartle and the Czech Jawa of František Šťastný. Redman also won the 250cc race ahead of a spirited challenge from Yamaha's Ito, the first of his three TT doubles. Ito's teammate Tony Godfrey made headlines when, after crashing heavily at Milntown, he was the first rider to be taken to hospital by helicopter.

The Gileras were more competitive in the 500cc class, particularly in the hands of Hartle, and Hailwood's lead in the Senior race was only 8s after the first lap. A new lap record of 106.41mph, however, saw him pull clear and Hartle and Read had to settle for second and third respectively. The Gileras were put back into mothballs at the end of the season.

Honda had underestimated the challenge of Suzuki in the 50cc and 125cc classes, with Hugh Anderson winning the 125cc race and going on to win the world title ahead of Suzuki teammates Frank Perris and Degner. Anderson finished second in the 50cc race, which was increased from two laps to three, after leader Degner retired on the final lap, and Mitsuo Itoh etched his name in the record books as he became the first Japanese rider to win a TT.

Once again BMW dominated the Sidecar race as Florian Camathias/Alfred Herzig took the lead from teammates Fritz Scheidegger/John Robinson on the second lap.

▼  Leading British privateer Alan Shepherd (Matchless) was forced to retire from fifth place on the final lap of the 1963 Senior TT.

Swain Becomes First Female Solo Competitor
1962

Although the Isle of Man TT Races first fired into life in 1907, it wasn't until 1954 that the first female competitor appeared, when German Inge Stoll partnered Jacques Drion to a fine fifth place in the Sidecar TT. It would be another eight years before the TT saw a female rider contest a solo race for the first time.

That honour fell to London's Beryl Swain. Born in Walthamstow in 1936, Swain worked as a senior secretary at P&O in the City. In 1958 she married Edwin Swain, a motorcycle shop owner, and from that point her passion for bikes developed rapidly.

Swain was a regular competitor in the 50cc class at Brands Hatch and Snetterton, the bike being ideal for her diminutive stature, and when the TT hosted the first ever 50cc World Championship race in 1962, Swain swiftly entered.

▲ The history-making Beryl Swain rounds Governor's Bridge on her Itom during the 1962 50cc race.

The move wasn't without controversy; indeed, Swain faced many hurdles from within the male-dominated world. But there was no rule to say a female couldn't compete, so she duly lined up on Glencrutchery Road on her 50cc Itom and went on to finish twenty-second out of 25 finishers. She would have finished higher too, had the Itom not lost the top gear of its three-speed transmission on the second lap.

However, this wouldn't represent the start of an international career for Swain, as organisers quickly moved to prevent Swain or any other female competitors entering. Swain's licence was revoked and the organisers introduced a new minimum weight rule in 1963, stating that the TT was too dangerous for women. Swain appealed the decision to no avail.

Unable to meet the weight limit, Swain had no option but to retire, and the ban on female solo riders at the TT continued until Hilary Musson contested the Formula Three race in 1978. Swain's racing career dwindled away and she went on to work for Sainsbury's as a departmental manager in London. She died in 2007 aged 71.

▲ Fritz Scheidegger/John Robinson (500cc BMW) finished second in the 1963 Sidecar race but would go on to win three years later.

The format for 1964 remained the same with two races each day – Monday, Wednesday and Friday – but both Camathias and Scheidegger were out of luck in the Sidecar race and reigning world champions Deubel/Horner repeated their 1961 victory.

Yamaha now had a greater presence in the 125cc and 250cc classes, having signed Read and Canadian Mike Duff; Read would go on to become world champion in the larger-capacity class after a year-long battle with Redman. At the TT, though, Redman came out on top after Read retired from the lead on the fifth lap, and Alan Shepherd (MZ) and Alberto Pagani (Paton) finished second and third.

Redman also won the Junior race, where Hailwood was a non-starter due to illness, in a stunning field of 103 entries. Read and Duff, riding private AJS machines in the 350cc class, joined Redman on the podium and Honda also won the 125cc race with Taveri leading home team leader Redman – by just 3s – and Northern Ireland's Ralph Bryans.

Bryans had to settle for second in the 50cc race, where Suzuki's Anderson was victorious. Hailwood was passed fit for the Senior, and in a comfortable race he led from start to finish, his eventual winning margin over Minter more than three minutes.

The 50cc class was arguably the most innovative of the time, with a fierce battle raging between Honda and Suzuki. The smaller the engine, the narrower the powerband; ten-speed gearboxes were common, and 15 or even 18 speeds were not unheard of.

At the 1965 TT Honda were back on top as Taveri defeated the Suzukis of Anderson and Degner, although seven finishers highlighted just how fickle the tiny machines were around the Mountain Course.

Jim Redman

▲ Jim Redman, with son Jimmy, after winning the 1964 Junior race.

From	Bulawayo, Rhodesia (now Zimbabwe) (born: London, England)
Years Active	1958–1965
Wins	6
Podiums	9
Fastest Lap	101.8mph
Manufacturers	Honda, Norton

Redman was born in London in 1931 and emigrated to Rhodesia when he was 18. After winning the 1957 South African 350cc Championship, he returned to Britain the following year armed with a pair of Nortons.

He made little impression initially and returned home in 1959 before returning for another try in 1960, when it was a case of second time lucky. Redman got a break with Honda after Tom Phillis was injured during practice at the 1960 Dutch GP, and never looked back.

Having finished in the top 20 of the Senior race on his TT debut in 1958, Redman claimed his first TT podium with Honda, placing third in the 1961 Lightweight race. He quickly became team captain at Honda, renowned for his astute and shrewd leadership.

A clever rider and a tough negotiator, Redman contributed greatly to Honda's success, both on and off the track, taking six World Championships and six TT victories. The latter was a unique treble-double, with victory in both the Lightweight and Junior races between 1963 and 1965. Many of those battles were with Yamaha's Phil Read, and although the Yamaha was quicker than the Honda, Redman's skilful and intelligent riding meant he was always in the hunt.

Professional and stylish, Redman never travelled faster than was necessary to win or took unnecessary risks, tactics he fully utilised at the TT. In 1966 he had designs on the 500cc World Championship, but after victories in the first two rounds a crash in the third left him with a broken forearm, and he announced his retirement at the end of the season.

▲ Max Deubel/Emil Horner and their BMW won three Sidecar TT races on the Mountain Course between 1961 and 1965.

This year saw Manx Radio provide full race commentaries for the first time and it was also when Yamaha claimed their first victory, with Read defeating Taveri in the 125cc race by just 5.6s, while Duff's Yamaha finished third. Suzuki's Anderson set a new lap record of 96.02mph while Deubel/Horner won their third Sidecar TT.

Read was also flying in the 250cc race, his opening lap of 100.01mph the first ever 100mph lap on a 250cc machine. However, his race ended at the Mountain Box on lap two and Redman went on to take a comfortable win – by more than three minutes – from Duff, the first victory on the island for the legendary six-cylinder Honda. Redman then beat Read in the Junior race to make it a unique hat-trick of 250cc and Junior wins.

MV Agusta and their new and exciting Italian star Giacomo Agostini, on his Isle of Man TT debut, took third in the Junior race. It was an impressive first-time

appearance by the 22-year-old, but he was caught out by a wet patch in the Senior when he fell near Sarah's Cottage on the second lap.

The race was held in poor conditions with intermittent rain showers throughout and, amazingly, exactly a lap after Agostini crashed, Hailwood came to grief at the same spot. The windscreen of his MV was smashed and the handlebar bent but Mike remounted, made some repairs at his next pit stop and still won by more than two minutes! Many considered it to be one of his finest TT victories.

In 1966 Honda decided to increase their racing activities, not only doubling their efforts in the smaller classes but also contesting the 500cc class for the first time. Taveri and Bryans entered the 50cc and 125cc races and long-time team leader Redman the bigger classes. The 500cc World Championship was his clear aim in what he'd stated would be his final season.

Honda's intent was further underscored by the recruitment of Hailwood. Like Gary Hocking before him, he'd become increasingly frustrated with the restrictions placed upon him by MV Agusta in terms of what he could ride and where – primarily only the 500 – whereas Honda let him contest the 250cc, 350cc and 500cc races.

> the 1966 TT would take place at the end of August and not June, because of a national seamen's strike

The biggest talking point, though, was that the 1966 TT would take place at the end of August and not June, because of a national seamen's strike. This meant a hectic month of practising and racing on the Isle of Man, with the TT and Manx Grand Prix being held back to back.

By that time Redman was out after crashing heavily at Spa, Belgium, breaking his forearm. When it became clear the injury wasn't going to heal he stuck to his decision to retire. Hailwood led the charge on the fast but ill-handling Honda-4 and duly won the Senior TT with a new lap record, although Agostini and MV would win the world title, the first of 15 for the Italian.

Hailwood also won the 250cc race at the TT that year and Agostini took his first win around the Mountain Course in the Junior after Hailwood retired at Bishopscourt on the opening lap. Honda won the 50cc race with a new lap record of 85.66mph, helping Bryans beat teammate Taveri, but it was Yamaha who dominated the 125cc race with new signing Bill Ivy.

But the closest and most controversial race in 1966 was the Sidecar. Regular sparring partners Scheidegger/Robinson and Deubel/Horner battled closely throughout, and in one of the closest TT finishes ever, Swiss ace Scheidegger got the verdict by just 0.8s.

Further drama came when he was excluded for a fuel technicality and his initial appeal was turned down. He appealed again, and it was months before he was finally awarded the victory, his first TT win. The points helped him secure his second successive world title.

◀ Factory Suzuki rider Ernst Degner rounds Governor's Bridge during the 1965 50cc race. The German rider finished in third place.

By the start of the 1967 season, Honda's interest was beginning to wane, and it was only the thought of success in the 500cc class that drove them on. It was factory policy to build and race only four-strokes, and with two-strokes continuing to be in the ascendancy they were having to spend more to try to stay ahead. The cost of developing new engines, particularly those with more cylinders, was astronomical.

The Isle of Man government weren't losing interest, though, and to celebrate the sixtieth anniversary of the TT in 1967, a special ceremony was held at the Grandstand on the Saturday evening. The Diamond Jubilee meeting also saw the introduction of the Production races for 250cc, 500cc and 750cc machines, held over three laps and run concurrently with a massed start.

These new races kick-started the week and John Hartle returned to the island after a four-year absence to lead the 750cc class from start to finish on his Triumph twin. Neil Kelly did likewise in the 500cc class to become just the second Manxman to win a solo race after Tom Sheard's two victories in the 1922 Junior and 1923 Senior.

The 250cc class was a much closer-fought affair, though, with Tommy Robb and Bill Smith never more than yards apart on their identical Bultacos. On the run to the line it was still anyone's race, but Smith took the win by just two-fifths of a second.

The 50cc race also had a mass start, with victory going to Suzuki's Stuart Graham, effecting the first ever father-and-son combination to win a solo TT race, as he emulated the 1953 victory of his father Les. The Sidecar race saw BMW take their thirteenth successive victory, with the new partnership of Siegfried Schauzu/Horst Schneider getting the better of Klaus Enders/ Ralf Engelhardt in just their second appearance at the TT.

The rest of the programme was expecting to see the heavyweights of Honda, Yamaha and MV Agusta do battle, and first blood went to Honda and Hailwood in the 250cc race, a new lap record of 104.50mph helping Mike to a comfortable victory over Read's Yamaha. Phil got his win in the 125cc race, though, defeating Suzuki's Graham by just 3.4s.

Hailwood then not only broke the Junior lap record from a standing start but also the outright lap record, with a speed of 107.73mph. Another 107mph lap second time around gave him a lead of more than a minute over Agostini, and he eventually won by more than three minutes, the MV clearly being no match for the Honda. Victory also moved Mike onto 11 TT wins, breaking the long record of ten that had been held by Stanley Woods since 1939.

That just left the Senior, and what a race it turned out to be – almost 60 years later it is still talked about as being one of the greatest ever to take place on the Mountain Course. Hailwood and Agostini repeatedly broke the outright lap record on their respective Honda and MV mounts, and a second lap of 108.77mph by Hailwood reduced Ago's lead to 8s.

The lead was reduced further to just 2s as the two riders pitted and Mike used a hammer to bash a loose twistgrip into place. By the end of lap four Agostini's lead was back up to 12s, but hopes of a fairytale win were dashed a lap later when the MV's chain broke and he coasted back to the pits in tears. Hailwood duly took his twelfth TT win from Peter Williams by almost eight minutes.

BMW
1937–present
53 wins

BMW is the manufacturer to beat in the modern era of the Isle of Man TT, but some might be surprised to learn that its history on the island actually began back in 1937. It took the German marque just two years to climb the top step of the podium, when Georg Meier won the Senior TT aboard the supercharged RS 255. Meier's win made him the first non-British rider to win the blue riband Senior.

After the Second World War, BMW's presence on the island was sporadic, and although Walter Zeller finished fourth in the 1956 Senior, it was Helmut Dähne's 1976 1000cc Production victory with Hans-Otto Butenuth on the R90 S that remained the highlight for the brand in the solo classes.

However, if solo success was scarce, the opposite was the case in the Sidecar class. BMW took no fewer than 26 victories between 1955 and 1975, by riders including Walter Schneider, Max Deubel, Klaus Enders and Siegfried Schauzu. The 500cc powerplant also dominated the three-wheel World Championship before two-stroke engines took over.

Dave Morris returned BMW to winning ways on two wheels, taking three successive Singles victories between 1997 and 1999. Fast forward to the twenty-first century, and BMW began to establish itself as the manufacturer to beat in the big bike classes thanks to the introduction of the S1000RR. This bike transformed BMW's fortunes in racing across the globe, ushering in a new golden era of success.

Michael Dunlop took the brand's first win in almost two decades in 2014, winning the Superbike, Superstock and Senior races, then repeating his Superbike and Senior successes in 2016, while Ian Hutchinson added the Superstock victory that same year. Further wins came in 2017 at the hands of Hutchinson, and in 2018 from Dunlop and Peter Hickman, who has arguably become the rider most synonymous with BMW in recent years. Indeed, all Hickman's 1000cc wins, as well as his outright lap record, have come with the German manufacturer. With Davey Todd adding to the success story, BMW have now collected 53 victories across more than 80 years of TT competition.

▲ Davey Todd spectacularly leaps Ballaugh Bridge on his Superstock-spec BMW M1000RR.

Honda's much anticipated withdrawal from racing came at the start of the 1968 season, with Suzuki joining them. Just as the loss of Moto Guzzi, Gilera and Mondial had cast a shadow over the sport some ten years before, this did too.

Now MV Agusta's only opposition in the 1968 Senior was Norton and AJS machinery straight out of the 1950s, and Agostini had a comfortable win without having to get near lap or race records. His cause was aided by Hartle, back on an MV, crashing at Cronk-ny-Mona, and Ago won by a whopping eight and a half minutes. The battle for second was substantially closer, though, as Brian Ball edged out Barry Randle by just 0.4s.

The Junior followed a similar pattern, Agostini winning this time by almost three minutes for his first Senior-Junior double, but the 125cc and 250cc races had a definite edge to them, largely due to the bitter rivalry between Yamaha teammates Read and Ivy. The two went at it hammer and tongs in the 250cc race, with Ivy setting a new lap record of 105.51mph.

However, Read led on the fourth lap, only to retire at the Bungalow with a rear-wheel puncture, and Ivy went on to claim his second TT win. Read got his

▼ Giacomo Agostini (350cc MV Agusta) takes the right-hander at Quarter Bridge during the 1967 Junior.

Giacomo Agostini

▲ A delighted Agostini after winning the 1972 Junior TT.

From	Bergamo, Italy
Years Active	1965–1972
Wins	10
Podiums	13
Fastest Lap	108.30mph
Manufacturers	MV Agusta

With dashing good looks and charisma in abundance, you'd have been forgiven for thinking Giacomo Agostini was a film star, but it was motorcycling that made him a national hero and international celebrity. His career saw him set countless records; 15 world titles and 122 Grand Prix wins make him the most successful rider ever in the history of the World Championships.

Agostini gained early experience in hill-climb events and Italian road races, and in 1964 he became Morini's lead rider. Having defeated the established Tarquinio Provini to the 250cc Italian Championship, he was signed by MV Agusta for the 1965 season, despite having no experience on anything larger than a 250cc machine.

The 350cc and 500cc MV Agustas could quite well have been a baptism of fire for Ago, but he was immediately quick, and nowhere was that seen more than at the TT, where he won in 1966 on just his second attempt. When Mike Hailwood moved to Honda, Agostini became MV's senior rider, and the duo frequently did battle.

Years of domination by Agostini and MV followed, including a total of ten TT wins. Agostini took a Junior-Senior double on no less than four occasions, and through no fault of his own found himself with little opposition. But when his close friend Gilberto Parlotti died in the 1972 125cc race, his love affair with the TT came to an end.

Agostini actively campaigned for the TT to be removed from the World Championship calendar, which it ultimately was. Time proved to be a healer for Ago, and he's been a welcome visitor to the island over the years, often parading one of his beloved MVs.

Phil Read

▲ With eight TT wins and eight World Championship titles, Read was one of Britain's all-time greats.

From	Luton, England
Years Active	1960–1982
Wins	8
Podiums	13
Fastest Lap	111.09mph
Manufacturers	AJS, Norton, Gilera, Yamaha, Suzuki, Honda, Benelli, Matchless, MV Agusta, Bultaco

Phil Read's career began in 1956 at the age of 17, and he went on to compete at international level for more than 25 years, continuing to take part in parade laps well into his 80s. His greatest success came with Yamaha and MV Agusta, winning eight world titles and 52 Grands Prix, standing on a Grand Prix podium 121 times.

Read also won eight races at the TT, including on his debut in the 1961 Junior, a year after he'd been victorious in the Senior Manx Grand Prix. His TT victory proved to be a career breakthrough, but it was when Yamaha signed him in 1964 to ride their 125cc and 250cc machines that he really shone.

Setting the first ever 100mph lap of the Mountain Course on a 250 in 1965, Read won the 125cc race that same year, and he repeated the feat in both 1967 and 1968. By then he was embroiled in a bitter feud with teammate Bill Ivy, and when Read heard Yamaha were withdrawing from racing at the end of the year he ignored team orders and walked away with both the 125cc and 250cc world titles.

Controversial at times, Read was a smooth and stylish rider, and further 250cc TT wins were taken as a privateer before he joined the likes of Giacomo Agostini and Barry Sheene in boycotting the TT, only to return in 1977 when he took a famous Formula One-Senior double. At his final TT in 1982 he finished fourth in the Senior.

Read faced the might of Mike Hailwood, Jim Redman, Agostini, Ivy and Sheene during his career, defeating them all, and he remains one of the UK's greatest ever riders.

▲ Pictured at Parliament Square, Phil Read won the 1968 125cc race ahead of Yamaha teammate and rival Bill Ivy.

revenge in the 125cc race, although Ivy went into the record books with the first 125cc 100mph lap at 100.32mph. Yamaha wanted Phil to win, though, and Bill mysteriously slowed on the final lap with engine problems that were never established, and that allowed Phil to take the victory.

The Yamaha factory wanted Ivy and Read to win the 250cc and 125cc World Championships respectively, but when Read got wind of Yamaha's pending withdrawal at the end of the season he decided the gloves were off and it was every man for himself. He went on to win both titles and Ivy retired, only to return to racing with Jawa in 1969 when he died in a practice crash at the Sachsenring, East Germany.

The 1968 TT concluded with victories in the Production races for Ray Pickrell, Ray Knight and Trevor Burgess, and Barry Smith won the final 50cc race to be staged. Meanwhile, organisers had recognised the popularity of the Sidecar class with an additional 750cc race, which ran concurrently with the 500cc World Championship class. Schauzu/Schneider were victorious in the 500cc, and Terry Vinicombe/John Flaxman (BSA) rode the first 750cc machine home.

With Yamaha quitting at the end of the year, MV Agusta were the only factory team left in 1969, save for Benelli's sole entrant in the 250cc class. Australian Kel Carruthers was their rider, and he won the 250cc TT from Frank Perris on a Suzuki and Santiago Herrero riding an Ossa. Carruthers also won the World Championship, the final 250cc title to be won by a four-stroke machine.

▲ Benelli were one of the few factory teams to contest the 1969 TT but Kel Carruthers gave them victory in the 250cc race.

Agostini had his expected comfortable victories in the Junior and Senior races, by more than eight minutes in each, and there's no doubt the loss of factory teams had an impact on the status of the TT on the racing calendar. More short circuits were being used in the World Championship, such as Jarama, Imola and Le Mans, and the need for riders to contest the TT for World Championship points was rapidly diminishing.

Dave Simmonds gave Kawasaki their first TT victory when he won the 125cc race, one of eight he won that year on his way to the world title, and because the 50cc class was dropped, separate 500cc and 750cc Sidecar races were held. Schauzu/Schneider took their third successive win in the 750cc race, but they were edged out by fellow Germans Enders/Engelhardt in the 500cc.

Bill Penny and Tony Rogers won the 500cc and 250cc Production races, but it was Malcolm Uphill who grabbed the headlines, setting the first 100mph lap by a Production machine on his way to victory in the 750cc class.

There can be no doubt the withdrawal of the major manufacturers and subsequent dominance of MV Agusta, in the larger-capacity classes at least, had a major impact on racing as a spectacle in the late 1960s and early 1970s. It wasn't MV's fault that their machinery was superior to the opposition, nor was it Agostini's that he was the best rider.

> The 1970 TT saw Agostini complete his third successive Senior-Junior double

The combination of man and machine was simply too good, and just as Ago was winning by minutes at the TT he was decimating the field in the shorter Grand Prix races on the Continent, often lapping the entire field. But one only has to remember his battles with Hailwood to realise just how good he was at the TT, especially as his Mountain Course career was in its infancy at the time.

The 1970 TT saw Agostini complete his third successive Senior-Junior double with Carruthers winning the 250cc race for the second year in a row, this time on a private Yamaha ahead of eventual world champion Rod Gould. The race was marred by Spanish ace Herrero dying from injuries he sustained in a crash at the thirteenth milestone. Herrero was leading the World Championship at the time, and his accident led to the Spanish federation refusing to issue a racing licence to any Spaniard wishing to compete at the TT.

Newcomer Günter Bartusch finished third for MZ in the 250cc race, as he did in the 125cc race two days later. In somewhat of a rarity, newcomers filled the first three places, with German Dieter Braun (Suzuki) winning ahead of Swede Börje Jansson (Maico).

Uphill, Frank Whiteway and Chas Mortimer won the Production races, the latter winning the first of eight TT races, with Schauzu/Schneider (750cc) and Enders/Wolfgang Kalauch (500cc) sharing the Sidecar spoils again.

Although the TT Races were deprived of manufacturer participation and star riders from overseas, instead relying on the hordes of British privateers to swell the entries, attendances remained high and race fans were privy to an extra race in 1971. The Formula 750 race, held on the Saturday evening, was added to the programme to cater for the new breed of superbikes, making it a busy week of eight races.

Triumph, Norton and BSA all had official entries, and it was Tony Jefferies on a Triumph 750 who won by 26s from BSA's Ray Pickrell. Pickrell got his revenge later in the week, though, when he comfortably defeated Jefferies in the Production 750 race, while John Williams and Bill Smith gave Honda success in the 500cc and 250cc classes respectively.

Jefferies' week got even better in the Junior race, reduced to five laps, after the unbelievable happened – Agostini's MV broke down at Ramsey on lap one, which was greeted by cheers from the crowds around the course!

Leader Phil Read retired at Glen Helen on the fourth lap, and poor conditions throughout caused Dudley Robinson, Rod Gould and Alan Barnett to crash, which meant Jefferies brought his 350cc Yamsel home for his second win of the week. After years of trying, Read finally won the 250cc race, his winning margin more than two minutes.

Conditions were terrible throughout the week, but Chas Mortimer gave Yamaha another victory in the 125cc race, which saw a certain Barry Sheene – competeing at the TT for the one and only time – crash out from second place at Quarter Bridge on the second lap. Sheene was hoping to take points off his World Championship rival Angel Nieto, but having also failed to finish in the 250cc Production race earlier in the week, he vowed never to return.

In the Sidecar class Schauzu, now with Wolfgang Kalauch in the chair, won his fifth TT after a superb battle with BMW teammates Georg Auerbacher/Hermann Hahn. The gap between the duo after three laps was just 5.6s, but Auerbacher had had his moment of glory earlier in the week when he took a comfortable victory in the 750cc race.

The programme remained the same in 1972, a year that would prove to be a major turning point in the history of the TT, and particularly its status within the World Championship. In the 125cc race, Italian newcomer Gilberto Parlotti, who was a close friend of Agostini and leading the World Championship at the time, crashed at the Verandah in atrocious conditions, sustaining fatal injuries.

Agostini expressed a desire to withdraw from the Senior race, which followed on the same day, and it was only after some frantic phone calls between the MV factory and the Italian star that both he and teammate Alberto Pagani decided to race. Ago duly came home ahead of Pagani for an MV 1–2, but it was the last time they raced at the TT, and other big names, including Read and Gould, also joined the boycott the following year.

This all unfolded on the final day of the event, but earlier in the week it had been plain sailing for Agostini in the Junior race when he took another win, this time by more than four minutes, from Yamaha privateers Tony Rutter and Mick Grant, both of whose successful TT careers were just beginning to flourish. Grant also finished third in the Senior.

Pickrell and his 750cc Triumph won both the Production 750cc and Formula 750 races, making it four TT wins in total for the Middlesex rider, with victory in the 500cc and 250cc Production classes going to Stan Woods and John Williams.

Read and Mortimer repeated their 250cc and 125cc success from the year before with Schauzu/Kalauch winning both the 750cc and 500cc Sidecar races.

Siegfried Schauzu

▲ A smiling Siegfried Schauzu after winning the 1969 Sidecar 750cc race.

From	Silesia, West Germany
Years Active	1966–1976
Wins	9
Podiums	14
Fastest Lap	99.72mph
Manufacturers	BMW, Aro

In a career which spanned some 20 years, German Siegfried Schauzu never managed to win the World Championship, finishing second once and third five times, but he was the dominant force at the Isle of Man TT, winning an impressive nine races.

Schauzu first competed in solo grass track racing but he soon moved onto the tarmac, winning the 1963 West Germany Junior Championship. Three years later he made his TT debut with Horst Schneider, the pairing finishing an excellent fourth place.

From then until his final TT in 1976, the popular Schauzu was almost always in the top three, enjoying partnerships with two excellent passengers. He competed with Schneider from 1966 to 1970 and then Wolfgang Kalauch from 1971 to 1976.

The combination of Schauzu, BMW and Schneider or Kalauch yielded countless wins and podiums at almost all the circuits in Europe, especially the TT, with his first victory in 1966. Schauzu's tally of 14 podiums was an exact 50/50 split between Schneider and Kalauch, while four wins were taken with Schneider in the chair and five with Kalauch.

Affectionately known as 'Sideways Sid' due to his masterful control of a three-wheel drift, Schauzu's total of nine TT wins was only bettered at the time by Mike Hailwood, Stanley Woods and Giacomo Agostini. It remains the joint fourth-highest of all time in the Sidecar class, a clear indication of just how talented he was around the Mountain Course.

In 1976 Schauzu's final TT saw him finish second and fourth, the latter on the two-stroke Aro, but he continued to contest the World Championship and retired at the end of the 1979 season, having finished fourth overall.

▲ Runner-up Börje Jansson (left) congratulates 1971 125cc race winner Chas Mortimer.
▶ The 1972 Junior race saw Giacomo Agostini claim his ninth TT victory.

The fallout from Parlotti's accident was evident in the 1973 entry. No Agostini, no Read, no MV Agusta and hardly anyone lying in the top ten of any of the solo World Championships after the opening rounds of the season.

The risks of competing at the TT for World Championship points were no longer deemed acceptable or viable for the leading road racers in the world, especially as the rewards were minimal. Winners of the 350cc, 250cc and 125cc races would receive just £600, £500 and £200 respectively, with the Senior victor receiving the slightly higher figure of £1,000.

Apart from a few foreign riders, the solo TT entry was now made up of British privateers. Fortunately, the two-stroke era was really beginning to kick in and many competitors were able to contest several races on their 250cc and 350cc Yamahas, the latter being eligible for the Junior, Senior and Formula 750 races.

In a way, the lack of star riders made for better racing. With no MV or Agostini, the Senior and Junior races were wide open, and it was Australian Jack Findlay, who'd been trying to win a TT since 1959, and Rutter who prevailed. For Rutter, it was the first of his seven TT victories, while Findlay's success gave Suzuki their first 500cc Grand Prix and Senior TT win.

Former factory Yamaha and Honda rider Tommy Robb, whose TT career started a year before Findlay's, was a popular winner of the 125cc race, and it was a similar scenario in the Formula 750 race; Peter Williams, who had seven second-place finishes to his name, was victorious.

In a year of firsts, Charlie Williams claimed his maiden TT wins in the Production 250cc and 250cc races, but the experienced Bill Smith won the Production 500cc encounter, with Jefferies also taking another win, this time in the Production 750cc race.

The sidecars, meanwhile, still retained the support of the BMW factory and the World Championship stars, and both the 500cc and 750cc races were won by Enders/Engelhardt. Enders had retired at the end of 1970 to try his hand at car racing which proved unsuccessful, so he returned to sidecars and set a new lap record of 96.86mph on his way to victory.

Enders was out of luck in 1974 as he had to retire while leading the 500cc Sidecar race, allowing Heinz Luthringhauser, who had made his TT debut in 1961, to take the win. He was partnered by Hermann Hahn, who'd been victorious three years earlier with Georg Auerbacher.

Schauzu/Kalauch took the 750cc race, and all the time the lap record was nudging closer to 100mph, with Rolf Steinhausen, who made his debut the year before, lapping at 98.18mph.

> it was Clive Horton who had the honour of being the last ever 125cc race winner

Bad weather had affected the programme at the beginning of the week, when Rutter took his second successive Junior race victory ahead of Grant. With the overseas stars absent, riders such as Rutter, Grant, Mortimer and John and Charlie Williams were now the men to beat; British privateers were running at the front in all classes.

Charlie Williams repeated his 250cc race win from the year before and Grant made it six wins in a row for Triumph in the Production 1000cc category. Keith Martin and Martin Sharpe were the respective winners of the 500cc and 250cc races.

The Formula 750 and 125cc races, meanwhile, were run for the final time, the former being dominated by over-bored 350cc machines after all the full-blown 750cc machines ran into trouble. Mortimer was the winner from Charlie Williams and Rutter, and it was Clive Horton who had the honour of being the last ever 125cc race winner.

The demise of the 125cc event allowed race organisers to run a ten-lap Production race in 1975, the longest ever race in TT history with each machine ridden by a team of two riders. The Formula 750 race was replaced by the Open

Klaus Enders

From 1955 until 1974, BMW dominated sidecar racing with their superior, low-torque outfits, and that period saw them win all but two of the World Championships; only two of the individual titles were won by non-German drivers, the exception being Swiss ace Fritz Scheidegger.

From	Wetzlar, West Germany
Years Active	1966–1974
Wins	4
Podiums	5
Fastest Lap	96.86mph
Manufacturers	BMW

At World Championship level the best driver – or at least the most successful – was Klaus Enders with six World Championship titles, a record that remained unbroken until 1994, when Swiss driver Rolf Biland won his seventh.

Enders was born in 1937 and entered the sport just as two of the finest talents, Scheidegger and Max Deubel, saw their careers end. With this formidable opposition out of the equation, Enders won his first world title in 1967.

That victory came a year after Enders had made his TT debut, when he finished a fine fourth behind Scheidegger, Deubel and Georg Auerbacher. Having gained the services of renowned engine tuner Dieter Busch, who also excelled at chassis design and development, Enders's first World Championship-winning year of 1967 also saw him claim his first TT win, with Ralf Engelhardt in the chair.

After a lacklustre 1968, further TT wins came in 1969 and 1970, the latter with Wolfgang Kalauch as passenger, and although he briefly tried four wheels in 1971, Enders was back in the sidecar paddock the following year.

Back with Engelhardt, Enders took three more Sidecar World Championship titles between 1972 and 1974, with another TT win in 1973. His success in the latter years came despite strong opposition from the new four-cylinder Königs. When he retired for good at the end of the 1974 season, Enders was the most successful sidecar driver ever.

▲ The combination of Enders and Engelhardt was victorious on three occasions.

Classic which replaced the Senior as the finale of race week. The Senior moved to Monday instead.

The Production race got proceedings underway, and it proved to be an exciting event with lap records in two of the three classes, Alex George and Dave Croxford giving the famous 'Slippery Sam' Triumph yet another victory. Charlie Williams and Eddie Roberts won the 500cc class and Mortimer and Billy Guthrie took the 250cc honours, the small 250cc machines doing the slightly shorter distance of nine laps.

Mortimer and Williams were rapidly becoming the men to beat in the smaller-capacity classes, and they won the 250cc and Junior races respectively. Rutter was out of luck on each occasion; however, he made history in the Classic race as he set the fastest ever lap by a 350cc machine at 107.88mph, although luck again deserted him as the chain came off at Ballaugh Bridge on the penultimate lap.

The same fate befell Grant at the Gooseneck on lap three, but not before he finally broke Mike Hailwood's longstanding outright lap record with a lap of 109.82mph on his 750cc Kawasaki. Those retirements helped John Williams

▼ Peeling into the Creg-ny-Baa, Mick Grant (750cc Kawasaki) set a new outright lap record of 109.82mph during the 1975 Classic race.

take the win and the £1,500 prize, and it wouldn't be long before he was in the history books himself.

Grant had better fortune in the Senior race, which he won by half a minute from John Williams and Mortimer. With Enders having retired from racing, Steinhausen took over as the 500cc Sidecar world champion, his cause aided by a maiden TT victory. In the 750cc class, Schauzu took his ninth TT win and increased the lap record further to 99.31mph.

1976 proved to be a watershed moment for the Isle of Man TT as it hosted its last ever round of the World Championship. The FIM, the World Championship organising body, felt the TT was no longer relevant on their calendar.

But that was yet to come, and 1976 saw another milestone achieved with the first ever 110mph lap. Many thought it would come from Grant and Kawasaki, given their exploits the year before, but it was John Williams and the factory Heron Suzuki team who achieved the mark in the Senior race.

> 1976 proved to be a watershed moment for the Isle of Man TT as it hosted its last ever round of the World Championship

Williams had been recruited to the team because lead rider Barry Sheene had no interest in competing at the TT, where Williams was already excelling. Williams was a good back-up to Sheene in the World Championship, which Sheene eventually won, and he ensured Suzuki would grab the glory at the TT. Williams stormed into the lead of the Senior race straightaway, his opening lap of 110.71mph seeing him enter the history books forever.

Next time around, Williams lapped at a mighty 112.27mph, and by the end of the penultimate lap he led by three minutes. However, he'd been experiencing various issues with the Suzuki during the race and he gradually got slower around the last lap, eventually stopping at Governor's Bridge and pushing the big Suzuki home.

This dropped Williams down the order to seventh, and so Tom Herron won the race, his first TT victory, by just 3.4s from Ian Richards. Herron made it a double later in the week when he won the 250cc race from sensational newcomer Takazumi Katayama and Mortimer, while Williams made up for his Senior disappointment by taking a comfortable Classic race win.

Mortimer had been victorious in the Junior, the opening race of the week, with Rutter 7s adrift at the chequered flag. On his 250 Yamaha, Mortimer shared the Production race win with Bill Simpson, Rutter again having to settle for second, alongside Dave Hughes.

Steinhausen/Josef Huber won the 500cc Sidecar race for the second year in a row, their Konig outfit too fast for the Yamahas of Brits Dick Greasley/Cliff Holland and Mac Hobson/ Mick Burns. Hobson/ Burns had their moment of glory in the 1000cc race, though, winning in record speed from Schauzu/Kalauch – in their final TT race – and coming mightily close to the first ever 100mph Sidecar lap at 99.96mph.

▲ Every vantage point is taken at the Creg-ny-Baa during the 1976 Production race.

Later in the year the FIM dropped their bombshell. Since the events of 1972, the TT had been clinging on to its World Championship status, but its place on the calendar had been reducing in importance each year. Riders in the leading positions of the World Championships didn't need to contest the TT any more, and with none of their rivals at the TT they could pick up the necessary points elsewhere.

The FIM felt the Mountain Course was simply too dangerous and so the British round of the series switched to the Silverstone airfield circuit instead. Montjuich Park in Spain was also scrapped at the end of the year and Clermont Ferrand had gone in 1974. With many of the old road circuits from the 1950s and 1960s, including the Sachsenring and Dundrod, having already fallen by the wayside, the likes of Imatra, Brno and the Nürburgring only had a few years left.

The World Championship scene had moved on – it was out with the public road courses and in with the custom-built short circuits. The TT was facing a rocky future – could it survive without its World Championship status?

John Williams Sets First 110mph Lap
1976

When Mick Grant lapped at 109.82mph in the 1975 Classic race, breaking Mike Hailwood's eight-year-old lap record, hopes were high that the following year would see the first 110mph lap of the Mountain Course.

John Williams had won that Classic race, and with the Cheshire rider deservedly getting an opportunity with the factory Heron Suzuki team, he was in pole position to put his name in the record books.

However, the season hadn't started well, with crashes at the Daytona 200 and French and Austrian Grands Prix, and he was also struggling to come to an agreement with the ACU regarding his TT start money. Nevertheless, a lap of 107.51mph in practice made him the favourite for the Senior TT, despite problems with the 500cc Suzuki seizing regularly.

The race saw him grab an immediate lead, and at the end of the first lap, Williams clocked not only a new 500cc lap record but also a new outright one too – his lap of 110.71mph etched his name in history as he became the first man to lap the 37.73-mile Mountain Course at more than 110mph.

Williams's second lap was a sensational 112.27mph, but it was far from trouble-free as the clutch failed at Ballacraine on the opening lap, and with less than two laps to go his steering damper broke.

His lead was almost three minutes, but a selector fault then made it almost impossible to change gear. By good fortune he was able to find bottom gear for both Ramsey Hairpin and the Gooseneck, but at Governor's Bridge on the final lap and with the chequered flag within sight the engine stalled.

Williams had to push the big Suzuki for the final 600 yards and he collapsed at the line totally exhausted, taking seventh place rather than the coveted race win. Later in the week, luck was finally on his side as further 110mph+ laps saw him take the Classic TT victory.

▶ Pictured during the 1978 Formula One race, John Williams made history two years earlier with the first ever 110mph lap.

CHAPTER FOUR

1977–2000

The news that the Isle of Man TT would no longer be the British round of the FIM World Championship in 1977 was a crushing blow that many felt it would never recover from. However, ever since Giacomo Agostini, Phil Read and the factory teams had quit the TT so publicly, the event had ceased to attract world-class international competitors in large numbers anyway. The only exception was the Sidecar class, where the world's best continued to compete.

Nevertheless, the loss of Grand Prix status, in prestige at least, meant a huge gap needed filling. Vernon Cooper of the Auto Cycle Union, the UK's governing body, recognised this and worked hard to save the event. The FIM acknowledged the TT's special status by quickly sanctioning a new World Championship series. And so, the Formula One, Two and Three World Championships were born, and the first races took place in 1977 when the TT celebrated its seventieth anniversary.

The series provided a direct link between road and track, using machinery developed from ordinary production motorcycles. There were to be no factory bikes or factory teams in the Formula One class – the flagship event – in the early days at least.

Numerous rules and regulations were laid down to even the playing field, but that didn't stop Honda Britain having an official entry. Their team was already enjoying success in Europe's booming endurance series.

Honda employed none other than seven-time world champion Read, who controversially returned to the Mountain Course after a five-year absence. Read always maintained he had no issue with racing at the TT – it was something he enjoyed immensely – but the financial rewards when it was part of the World Championship, or lack of them, were the issue. Thankfully, both start and prize money had soared since 1972.

Although the race was blighted by poor weather, Welshman Roger Nicholls on the Sports Motorcycles Ducati led Read by 20s as the rain lashed down. At the end of lap three it was announced that the race would be shortened from five laps to four. By that time Nicholls had already made his fuel stop, but Read went straight through, his Honda team aware of the change before the announcement, and took the victory and the World Championship by almost 40s.

Read was also in sparkling form in the Senior, where deteriorating weather saw it cut from six laps to five. With a 14s lead at the end of the opening lap, Read became just the third rider to lap the Mountain Course at over 110mph, and when second-placed Alex George crashed out at the Black Hut, Tom Herron claimed the runner-up position.

The chances of a Read hat-trick in the Classic race disappeared when he broke his collarbone in a crash at Brandish Corner during unofficial testing the previous day. That race was dominated by Mick Grant on the factory KR750

> That race was dominated by Mick Grant on the factory KR750 Kawasaki, who set a new outright lap record of 112.77mph

▲▲ Joey Dunlop (750 Honda) rounds Keppel Gate during his winning ride in the 1984 Formula One race.

Kawasaki, who set a new outright lap record of 112.77mph on his way to victory by more than three minutes, with Charlie Williams and Eddie Roberts joining him on the podium.

Williams had taken the Junior race earlier in the week, while the final solo race of the week, the one-off Jubilee race to celebrate the Queen's Silver Jubilee, was won by Joey Dunlop, or Joe Dunlop as he was known then. Relatively unknown outside of Northern Ireland, Dunlop lapped at a mightily impressive 110.93mph and even had time to stop at Parliament Square to check the wear on his rear tyre. He won the race from George Fogarty, father of future TT winner and World Superbike Champion Carl.

There were also record-breaking feats in the Sidecar class. Speeds, naturally, had been increasing all the time, and Mac Hobson/Mick Burns had come close to the first ever three-wheel 100mph lap in 1976, but 12 months later the milestone was reached.

George O'Dell/Kenny Arthur achieved the mark in practice, but the official honour went to Dick Greasley/Mick Skeels, who lapped at 100.59mph on the opening lap of the first race. O'Dell/Arthur won the race, though, setting a new lap record of 102.80mph on the final lap. More 100mph+ laps were set in race two by race winner Hobson, Rolf Steinhausen and, amazingly, Swiss newcomer and future World Champion Rolf Biland.

The following year would be remembered for both the good and bad sides of the TT. Read and Honda Britain returned for the Formula One race, with John Williams as his teammate, and interest in the series was growing rapidly. Nicholls was back on a 900cc Ducati along with two teammates: Fogarty and, sensationally, Mike Hailwood.

Since retiring from full-time racing at the end of 1967, Hailwood had only had the occasional outing and instead had forged a career on four wheels, winning the 1972 European Formula Two Championship. He finished eighth in the Formula One World Championship that same year and took second behind eventual world champion Emerson Fittipaldi at the Italian Grand Prix.

However, Hailwood's Formula One career ended two years later after he was badly injured in a crash at the German Grand Prix. Retiring to New Zealand, Hailwood disappeared from racing before privately making plans for a return to the TT towards the end of the 1977 season, despite it being 11 years since he'd last competed there.

The racing world had changed considerably, but in a sporting comeback that continues to be talked about to this day, it was just like old times as Hailwood and Read went head to head. The duo treated the thousands of fans to an on-track duel, but it proved too much for Read's Honda, which stopped at the eleventh milestone with an oil leak on lap five, allowing Hailwood to complete a fairytale win.

The rest of Hailwood's campaign, which saw him ride Martini-sponsored Yamahas, was hugely disappointing, and it was Herron who claimed the Senior race honours after battling with fellow 500cc Suzuki riders John Williams and American Pat Hennen.

Hennen, who finished fifth on his TT debut in 1977, was leading the 500cc World Championship at the time for Heron Suzuki, but was believed to be under

Joey Dunlop

▲ Joey Dunlop celebrates his fourth successive Formula One race win in 1986.

From	Ballymoney, Northern Ireland
Years Active	1976–2000
Wins	26
Podiums	40
Fastest Lap	123.87mph
Manufacturers	Yamaha, Honda, Benelli, Suzuki

When Joey Dunlop finished sixteenth and eighteenth on his TT debut in 1976, few would have thought he'd go on to become one of the greatest TT riders of all time. And for many, only Joey and Mike Hailwood come into that conversation.

A year after his debut, it wasn't so much victory in the 1977 Jubilee race that caught everyone's attention but his lap of 110.93mph, the third-fastest ever at the time. However, Dunlop struggled to live up to the hype for the next two years, managing just two top ten finishes until a second victory cemented his arrival; in the 1980 Classic race he defeated the works Honda pairing of Mick Grant and Ron Haslam on a battered-looking TZ750 Yamaha and set a new outright lap record.

Suzuki briefly secured Dunlop's services after his Classic TT victory, but Honda realised a gem lay within and signed him for the 1981 season – he'd ride for the Japanese giant for the remainder of his career.

Dunlop won at regular intervals and on all machinery – his win in the 2000 Formula One race, aged 48, is still talked about today – but what made Joey stand out wasn't just his performance around the Mountain Course, but his demeanour off it. Humble, shy and one of the people, there were no airs or graces with Joey, and even though he was a factory Honda rider he loved nothing more than getting his hands dirty.

Dunlop loved the Mountain Course, and the Isle of Man loved Joey. He sadly died in a race in Tallinn, Estonia, but is revered as much today as ever. A true racing legend.

▲ American Pat Hennen, seen here at Signpost Corner, created TT history in 1978 but a crash curtailed his promising career.

pressure to contest the TT, such was its importance to both the manufacturer and the team. Nevertheless, he said he was happy to race and made history on the fifth lap when he became the first rider to lap the Mountain Course in under 20 minutes.

He trailed Herron by 19s going into the final lap and, perhaps trying too hard to make up the time, he crashed heavily at Bishopscourt. Reports differ as to whether he hit a bird or clipped the kerb, but the spill left him with serious head injuries, and although he recovered he never raced again.

Further tragedy hit the event in the opening Sidecar race, when Mac Hobson and passenger Kenny Birch were killed instantly in a horrific crash just after the top of Bray Hill, seconds after the start. The accident was said to have been caused by a raised manhole cover, which had had yellow lines painted on the road to highlight the issue. Swiss driver Ernst Trachsel was killed in a separate accident at the bottom of Bray Hill minutes later.

Biland, with Kenny Williams in the chair of his revolutionary Beo outfit, carried on after the accidents, and in just his second year at the TT he set a stunning new lap record of 103.81mph. With a clear lead, hopes of a maiden TT win disappeared on the third and final lap though, when his outfit shed its chain at Laurel Bank. That allowed Greasley/Gordon Russell to take the win from Scottish newcomer Jock Taylor and his experienced passenger Kenny Arthur.

The second race later in the week was held in damp conditions, and Rolf Steinhausen/Wolfgang Kalauch won from Mick Boddice/Chas Birks, with third place giving Taylor the overall title. Biland had returned home after the tragedies of the first race.

Elsewhere, Chas Mortimer got the better of Charlie Williams in the Junior race, with Alan Jackson and veteran Bill Smith claiming the top spots in the Formula Two and Formula Three races, respectively.

After the tragic events earlier in the week, the 1978 meeting ended positively with the Classic race living up to its title, as Grant and Kawasaki dominated proceedings again to take a start-to-finish victory. Upping his outright lap record to 114.33mph, Grant came home almost a minute clear of John Williams, with Alex George in third and Read just missing the podium in fourth.

Read was absent in 1979, and George replaced him at Honda Britain, but Hailwood returned, now with a works 500cc Suzuki to complement his Formula One Ducati, which was far from competitive this time, and he finished a distant fifth. George set a new lap record of 112.94mph to get the better of Charlie Williams and the second Honda of Ron Haslam. Meanwhile, New Zealand newcomer Graeme Crosby put in a superb ride on his Moriwaki Kawasaki to finish fourth.

With the Isle of Man celebrating a thousand years of its historic parliament, Tynwald, the Senior race was very different for Hailwood. Grant led the early stages, despite riding with a cracked pelvis that he'd sustained in a spill at the North West 200 a few weeks before, but his pace understandably slowed, allowing Hailwood to take over at the front and sweep home for his fourteenth TT victory, with fellow Suzuki riders Tony Rutter and Dennis Ireland joining him on the podium.

> Upping his outright lap record to 114.33mph, Grant came home almost a minute clear of John Williams

Charlie Williams got back to winning ways in the Junior race, with another impressive newcomer, Australian Graeme McGregor, taking a stunning second, while Alan Jackson took the Formula Two race for the third successive year. Another Australian, Barry Smith, claimed the honours in the Formula Three race, 11 years after he'd been victorious in the 50cc race.

Meanwhile, both Sidecar races went the way of Trevor Ireson/Clive Pollington, although the first race was extremely close with just 7s separating them, Greasley/John Parkins and Boddice/Birks after two laps. Greasley almost ran out of petrol on the final lap but limped home for second with Boddice stopping at the Creg-ny-Baa after his chain worked its way loose.

George and Hailwood then had a titanic battle in the closing Classic race, with little to choose between them for the entire six laps. The duo set identical lap speeds on their third lap, and as they started their final lap Hailwood led by just 0.8s, but he increased his advantage to 2s at Ballaugh.

▶ Honda Britain's Mick Grant finished second to Joey Dunlop in the 1980 Classic TT.

Jock Taylor

Few sidecar racers have left a bigger or more favourable impression at the Isle of Man TT than Jock Taylor. More than 40 years after his last race, many still consider the Scot to be the greatest three-wheel exponent to have graced the Mountain Course.

From	Pencaitland, Scotland
Years Active	1978–1982
Wins	4
Podiums	7
Fastest Lap	108.29mph
Manufacturers	Yamaha

Taylor's first sidecar outing was as a passenger in 1974, aged 19, but the following year he took to driving. He had his first foray into the World and British Championships in 1978 and his debut at the TT the same year.

Recruiting the experienced Kenny Arthur as passenger, Taylor had a superb debut. He took the overall title with second- and third-place finishes and a lap of 102.51mph. It would be 30 years before another newcomer stood on the podium at their first attempt.

Joining forces with sponsor Dennis Trollope proved to be a masterstroke, and although the 1979 TT was disappointing, the following year was the opposite. With a new passenger, Benga Johansson of Sweden, Taylor took the World and British Championships and finished first and second at the TT, adding almost 3mph to the lap record, upping the mark to 106.08mph.

Combining his own natural talent with devastating pace, Taylor was breathtaking around the Mountain Course, and he claimed a double victory and new lap record in 1981, adding another in 1982. Taylor was almost untouchable; that year saw him raise the lap record further to 108.29mph, and it's clear he was on course to post the first 110mph lap around the Mountain Course.

Sadly, it wasn't to be, as 1982 proved to be his last TT. Less than two months later Taylor died after crashing in atrocious conditions at the Finnish Grand Prix.

▲ Jock Taylor, with Gordon Russell in the chair, exits the Waterworks in 1979.

However, George was in the ascendancy, and a final lap of 114.18mph gave him a narrow 3.4s victory. Amazingly, it was the first time Hailwood had finished second in his illustrious TT career, and it would be the last time he'd race on the Mountain Course, retiring for good this time.

By the turn of the 1980s, the loss of the British Grand Prix was a thing of the past. Spectator interest was as high as ever and the manufacturers were returning, primarily due to the World Formula One series. Both start and prize money were increasing all the time, with a start-to-finish victor of the Classic race now getting £10,000, the equivalent of a cool £55,000 in 2025's money.

George was joined at Honda Britain by Grant and Haslam, but the Scot crashed heavily during practice at Ginger Hall and was a non-starter. Suzuki now fielded an official team, with Crosby on board after his stunning newcomer exploits the previous year.

However, controversy reigned after Crosby, due to start at number three, moved to George's vacant number 11 to start alongside the more experienced Grant in the Formula One race. Honda objected, but the change was approved.

> After a lacklustre 1979, Jock Taylor was back to the form he had shown as a newcomer in 1978

Held in damp conditions, a thrilling race followed with Grant getting the win by 10.8s, but a protest was lodged that the Honda's tank was bigger than the 24-litre limit. It turned out to be 28 litres and had air-filled bottles and ping pong balls inside to reduce capacity, and Grant sparked further controversy by banging the tank after crossing the line in an attempt to reduce its size. After two days' deliberation, the result stood.

After a lacklustre 1979, Jock Taylor was back to the form he had shown as a newcomer in 1978. After he finished second to Ireson/Pollington in a damp first Sidecar race, the Scot turned the tables in the second race to take his maiden TT victory. In a sign of things to come, he and passenger Benga Johansson set both lap and race records, the lap record now an impressive 106.08mph.

Charlie Williams, a TT competitor for a decade now, was still at the top of his game and achieved the rare feat of winning two races in a day; the Mitsui Yamaha rider won both the Junior and Formula Two races, while Barry Smith took a second successive Formula Three win.

The mid-week Senior race saw a battle royal between the 500cc Suzukis of Crosby and Ian Richards, and it wasn't until the end of the fifth lap that Crosby took the lead. A thrilling finish was denied when Richards' gearbox locked solid on the final approach to Ballacraine, and Crosby took his first TT win by more than 50s from Steve Cull and Steve Ward.

That just left the Classic, a race that would prove pivotal in the career of Joey Dunlop. Since winning the 1977 Jubilee race, Dunlop's TT career had stalled with just one top-six finish. His close friend Frank Kennedy and brother-in-law Mervyn Robinson had both died in separate accidents at the North West 200, and the latter hit Dunlop so hard he almost pulled out of the 1980 TT.

After a last-minute change of heart Dunlop made his regular fishing boat trip to the island, but after a low-key week few could have anticipated what would happen in the Classic race, where the factory Honda Britain machines of Grant and Haslam were clear favourites. Riding the somewhat scruffy-looking Rea Racing TZ 750 Yamaha, Dunlop had other ideas and fitted a borrowed fuel tank that he then had enlarged to the maximum-permitted 32 litres by a local welder to ensure he only had to make one fuel stop compared to the two needed by the thirsty 999cc Hondas.

Dunlop led by 6s after the first lap and he'd increased it to 23s after lap three. It took 53s to fill the big tank at the fuel stop, though, and with Grant's quick filler doing it in just 12s, he took the lead on lap four. However, despite the big tank coming loose when one of the retaining straps broke, Dunlop broke the outright lap record on lap five and went quicker still on the final lap at 115.22mph, to take a famous victory by 20.4s.

It was a turning point in his career, and after a brief dalliance with Suzuki, Dunlop signed with Honda for the 1981 season, where he lined up alongside Haslam. Grant was now teammate to Crosby at Suzuki; Crosby missed his starting position in the Formula One race after a late decision to fit a slick rear tyre and started from the back of the grid, without a time allowance.

Dunlop led for the first four laps, and after Grant retired, Haslam moved into second and then first when Dunlop pitted for a new tyre, the first rear-wheel change in a TT race. Crosby was flying through the field, and a new lap record

▼ The 1980 Classic TT race was a career-defining moment for Joey Dunlop, pictured at Sulby Bridge on the 750cc Rea Racing Yamaha.

▲ Taking the right-hand Douglas Road Corner – 1981 saw Mick Grant switch from Honda Britain to Heron Suzuki.

of 113.70mph elevated him to third. Haslam thought he'd taken his first TT win, but hours later Crosby was declared the winner as Suzuki protested about him not getting a time allowance. Despite a counterprotest, Crosby eventually got the verdict over Haslam and Dunlop.

Grant had better luck in the Senior race, but there was controversy there, too. The initial race was stopped at the start of lap three due to deteriorating conditions, when privateer Chris Guy, running with unlucky number 13, was leading. He crashed out in the rerun, and Grant revelled in the mixed conditions for another TT win. Another veteran was smiling when Tony Rutter won the Formula Two race on his Ducati, and Barry Smith made it a hat-trick of wins in the concurrently run Formula Three race.

Steve Tonkin broke the Yamaha domination of the Junior race to win on his Randle Armstrong; reigning 350cc world champion Jon Ekerold ran inside the top three after the first two laps before being forced to retire. Organisers had enticed Ekerold back to the TT for the first time since 1976 while, controversially,

▲▲ Rounding Stella Maris, reigning 350cc World Champion Jon Ekerold was a welcome returnee to the TT in 1981.
▲ Race winners in 1979 and 1980, Trevor Ireson/Clive Pollington retired from both Sidecar races in 1981.

▲ Joey Dunlop (1123cc Honda) set a new outright lap record during the 1981 Classic TT but Honda's black protest backfired.

also paying big money to Daytona 200 winner Dale Singleton and 500cc Grand Prix race winner Boet van Dulmen.

Many felt the money should be going to the established runners instead, and their concerns were proved to be right, as although Ekerold was highly competitive and gave 100 per cent, the others didn't and quite literally took the money and ran.

The Sidecar races were dominated by Taylor/Johansson, who arrived on the island as reigning world champions. They lived up to that tag with two more wins, upping their own lap record to 108.12mph in the first, just 7mph down on Dunlop's outright lap record.

After the Formula One race controversy, Honda's response was to run all-black machines in the Classic race, with Dunlop, Haslam and Alex George in similarly coloured leathers with yellow numbers on the back, like the old days. Honda argued that although it was 1981 the organisers were running the event in an old-fashioned, antiquated manner.

It was a protest that backfired, though, as although Dunlop upped his outright lap record to 115.40mph on lap two, he ran out of fuel on the third lap, and Haslam also retired. Crosby, who was only 0.8s slower than Dunlop after his own lap of 115.32mph, took over the lead and led Grant home for a Suzuki 1–2. George took third on the only remaining Honda.

Graeme Crosby

▲ Crosby made a superb TT debut in 1979, finishing fourth on his Moriwaki Kawasaki in the Formula One race.

From	Renwick, New Zealand
Years Active	1979–1981
Wins	3
Podiums	4
Fastest Lap	115.32mph
Manufacturers	Suzuki, Moriwaki Kawasaki

New Zealand's Graeme Crosby had a brief but exciting TT career; although he only competed in eight races, he won three of those, and after his final race he was the second-fastest rider to have lapped the Mountain Course.

Crosby established himself as a formidable four-stroke competitor during the late 1970s in both his homeland and Australia, and when he arrived in the UK in 1979 he made an instant impression. He was a natural on the roads, and a sensational TT debut on the Moriwaki Kawasaki saw him finish fourth in the Formula One race.

Signed by Heron Suzuki for the 1980 and 1981 seasons, Crosby won the World Formula One Championship on each occasion and finished a close second to Mick Grant in the 1980 TT Formula One race. He also won the Senior after a titanic battle with Ian Richards, proving he was master of the two-strokes too.

In 1981 he won both the Formula One and Classic TT races in race record times, setting a new lap record in the former. The Classic race also saw him lap at 115.32mph, just 0.8s outside the outright lap record set by Joey Dunlop in the same race.

That was his final TT race, as he decided to focus all his efforts on the World 500cc Championship where he was already competing successfully. In 1982 Crosby placed second overall, and he was also victorious at the Daytona 200, Imola 200 and Suzuka 8 Hours.

However, the fun-loving rider had become rapidly disillusioned with the politics within the sport and retired aged just 27. There's no doubt he would have won countless more TT races had he decided to continue.

Crosby decided to focus on the 500cc World Championship in 1982, and Haslam's moment of glory came when he deservedly won the Formula One race ahead of teammate Dunlop. Both riders retired from the Classic race, along with many of the fancied runners, and it was Dennis Ireland who got the win, just edging out a determined Ekerold and Rutter.

South African Ekerold had finished in a similar position in the Senior race, which saw Grant crash out at Doran's Bend after tangling with a slower rider. Northern Ireland's Norman Brown, competing in his first TT after winning the 350cc Newcomers Manx Grand Prix the year before, took a memorable win on the Hector Neill Racing Suzuki.

Ekerold also retired from the Junior race, as did Tonkin, Williams and McGregor, leaving Con Law to take the win on the 250cc Waddon-Ehrlich machine. Rutter took a second successive Formula Two victory while Gary Padgett won the final Formula Three race.

In the first Sidecar race, Taylor/Johannsson stopped at Alpine Cottage to make adjustments on the first lap of the opener, eventually finishing eighteenth, which allowed regular sparring partner Ireson to take the win. The Scottish–Swedish pairing had no such trouble in the second race, winning by more than a

▼ Dennis Ireland was a surprising but popular winner of the 1982 Classic race.

minute after setting yet another lap record, this time 108.29mph. Julia Bingham became just the second female to stand on a TT podium, after Rose Arnold in 1968, when she finished second with husband Dennis.

Sadly, and with a 110mph lap well within his grasp, it would prove to be Taylor's final TT outing as he was killed at the Finnish Grand Prix later that year.

Haslam followed Crosby onto the world stage in 1983, and Roger Marshall replaced him at Honda while talented youngster Rob McElnea joined Grant at Suzuki. A new lap record of 115.73mph meant Dunlop was untouched in the opening Formula One race, which he won by 53s on the all-new RS850cc V-Four. Grant and McElnea took second and third.

Law repeated his Junior success of 12 months before, this time on Dr Joe Ehrlich's EMC, with McGregor and Brown taking second and third respectively. In the reintroduced 350cc race, popular Yorkshireman Phil Mellor claimed a first TT victory. Rutter took a third successive Formula Two race win and the Sidecar races were shared between Greasley/Stewart Atkinson and Boddice/Birks, Boddice taking his first TT win 17 years after making his debut.

There was an unpopular change in 1983, as the Senior and Classic races were merged into one, meaning race week closed with the imaginatively titled Senior Classic TT. Dunlop could only manage third, and instead Brown set a scorching pace. He led from the off on his 500cc Suzuki, and second time around he extended his lead with a new outright lap record of 116.19mph.

However, Brown ran out of fuel on the third lap and retired at Creg-ny-Baa, and McElnea took over the lead on his 997cc Suzuki, which he held until the chequered flag. Law capped another strong week of racing by taking second on the 500cc Millar Racing Yamaha. Tragically Brown, with a bright TT career ahead of him, died two months later in the British Grand Prix at Silverstone.

> McElnea took over the lead on his 997cc Suzuki, which he held until the chequered flag

There were further changes in 1984, with an ambitious schedule of nine individual races and 12 TT winners to be crowned. The Formula One race had its capacity reduced from 1000cc to 750cc, and the Production race – with three separate classes – was reintroduced for the first time since 1976. The Senior and Classic were individual races once more and the 350cc class was merged back into the Senior race.

The booming Classic racing scene was also catered for, with Historic 500cc and 350cc races taking place, and Cull was the latest Northern Ireland rider to taste success, with victory in the 350cc category. History was made in the 500cc race when Dave Roper became the first American rider to win a race on the Mountain Course.

In the Formula One race, Dunlop took his second straight win after a close tussle with teammate Marshall, the latter leading by 2s as they started the final lap. Dunlop had stopped earlier due to exhaust problems but flew on the sixth and final lap, a new lap record of 115.89mph helping him win by 20s. The Suzukis of Grant and McElnea both retired, allowing Ducati's Rutter to take third.

▲▲ Rob McElnea's TT career was brief but spectacular and he won three of the four races he finished.
▲ First and third in the two Sidecar races of 1984 gave Steve Abbott and Shaun Smith overall victory.

Boddice/Birks took the opening Sidecar race and the Binghams claimed a third successive podium, but they both retired from the second race, allowing Steve Abbott/Shaun Smith to take the win. Third in the opener meant they claimed the overall title before turning their attention to the World Championship.

The Senior race was one of the finest seen at the TT as Dunlop and McElnea had a fierce battle on their respective 500cc Honda and Suzuki mounts. Dunlop led initially before McElnea shattered the outright lap record second time around with a speed of 118.24mph. He stopped for fuel twice compared to just once for Dunlop, who set another lap record of 118.48mph, giving him a lead of 40s going into the final lap.

However, the one stop proved too much for his Honda, and he retired on the mountain, allowing McElnea to win in record time by more than three minutes from Marshall's Honda. Switching to the four-stroke 997cc Suzuki for the Classic, McElnea made it a double as he edged out Dunlop by 14s, with Grant in third.

Australian ace McGregor finally won a TT race, taking a record-breaking victory on his EMC in the Junior. Dunlop, on the only 250cc Honda outside of Japan, retired on the final lap, and that allowed Charlie Williams, in his final TT, to take a twentieth podium. McGregor then made it two wins in a day as he halted Rutter's dominance of the Formula Two category.

The three-lap Production races proved to be an instant hit, with Geoff Johnson, Trevor Nation and Mellor winning the 1500cc, 750cc and 250cc categories respectively. The popularity of these races would increase over subsequent years, with close racing guaranteed.

As had become the norm, success around the Mountain Course paved the way for a factory ride in the 500cc World Championship, and in 1985 McElnea was the latest to move away from the TT. That meant Dunlop's biggest rival would be his Honda teammate Marshall.

There was drama before the meeting got underway, though, as the fishing boat Dunlop and others, including younger brother Robert, were using to travel to the island sank in stormy weather in Strangford Lough. Joey was instrumental in saving his fellow passengers, and all 12 were safely rescued, although several machines had to be recovered from the Lough.

Fortunately Honda, now sponsored by Rothmans, had flown their RVF750 for Dunlop straight to the Isle of Man. He put the traumatic experience behind him to win his third successive Formula One race, with a winning margin over Rutter of more than five minutes.

The Junior race was a close-run affair, though, with Dunlop and his Honda doing battle with the EMC of fellow countryman Brian Reid. The duo frequently exchanged the lead, but a new lap record of 112.08mph looked to have given Reid the edge. However, he ran out of fuel at Hillberry on the final lap, less than two miles from home, allowing Dunlop to claim his second win of the week. He then completed his hat-trick in the Senior, becoming only the second man, after Mike Hailwood, to win three races in a week. Marshall took second after setting the fastest lap of the race.

Reid was also out of luck in the Formula Two race, retiring from the lead, which meant Rutter took yet another TT win, and another veteran, Grant, came out on top in the 750cc Production race on the all-new GSXR750 Suzuki. These

Suzuki
1960–present
47 wins

Few manufacturers boast a TT legacy that is as rich and varied as that of Suzuki. The Japanese marque made its debut at the Isle of Man TT in 1960, when it entered under its original name of Colleda, and it would rise to prominence through the decades.

Suzuki's breakthrough came in 1962 when Ernst Degner took victory in the 50cc class; the German brought his own engineering expertise and that of MZ with him after defecting from East Germany in September 1961.

▲ TAS Racing team owner Hector Neill with riders Bruce Anstey (left) and Adrian Archibald (right) – the team won 15 races with Suzuki machinery.

Degner won the 50cc world title that year, Suzuki's first, and in 1963 the brand claimed another TT victory with Mitsuo Itoh emulating Degner's feats, the first and only TT win by a Japanese rider. They did even better in the 125cc, with New Zealander Hugh Anderson winning ahead of teammates Frank Perris and Degner. Anderson won again in 1964, with Stuart Graham, son of 1953 victor Les Graham, taking the 1967 125cc race.

Suzuki continued to rack up victories across various classes during the 1970s, most notably by Jack Findlay, who won the manufacturer's first Senior race in 1973. That marked the start of a prosperous era for the brand, which saw an incredible streak of success between 1976 and 1984, with John Williams, Phil Read, Tom Herron, Mike Hailwood, Graeme Crosby, Mick Grant, Norman Brown, Dennis Ireland and Rob McElnea all winning on the iconic RG500.

Although the 1990s proved a somewhat lacklustre decade for Suzuki at the TT, as the Millenium dawned the TAS Racing team helped transform their fortunes. David Jefferies took all three 'big bike' wins at the 2002 TT, while Adrian Archibald claimed Superbike and Senior wins with the squad in 2003 and another Senior in 2004.

As the noughties drew to a close, Bruce Anstey, Cameron Donald and sidecar duo Dave Molyneux and Dan Sayle added their names to the Suzuki winners list, cementing the GSX-R range as one of the most successful in TT history.

In more recent years, Michael Dunlop has flown the Suzuki flag highest. His remarkable Senior TT win in 2017 on the new GSX-R1000 gave Suzuki their first blue riband victory in over a decade and marked one of the standout performances of the modern era.

were their final TT wins, as Grant retired at the end of the season and a serious crash at Montjuich Park ended Rutter's competitive career. Johnson retained his 1500cc title and road tester Mat Oxley took the honours in the 250cc category.

Boddice/Birks took first and second in the Sidecar races, the latter result coming after their chain came off at Governor's Bridge on the final lap. As they limped home, Dave Hallam/John Gibbard swept through for the victory.

Poor weather proved to be an issue at the beginning of the 1986 meeting, with the Formula One and Two races both cut from six laps to four. Irish eyes were smiling, though, as Dunlop and Reid came out on top.

That would be as good as it got for Dunlop, though, as he was uncharacteristically out of sorts, his brother Robert's crash in the Formula Two race understandably unsettling him. Joey had his own crash – the only one he suffered at the TT – at Sulby Bridge in the Junior, and although he remounted, he retired shortly afterwards.

Sadly the race will always be remembered for the wrong reasons, as it made national headlines after one of the most horrific accidents ever seen at the TT. Reid crashed at Ballaugh Bridge on lap two, breaking his collarbone, and when the medical helicopter landed to take him to hospital a horse was frightened enough to jump over several fences before making its way onto the course.

Fifth-placed Gene McDonnell burst onto the scene flat out, and although he hit the brakes and steered away from the horse, it walked straight towards him instead. Both rider and horse were killed instantly, with McDonnell's EMC

▼ Two laps in and there's been plenty of change on the famous TT scoreboard in the opening Sidecar race in 1986.
▶ 1984 saw the Production races back on the schedule for the first time since 1976.

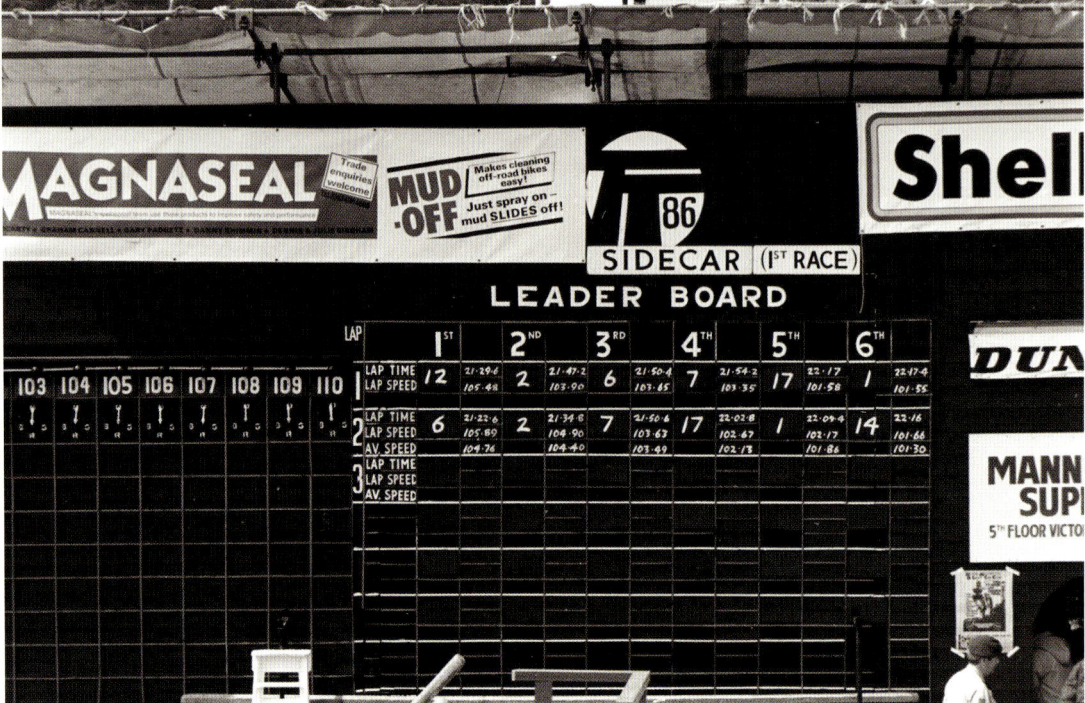

hitting a car on a garage forecourt before bursting into flames. Somehow the race continued, with Cull taking the win, although there was nothing to celebrate, and his victory was instead filled with sadness after the loss of a friend and countryman.

The Production races were now expanded to four classes split into two races, and speeds continued to increase, as did manufacturer interest, with lap records set in each category. Suzuki won all four races, which no doubt boosted showroom sales figures, as Nation and Mellor took the 1300cc and 750cc categories, while Gary Padgett and Barry Woodland won the 600cc and 400cc classes.

History was made in the opening Sidecar race as Lowry Burton/Pat Cushnahan became the first Irishmen to win the class with victory in race one. More history was made in the second encounter when Nigel Rollason/Donny Williams won on the British-built Barton Phoenix machine, the same engine used in the film *Silver Dream Racer*. Boddice was out of luck, though, when his passenger Birks fell out of the chair at Greeba Castle in race two and suffered a badly broken leg.

Dunlop could only manage fourth in the closing Senior race, in which his young Rothmans Honda teammate Roger Burnett was victorious. Nation led

▼ Honda Britain's Roger Burnett leads German Helmut Dähne during the 1986 Formula One race. Burnett would win the Senior race later that week.

▲ Competing with husband Dennis, Julia Bingham's five podiums make her the most successful female TT competitor on the Mountain Course.

Marshall in the early stages but retired on lap three, and Marshall had a lengthy pit stop to adjust his chain, eventually finishing sixth. That allowed Burnett to surge clear with his own 116mph+ laps, and he went on to win the British Championship before following Crosby, Haslam and McElnea onto the world stage.

The weather was again an issue in 1987, and for the first time in TT history a race was cancelled, with the Production A and C races scrapped. The Senior race was cut from six laps to four, and many say that it too should have been abandoned. After new Suzuki signing Mellor crashed at the Nook, Dunlop, riding his 500cc Honda, won by almost a minute from the factory Yamaha and Suzuki of Geoff Johnson and Marshall.

Earlier in the week, Dunlop had won a fifth successive Formula One race, this time on a more standard VFR750 Honda rather than the factory RVF model, much to his annoyance. Mellor, who'd unofficially broken the lap record in practice, had to settle for second.

Boddice, with Donny Williams in the chair, won the opening Sidecar race with Burton/Cushnahan repeating their 1986 victory in race two. Johnson took the Production B race for 750cc machines, after his Yamaha teammate Nation ran low on fuel in the closing miles. Woodland won the concurrently run Production D race.

The meeting also unearthed a future star in the shape of relatively unknown Steve Hislop, the 25-year-old Scot having a best finish of sixth from his previous two TT campaigns. Riding a privately entered 350cc Yamaha, he led the Junior race by more than two minutes before his bike's ignition expired, leaving Dublin's Eddie Laycock to take the win. There were no such issues in the Formula Two race. In what would be the last time the race was run, Hislop defeated Laycock by 17s. Hislop was in demand for the 1988 season, but it was Honda who secured his signature.

The Japanese manufacturer unveiled their 750cc RC30 machine at the start of the season, and the bike was a world-beater in all formats. Some riders, like Dunlop and the returning Burnett, were issued with factory-spec machinery, with Hislop, Brian Morrison and Carl Fogarty receiving highly competitive kitted versions, essentially a privateer machine with a few added extras.

The Formula One race was moved from its traditional Saturday slot to Monday, and it was the concurrently run Production C and D races that opened proceedings on the last day of practice week. Just as the RC30 dominated the big bike races, the CBR600RR Honda dominated the Production C race, and Morrison took the win as Hislop and Dave Leach took third and fourth, with only the Kawasaki of Roger Hurst spoiling the party in second. Woodland made it three straight wins in the D class on his FZR400 Yamaha.

The four-lap 750cc Production race was held on Saturday afternoon, and despite having to pit for fuel at the end of each lap, the RC30 was head and shoulders above the opposition. Hislop took the win from Morrison, and Dunlop was in fifth behind Yamaha's Johnson and Suzuki's James Whitham.

Dunlop took his sixth straight Formula One race win, increasing the outright lap record to 118.54mph, which highlighted the RC30's prowess. Hislop, starting

▼ Steve Cull (500cc Honda) led the 1988 Senior after setting a new lap record but heartbreak followed when the bike burst into flames.

Steve Hislop

Like Jimmie Guthrie, Steve Hislop hailed from Hawick, Scotland, and was one of the most naturally talented riders ever to come out of the UK and compete on the Isle of Man's legendary Mountain Course. Making his TT debut in 1985, Hislop quickly made an impact with his smooth yet aggressive riding style, earning admiration from fans and rivals alike.

From	Hawick, Scotland
Years Active	1985–1994
Wins	11
Podiums	19
Fastest Lap	121.34mph
Manufacturers	Yamaha, Honda, Norton, Cotton/Rotax

Hislop's breakthrough came in 1987 with his first TT victory in the Formula Two class, which led to him signing for Honda, with whom he'd enjoy much of his TT success. He claimed an impressive total of 11 TT wins and 19 podium finishes over his nine-year TT career, firmly establishing himself as one of the event's greats.

Riding Honda's iconic RC30 in 1989, Hislop was the first rider to lap the TT course at over 120mph, a landmark moment in TT history that confirmed his place at the top of the sport. He claimed a hat-trick that year and repeated the feat in 1991 with another treble.

Arguably his most iconic moment came in the 1992 Senior TT, when he rode the distinctive rotary-powered Norton to a dramatic victory over Carl Fogarty. The race, decided by just 4.4 seconds, is still considered one of the greatest TT battles of all time.

After a year away, Hislop claimed his final two TT wins in 1994, with victory in the Formula One and Senior races on the all-new 750cc RC45 Honda, before announcing his retirement to focus on short circuit racing. He went on to win the 1995 and 2002 British Superbike Championships but tragically died in a helicopter crash in 2003, aged just 41.

▲ Steve Hislop, flanked by Robert Dunlop (third) and Carl Fogarty (second), after winning the 1992 Senior TT.

Honda

1959–present
200 wins

When it comes to TT history, arguably no manufacturer's name is more deeply entwined with the Isle of Man than Honda. The Japanese giant made its debut at the event in 1959, entering multiple riders into the 125cc class. While that first year proved a baptism of fire for the brand, it ignited a spark that would see Honda return year on year, dominating many times.

Just two years later, in 1961, the legendary Mike Hailwood gave Honda their first TT victory, taking the Ultra-Lightweight 125cc race by just under eight seconds, a landmark moment that heralded a new dawn.

The rest of the 1960s saw Honda rapidly evolve from a plucky newcomer to an unbeatable force, with Hailwood claiming notable victories in the 125cc, 250cc, Junior and Senior races; iconic riders such as Jim Redman and Luigi Taveri were also victorious.

As Honda's innovative engineering department pushed the boundaries of motorcycling and strengthened its commitment to racing, the brand continued to set new standards. Throughout the 1970s and 1980s their supremacy continued, with stars such as Phil Read, Alex George, Mick Grant and Ron Haslam all claiming victories.

Joey Dunlop became most synonymous with Honda during the 1980s and 1990s, with all but two of his 26 TT wins with them. Dunlop's 2000 Formula One victory cemented a partnership that has become the stuff of racing folklore. Honda's success continued at the turn of the millennium, thanks in part to John McGuinness, who claimed 16 wins with them, including the memorable Senior TT win in 2015, his last TT win to date.

In addition to McGuinness, Ian Hutchinson, Bruce Anstey and Michael Dunlop have all taken solo wins with Honda in the modern era, while the Birchall brothers have dominated on their Honda-powered sidecar.

More recently, Dean Harrison ended Honda Racing's winless drought with two dominant wins in the 2025 Superstock races, taking Honda's tally to 200 wins and ensuring no other brand has enjoyed more success on the Mountain Course.

▶ Honda Racing's Dean Harrison won both Superstock races in 2025.

▲ Joey Dunlop enters the Gooseneck during his race-winning ride in the 1988 Senior TT. It was his thirteenth TT victory.

at number 32, had superbly worked his way up to second before retiring on the fifth lap, meaning Nick Jefferies on another RC30 claimed second. Burnett, returning to the TT after missing 1987, suffered a rear-wheel puncture on the second lap and dropped back to tenth, but he fought back superbly to take third with Fogarty fourth.

The Senior – which saw Norton make a low-key return – gave the RC30 its chance of completing its hat-trick. Dunlop had an epic battle with Steve Cull's RS500 Honda, and although he lapped at 118.77mph it was Cull who upped the outright lap record to 119.08mph to take the lead. No sooner had he done so than he ran into trouble: the expansion chamber cracked and he lost power before complete disaster struck on the final lap when the bike burst into flames.

Dunlop secured the win from Hislop, completing his second TT hat-trick and bringing his total wins to 13, adding to his victory in the Junior race earlier in the week, where he again engaged in a close battle with Reid. The other solo race, for the 1300cc Production machines, went the way of Dave Leach by just 0.8s as he held off a scarily fast last-lap charge of 116.55mph by Johnson.

The Sidecar races saw Boddice, reunited with Birks, do battle with Burton/Cushnahan and Kenny Howles/Steve Pointer in each three-lap encounter, but it

▲ Kenny Howles/Steve Pointer lead Lowry Burton/Pat Cushnahan and Dave Hallam/Steve Parker at the Graham Memorial in 1988's second Sidecar race.

was ultimately Boddice that came out on top, Howles losing the lead in race two on the final lap when his chain began to jump the sprocket.

There was a change in 1989 with just two Production races, for the 750cc and 1300cc classes, as the 600cc and 400cc categories had been upgraded to Supersport status instead. But Dunlop, chasing Mike Hailwood's record tally of 14 TT victories, was a spectator as he nursed injuries from a crash at Brands Hatch on Good Friday.

Hislop subsequently became Honda's number one rider on their factory RC30, and he took full advantage of the opportunity, sweeping to victory in three races, starting with a near-30s win over Leach in the Supersport 600cc race. Ireland's Laycock took the spoils in the Supersport 400cc race on his RGV250cc Suzuki.

But it was the Formula One race where Hislop cemented himself into the record books, shattering the outright lap record and becoming the first rider to lap the Mountain Course at more than 120mph.

Having stunned the island with a lap of 121.99mph in practice, almost 3mph quicker than Cull's record from the year before, hopes were high of it becoming official in the race, and Hislop duly delivered. An opening lap of 120.92mph was followed by 121.34mph, and with no need to go any quicker, Hislop controlled the race from there. Two more 120mph+ laps followed as he defeated fellow Honda RC30 rider Morrison, who also broke the 120mph barrier on the final lap.

Fogarty, on another RC30, came fourth, but he took his first TT win later in the week with a close victory in the Production 750cc race, his winning margin over Leach's Yamaha just 1.8s. The fine margin between success and failure was

Hizzy Cracks the 120mph Barrier
1989

Often considered one of the most naturally gifted road racers of all time, Steve 'Hizzy' Hislop had already taken several TT wins by the time the 1989 Isle of Man TT rolled around. His performance that year would cement him as one of the event's greats.

With 1989 marking 30 years since Honda made its Isle of Man TT debut, and as the sole Honda representative following Dunlop's withdrawal from injury, the pressure was on Hislop to see if history could be made with the first 120mph and sub-19-minute lap. The crowds trackside didn't have to wait long – Hizzy signalled his intentions with a 121.99mph lap during practice week.

However, as practice laps don't count towards lap records, all eyes were on the Formula One TT to see if he could repeat the feat in race conditions. Having already taken victory in the Supersport 600 race the night before, and with conditions around the course nearly perfect, the Scot was favourite for the win as he set off down Glencrutchery Road on his Honda RC30.

Dominating from the off, Hislop set a 120.92mph opening lap from a standing start, securing his name in the record books, but he wasn't finished there. The second circuit saw him go even faster, and while it might not have been quite as fast as he managed in practice week, a 121.34mph lap was enough to see him smash the existing outright record.

Two more 120mph laps on laps four and six saw Hislop secure the victory by over two minutes. Capping off an already impressive week, Hislop took a third win, this time in the blue riband Senior TT, where his fastest lap was 120.69mph. While he went on to clinch a total of 11 victories, including that legendary win on the Rotary Norton in 1992, it is his 1989 performance that arguably remains his defining moment.

◀ Hislop was Honda's number one rider in 1989, taking a hat-trick and setting the first ever 120mph lap.

The Snaefell Mountain Course

When the Isle of Man TT held its first race, it was not on the course that we know and love today. Instead, it was held on the St John's Short Course, which ran from the village of St John's through to Ballacraine, Kirk Michael, Peel and back. However, as speeds increased and technology advanced, organisers decided to create a longer and more challenging circuit, adapting the first iteration of the Snaefell Mountain Course in 1911 from a similar circuit already used for automobile racing.

The first major change came ahead of the 1920 TT, when the course was altered so competitors turned left at Cronk-ny-Mona and followed the A18 Mountain Road to Governor's Bridge, and the start/finish line was moved to Glencrutchery Road. 1922 saw further changes, with the widening of certain roads, a modification to Signpost Corner that rounded off the bend, and the adoption of a private road between Ramsey's Parliament Square and May Hill, which belonged to the Ballastowell Estate, thus avoiding a detour through the town's streets.

The next big change was in the mid-1930s, with the removal of both the East Snaefell Mountain sheep gate and a humpback bridge in Ballig, and further road widening and landscaping at key points around the course. Additional road widening, re-profiling and tweaks have occurred every decade since then, but the basis of the course has remained very similar for over 80 years.

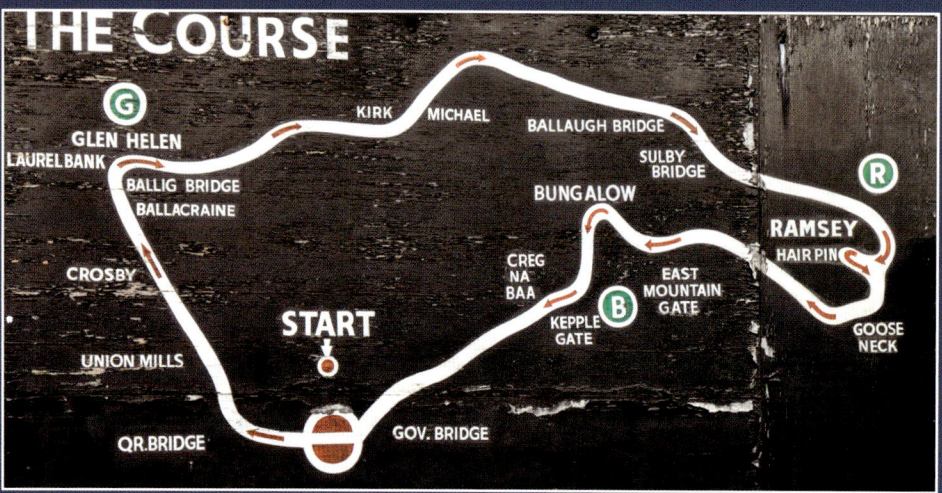

Sector one: The Grandstand to Glen Helen

A lap of the modern Snaefell Mountain Course gets underway under the now iconic starting arch, with the familiar tap on the shoulder from the race official. Accelerating down Glencrutchery Road, riders are immediately faced with the steep and daunting Bray Hill, with a blind entry and a plummeting descent that TV images don't do justice to. This section of the course is bordered tightly by homes and front gardens and is a very popular spot for fans, especially newcomers to the island looking for their first taste of the TT experience.

As Bray Hill bottoms out, riders immediately climb again to the famous Ago's Leap, named after the most successful Grand Prix rider of all time, TT legend Giacomo Agostini. The crest here is the first point on the course where riders become airborne, before beginning another descent down to Quarter Bridge, the first right-hander.

From there, the course winds its way past Braddan Bridge and Union Mills with speeds barely dropping below 140mph then increasing to over 190mph as riders blast towards Crosby village. Four miles into the course, the riders reach one of the most daunting corners of them all, the incredibly fast Ballagarey right-hander, or 'Ballascary' as it is affectionately nicknamed!

Things don't slow down once riders have negotiated the Crosby section, though, as they are straight into the 200mph Highlander sector – for many years the official speed trap was located here. From there, it's down a few gears into the Greeba Castle 'S' bends, named after the Gothic-styled building that was once home to British novelist Hall Caine.

As riders work past Appledene, Greeba Bridge and the popular Hawthorn pub their speeds begin to increase; the sweeping Gorse Lea is not for the faint-hearted but remains a must-visit spot for fans, where Harold's Farm is noted for its hospitality. Then it is hard on the brakes for Ballacraine, dropping from around 160mph to 70mph in mere metres.

From Ballacraine it's on to Ballig Bridge and Doran's Bend – named after Bill Doran, who broke his leg in a crash here during practice in 1952 – before the flowing section through Laurel Bank. This is a unique part of the course: the whole section is lined with trees, high banks and low walls. As riders power through Glen Helen they reach the first timing checkpoint, which gives an initial indication as to how the race is unfolding. The section of the Mountain Course between Ballacraine and Douglas Road Corner in Kirk Michael is the only part that remains of the original 1907 layout, and is critical to a fast lap.

Sector two: Glen Helen to Ballaugh

The second sector of the Mountain Course is a challenging ten-mile run. Both Ballacraine and Glen Helen were once radio commentary points, and while nowadays viewers can get livestreamed coverage of the entire race, historically the radio played a vital role in keeping spectators, teams and family members up to date with arrivals and race times.

From Glen Helen, riders first reach Sarah's Cottage, one of the most popular landmarks of this sector. It was named after a former resident who would keep fans and marshals fed and watered, and it continues to be a popular spot, with today's owners carrying on the tradition by opening up their garden for free to the many visitors.

▲ Dean Harrison emerges from the Bottom of Barregarrow, one of the most fearsome sections in sector two.
▼ The 37.73-mile Mountain Course.

Passing through Sarah's onto the Cronk-y-Voddy straight, the close confines disappear and open fields on either side give plenty of viewing spots of the bikes at incredible speeds. After passing through the eleventh milestone and Handley's Corner – named after four-time winner Wal Handley, who crashed here on the fourth lap of the 1932 Senior TT – the top of Barregarrow is up next. This is another high-speed left-hander, which leads to the bottom of Barregarrow – one of the most jaw dropping and must-watch vantage points, as the bottom of the fairing scrapes the ground as riders power through the left, inches from the wall.

Just under two miles further on from there is Kirk Michael village, a popular spot for pictures as riders race through a tunnel of homes and shops on either side of them. This is often the perfect image to showcase the TT, and for the fans trackside there is nothing quite like hearing the noise of the bikes echo off the walls.

After exiting Kirk Michael there is a series of high-speed kinks, such as Bishopscourt and Alpine Cottage, before another iconic landmark: Ballaugh Bridge. As riders crest the humpback bridge their bikes become airborne and they leap through the air – right in front of spectators enjoying the race from the Raven Hotel and pub.

Sector three: Ballaugh to Ramsey

Once over Ballaugh, it's back on the gas as soon as possible – but not before another huge airborne moment at Ballacrye – before entering the famous Quarry Bends. This was once a series of bumpy second- and third-gear corners, but it was remodelled in 1987 and is now a flowing, smooth and super-fast section that is vital to getting the speed onto the Sulby Straight.

The Sulby Straight is now home to the official speed trap, which flashes up on the timing screen. Modern riders are nudging 200mph and sometimes beyond – Josh Brookes was clocked at 206mph here in 2024. It's then heavy on the brakes over Sulby Bridge and past Ginger Hall, a popular viewing area and home to the pub of the same name that dates back to 1888!

The riders then enter the stretch from Ginger Hall to Ramsey, the bumpiest and most physical section of the entire course. Despite being only four miles in length, it no doubt feels a lot longer for the riders. The conker trees in the parish of Lezayre indicate the halfway mark of sector three, and are home to the famous 'K-Tree', which warns riders of a sticking-out kerb on the left side. The 'K' appeared when antiques dealer Joe Thornton painted it on while racing in the Manx Grand Prix in the 1960s, and the tradition continues to this day.

After the K-Tree comes Milntown, another spot offering spectacular views of the riders wrestling their machines through this challenging section. The bikes then fly past Ramsey Grammar School and round Schoolhouse Corner, where riders will often drift out into the bus lay-by to use every inch of the road. Then it's hard onto the brakes to one of the slowest corners on the circuit, Parliament Square. Fans trackside here will often hear the brakes and tyres squeal as the riders slow the bikes down for this tight right-hander.

▲ The sweeping right-hander of the Gooseneck.
◀ Ron Haslam leads Steve Parrish through Parliament Square in the 1982 Classic TT race.

Sector four: Ramsey to the Bungalow

Ramsey not only marks the start of the fourth sector, but also the beginning of the mountain climb, which some liken to a short circuit. British Superbike riders are always fast here, but others find it difficult to learn due to the wide-open spaces, similarity of corners and lack of reference points.

Once round the Ramsey Hairpin and through the winding Waterworks series of corners it opens out into one of the most picturesque parts of the course. The Gooseneck marks the start of the mountain properly, a tight right-hander that sits some 700 feet above Ramsey and offers spectacular views over the coast.

A further mile climb brings the riders to Joey's, the twenty-sixth milestone, which is named after the legendary Joey Dunlop and matches his tally of TT wins. This right-hander is critical to a fast lap and had extensive safety work carried out in 2007 following a serious accident there at that year's TT. In 2025 it was announced that the twenty-seventh milestone would be renamed MD's, a nod to Joey's nephew Michael Dunlop, who surpassed his uncle's once-thought unbeatable record in 2024.

In between the two milestones is the Guthrie Memorial, where Jimmie Guthrie retired in his final TT in 1937. MD's leads onto the Mountain Mile, through the Mountain Box and Black Hut, named for the marshal's post situated on that corner, and round the Verandah. This series of four bends is a high-speed part of the course and features a steep drop to the left. Anyone who has watched the documentary film *Closer to the Edge* will know it as the scene of Manxman Conor Cummins's big crash at the 2010 TT.

Having negotiated their way successfully around the Verandah, the riders come to the Bungalow, home to the Victory Café, the Joey Dunlop memorial statue and the halfway mark of the electric railway's journey to the summit of Snaefell. What makes this section of the course so unique is that riders have to cross over the tram tracks!

Sector five: The Bungalow to Cronk-ny-Mona

The fifth section begins at the Bungalow, taking riders through Hailwood's Heights and Duke's Bend, named after two more legends of the TT course, and onto Windy Corner. This fast right-hander is named after the strong gusts that can occur as wind from Laxey Bay is funnelled through the natural land tunnel, and riders need to be particularly careful when navigating this part of the track.

From here it's all downhill past Keppel Gate, which has seen various road re-profiling and safety works in recent years, and towards the iconic Kate's Cottage. This white cottage was originally known as Tate's Cottage, but a BBC commentator mistakenly referred to it as Kate's and the name has stuck ever since!

Powering past Kate's, it's onto the world-famous Creg-ny-Baa. This mid-speed right-hander draws huge crowds on race days, thanks not only to the pub of the same name but also the spectacular views and ability to get incredibly close to the bikes. The atmosphere here is particularly special on the final lap, as fans clap, cheer and wave programmes as the race leaders fly past for the last time.

Two fast straights follow Creg-ny-Baa, the first leading down to Brandish Corner and cited as one of the quickest parts of the course overall. Named after Walter Brandish who crashed and broke his leg in 1923, the corner was heavily re-profiled in 2007, changing from a second- or third-gear right-angled corner to a sweeping fifth-gear corner instead; there was a notable increase in speeds as a result.

Out of Brandish, the road drops down to Hillberry, which marks the end of the mountain and signals to the riders that the end of the lap is in sight as they head back into Douglas. This is a special spectator spot for those who want to get close to the bikes at high speeds, and hundreds of fans will pack in along the grass banking and stone wall.

The fast right-hander at Hillberry brings riders to Cronk-ny-Mona, the end of the fifth section and the start of the shortest of the whole course.

◀ Cameron Donald leads Suzuki teammate Bruce Anstey into the Creg-ny-Baa in 2008.
◀ The world-famous TT Grandstand and control tower.

Sector six: Cronk-ny-Mona to the Grandstand

As riders pass through Cronk-ny-Mona, a light on the scoreboard signals the teams in the pit lane to start preparing for a potential pit stop, simultaneously alerting everyone at the Grandstand that they are approaching.

For the riders, however, there are still nearly two miles to go before they're back at the Grandstand to take the chequered flag, refuel or fly by for another lap. With the mountain views long behind them, they're back in the midst of houses, and the first corner they have to negotiate is Signpost, a hard right-hand turn. This is another great spectating point, and in earlier times the race officials were based here and would telephone through to the scouts at the Grandstand to inform them to turn on the rider's light.

After Signpost comes Bedstead, rumoured to have got its name from the landowner making temporary repairs to his dilapidated farm using old bedsteads to keep the field stockproof. Once all fields, this area became home to a large housing estate in the 1990s. All that's left now is to navigate the Nook and then Governor's Bridge.

This tight and twisty section might be one of the slowest corners on the entire course, if not the slowest, but it has been the scene of many a drama over the years. At the notorious Dip it is very easy for riders to throw it all away or have their progress halted by fuel issues. Interestingly, this section is the only part of the modern course that is not used for everyday traffic. As it remains closed off for the rest of the year and is sheltered by the trees, the tarmac is notoriously slippery even on a sunny day.

Once clear, it's back on the gas, ready to blast back towards the Grandstand. The Grandstand has stood over the pit lane and start/finish straight for over 100 years. It first appeared at the 1920 TT and was rebuilt in 1986. With over 600 seats, it provides exceptional views of the start line and leaderboard and is often a popular spot for riders' friends and family to watch from.

And with that, a lap of the world's most iconic road race is complete. If you were on lap record pace, you would have covered the 37.73 miles in just over 16 minutes and 36 seconds, meaning you traversed the Isle of Man course at an average speed of 135.358mph!

highlighted in the Junior TT, though, when Hislop came to grief on his 250cc Honda, at more than 140mph at Quarry Bends, fortunately escaping injury.

Johnny Rea, father of future World Superbike Champion Jonathan Rea, went on to win ahead of Laycock, and Hislop bounced back in the Senior to win from Yamaha's Nick Jefferies and McGregor, who notched up his ninth podium, ten years after his first.

Local ace Dave Molyneux, with Colin Hardman in the chair, took the first Sidecar race by just 1.2s from Howles/Pointer, with the latter incorrectly being told they'd won in parc fermé. Later in the week, Boddice/Birks were victorious again, and they finally broke Jock Taylor's seven-year lap record, albeit by just 0.2s, with a lap of 108.31mph.

The 125cc class was flourishing on the short circuits, and 1989 saw its return to the TT schedule for the first time since 1974, giving the Dunlop family more success as Robert took his first TT win ahead of Ian Lougher and Fogarty.

However, the TT displayed its ugly side again in the Production 1300cc race. Leach beat Jefferies by 10s, Jefferies setting a new lap record of 117.27mph in the process, but lap two was catastrophic. Phil Mellor crashed his Suzuki at Doran's Bend and succumbed to his injuries later in hospital, and just nine miles later teammate James Whitham crashed at Quarry Bends.

Whitham was unscathed, but in trying to avoid the debris Mike Seward was badly hurt and Steve Henshaw was killed instantly. Several riders, including Morrison and Ray Swann, stopped to help and eventually pulled in. The loss of two of the sport's most popular riders proved to be a watershed moment for the Production class.

When the 1990 TT programme was announced, no one was surprised to see the Production class dropped in response to the tragedies. The stability of the powerful street bikes had been in question before the accidents, with several top riders not trusting their inferior handling.

> It was wisely agreed that the bikes were just too heavy and powerful to control

It was wisely agreed that the bikes were just too heavy and powerful to control around the 37.73-mile course at average lap speeds approaching 120mph.

The accidents resulted in changes elsewhere too. Riders no longer started in pairs; instead, they started on their own at ten-second intervals. The Senior also had a 750cc limit introduced, and the Sidecars weren't exempt from change either, with the class now for Formula Two-specification machines – 350cc two-strokes and 600cc four-strokes – all with the aim of reducing speeds and improving safety.

Honda remained the dominant force in the Formula One and Senior races, but it wasn't Hislop doing the winning. Brake issues on the opening lap of the Formula One encounter – now downgraded to FIM Cup status with the World Superbike Championship taking over as the premier four-stroke series – saw Hislop drop down the order to thirty-ninth, and although he shattered his own outright lap record with a final lap of 122.63mph, he had to settle for ninth.

It was Hislop's teammate Fogarty who celebrated victory, with Jefferies and Robert Dunlop joining him on the podium, the latter on board the hugely popular 588cc JPS rotary Norton. Brother Joey was back too after his crash at Brands Hatch the previous year and finished eighth as he continued to recover.

Poor weather in the Senior resulted in Hislop pulling in at the end of the opening lap, but Fogarty mastered the rain, his opening lap of 108.52mph showing just how treacherous the road conditions were. Norton was celebrating again with Nation taking second ahead of Leach.

Leach and Robert Dunlop had emerged victorious in the Supersport 400cc and 125cc races held earlier in the week, while Northern Ireland's Reid got back to winning ways in the Supersport 600cc race, his first victory since 1986, with Rea and Cull making it an all-Irish podium.

The race of the week was undoubtedly the Junior, where Hislop and Lougher repeatedly smashed the lap record. Hislop and his 250cc Honda led by 2.4s going into the final lap, and although he lapped at 117.37mph, Lougher upped the lap record to 117.80mph, the relatively unknown rider taking the victory by just 1.8s.

Dave Saville had been the pioneer for the Formula Two Sidecars, taking no less than seven class victories since they'd been introduced in 1984, and he was a clear favourite for victory in 1990. He didn't disappoint either, taking both wins with Nick Roche and setting the first ever 100mph lap by a Formula Two sidecar. Boddice, with new passenger Dave Wells, had no answer on his 600cc Honda and was a distant second in race one, and Geoff Bell/James Cochrane took the runner-up position in race two.

Despite a lack of terrestrial TV coverage, the TT continued to flourish as manufacturer interest remained high, which was clearly seen in 1991. Yamaha were celebrating their thirtieth year of TT competition and gave Morrison and Leach special 750cc OW01 machines, but Honda, keen to spoil their party, upped the ante further and flew over a pair of full-factory, hand-built RVFs for Hislop and Fogarty.

Said to cost around £500,000 each, the main advantage of the RVF was its weight and detailed engineering, and the combined weight/acceleration and handling advantage made it the most potent machine the island had ever seen. Yamaha didn't stand a chance.

In practice, the two Honda riders went head to head and approached mind-warping speeds. Hislop lapped at more than 124mph, prompting the Japanese bosses to tell them both to calm down. In the race, Hislop was never headed, lapping at 123.48mph on his way to defeating Fogarty by 1min 16s, with Morrison a distant third on the Loctite Yamaha.

That was Fogarty's only race of 1991, as he left to concentrate on his World Superbike Championship duties, and the RVF was handed to Joey Dunlop, now back to full fitness, for the Senior. But at almost 40, Dunlop had no answer to the younger Hislop and finished more than a minute adrift, despite breaking the 120mph barrier for the first time.

Hislop also won the Supersport 600cc race, 30s ahead of Cull, thus completing his second TT hat-trick, while Robert Dunlop not only won the 125cc race for the third year in a row but also the Junior, where he took a narrow win over Phillip McCallen, the latest in a long line of riders from Northern Ireland to make their mark at the TT.

▲ Carl Fogarty missed out on victory in the 1992 Senior but his outright lap record of 123.61mph stood for seven years.
▶ Johnny Rea, father of six-time World Superbike champion Jonathan, in action during the sun-kissed 1992 Senior race.

Elsewhere, Leach took his fourth TT win in the Supersport 400cc race, and the tide was beginning to turn in the Formula Two Sidecars as the 600cc four-stroke engines took over. Boddice/Wells won both races on their Honda Britain outfit, with race two not only giving the Kidderminster driver his ninth victory, equalling the record held since the 1970s by Siegfried Schauzu, but also seeing 600cc-powered outfits take a 1–2–3.

Hislop and Fogarty, especially, pursued World Championship opportunities in 1992, but the pull of the TT remained, particularly from a financial perspective, which, although not huge, would still help fund their aspirations on the world stage.

Yamaha had tempted Hislop to move away from Honda, but at the eleventh hour he jumped ship, sensationally taking a ride on a privately entered Norton. The budget was tight, and initially Hislop wasn't impressed with the unusual characteristics of the machine. In a strange quirk of fate, Fogarty took over the Yamaha ride.

Fogarty dominated the early laps of the Formula One race only to retire on the fifth lap, and with Hislop struggling to get to grips with the Norton, which was overheating in the warm June weather, McCallen took full advantage to claim his first TT win.

Hislop also had to settle for second behind McCallen in the Supersport 600cc race, with another runner-up spot taken in the Junior, this time to Reid, who also took the spoils in the Supersport 400cc race. Meanwhile, the two Sidecar races went the way of Geoff Bell/Keith Cornbill, the duo nudging up the Formula Two lap record to 102.54mph.

One of the biggest stories mid-week, though, was Joey Dunlop getting back on the top step of the podium, ending brother Robert's winning streak in the 125cc class. It was Joey's first win since 1988 and it moved him to a career total of 14, matching the record held by Mike Hailwood.

By the time of the Senior, Hislop had made changes to the Norton, nicknamed the 'White Charger', one of which was to remove the front mudguard to allow cooler air to reach the engine. What followed was one of the best TT races of all time as Hislop and Fogarty slugged it out. With Fogarty starting at number four and Hislop at 19, the duo never saw each other on the road but were never more than a handful of seconds apart on time.

At the end of lap one, Fogarty led by 1.2s, but Hislop took over at the end of lap two, with the gap now 2.8s. Fogarty regained the lead on lap three, but a superb lap of 123.27mph by Hislop fourth time around allowed him to surge 7.4s clear. Fogarty wasn't to be outdone, and despite his exhaust coming loose, he closed the gap.

The pair were riding so hard, neither wanting to lose to the other, that they lapped quicker than the RVF Hondas they'd ridden the year before, and Fogarty's final lap of 123.61mph broke the outright lap record. Hislop was also inside the record and took the win by 4.4s, Norton's first Senior win since 1961.

▼ Having made his Mountain Course debut in 1975, Nick Jefferies finally won his first TT race in 1993 with victory in the Formula One race.

Dave Molyneux

▲ Manx legend Dave Moyneux, the most successful sidecar TT racer of all-time.

From	Regaby, Isle of Man
Years Active	1985–2024
Wins	17
Podiums	31
Fastest Lap	116.785mph
Manufacturers	Yamaha, Kawasaki, Honda, Suzuki, KTM

Born in Douglas, Dave Molyneux is the most successful sidecar competitor in the history of the Isle of Man TT. A home-grown talent, Molyneux has built an extraordinary legacy on the Mountain Course, with a career spanning four decades.

'Moly' made his TT debut in 1985 and claimed his first victory four years later, setting the tone for an illustrious racing career. Since then, Molyneux has amassed 17 TT wins and 31 podiums, making him the most successful sidecar driver ever to compete at the TT and the fourth-most successful competitor overall in terms of victories, behind only Michael Dunlop, Joey Dunlop and John McGuinness.

Known for his technical acumen as much as his speed, Molyneux designed and built his own outfits, earning widespread respect for his engineering skills. His adaptability has also seen him win on both two- and four-strokes with all the major manufacturers and several passengers over the years, including Karl Ellison, Dan Sayle, Patrick Farrance, Rick Long, Craig Hallam and Colin Hardman.

Among Molyneux's most memorable triumphs was the 2007 double, which marked a popular comeback following a huge 140mph crash in practice the previous year. Further wins followed over the years, with his final victory coming in the second Sidecar race in 2014.

Constantly demonstrating grit, tenacity, determination and drive, the Manxman took his thirty-first and final podium in 2024, subsequently announcing his retirement. But anyone who knew Moly knew that would not be the end of his TT career, and he's now the Sidecar Liaison Officer and Technical Delegate for ACU Events Ltd, helping a new generation into the sport.

Both riders immediately said they were done with the TT, but Hislop's story hadn't quite come to an end.

Hislop and Fogarty stuck to their word and missed the 1993 event. McCallen had an RC30/RVF hybrid Honda, but he had to give way to Castrol Honda teammate Nick Jefferies in the opening Formula One race, the veteran finally claiming his first TT win on the older but reliable RC30.

Honda was the only manufacturer taking the TT seriously now, and Joey Dunlop made history when he won his second successive 125cc race, his fifteenth TT victory, making him the most successful TT rider in history. At the age of 41, the Ballymoney publican was getting back to the form he'd had before his 1989 accident, and retirement was the last thing on his mind.

Reid took another win in the Junior, and McCallen turned the tables on Jefferies in the Senior, which was now open to 250cc and 600cc riders to help swell the entry. Jim Moodie took a Supersport 400cc-600cc double, and Molyneux was back in the winner's circle with a Sidecar double and a new lap record, Karl Ellison his passenger on this occasion.

Honda sensationally talked Hislop into returning in 1994 as they launched their new 750cc Superbike, the RC45, and he again dominated proceedings, with McCallen trailing him by almost a minute and a half in the Formula One race. Joey Dunlop, on another Castrol Honda RC45, took third, but the race was marred by an accident involving Robert Dunlop on the exit of Ballaugh when the rear wheel on his Medd Honda RC45 collapsed, causing him serious leg and arm injuries.

Joey pressed on, winning his third successive 125cc race, which was run concurrently with a new class, the Singles. Moodie seized the opportunity and secured another win, while Dunlop also got the better of Reid in the Junior race to extend his TT tally to 17 wins. Moodie then took victory in the Supersport 400cc race only to crash out of the 600cc race two days later, with fellow Scot Iain Duffus emerging victorious.

Rob Fisher/Michael Wynn dominated both Sidecar races, pushing the lap record to 106.49mph and edging ever closer to Boddice's mark of 108.31mph set in 1989 on the TZ 700 Yamaha. Race week concluded with the Senior, where Hislop won his eleventh and final TT race. McCallen and Dunlop again made it a clean sweep for Honda on the podium.

Aside from Honda, the other leading manufacturers had started to stay away from the TT, preferring instead to focus on the British Superbike Championship. It was the same with the riders, as the leading short circuit stars no longer needed to contest the TT to secure a ride with a major team or manufacturer. This meant the event was now rapidly becoming the home for specialist road racers, particularly those from Northern Ireland.

Nowhere was this seen more than in 1995. With McCallen running his own team, Honda Britain's line-up comprised Joey Dunlop, Nick Jefferies and Steve Ward, all in their forties and having started their Mountain Course careers in the mid-1970s. With a combined age of 127, the press nicknamed them 'Dad's Army', but Honda needed success, and these three were the best available to do it.

◀ With Kate's Cottage behind him, Joey Dunlop gets set for the Creg-ny-Baa. He led the 1994 250cc race from start to finish.

The lack of young talent emerging was clearly evident, but the TT was managing to survive without the big-name superstars from the World or British Championships, even if the event was becoming increasingly disconnected from what was happening elsewhere. The fans didn't mind, though, and continued to flock to the Isle of Man in their thousands, with the TT now becoming as much about the festival as it was about the racing.

McCallen took the Superbike race from Dunlop, and with McCallen absent from the Senior due to commitments in the World Thunderbike Championship, Joey won his first 'big bike' race since 1988. Ward finished third and set the fastest lap of the race at 121.73mph to fully vindicate Honda's decision to give him a factory ride so late in his career.

Dunlop also won the Lightweight 250cc race but had retired from the 125cc race earlier in the day. A three-way battle for victory raged between Mick Lofthouse, James Courtney and Mark Baldwin, with Lofthouse leading on the first three laps, despite crashing at Parliament Square on lap two.

Lofthouse quickly remounted and led by 5.6s as he started the fourth and final lap. However, he mistakenly thought his advantage was bigger and eased off slightly on the final run down the mountain. Baldwin was pushing, and a new lap record of 109.01mph meant he edged out Lofthouse by 0.6s, the closest margin of victory ever in an interval start.

Fisher, with new passenger Boyd Hutchinson, cemented his status as the best Sidecar driver of the time with another double victory, overcoming a spill in practice at May Hill, and Rob Holden won the Singles race. Sadly, the popular Holden and Lofthouse both died in the same practice session the following year.

▼ Head down as always, Phillip McCallen rounds Glen Helen 1 during the 1996 Formula One race.

▲ Popular Irishman Gary Dynes (125cc Honda) rides through Ballaspur during practice in 1996.

McCallen, meanwhile, blotted his copybook when he crashed out on the final lap of the Junior 600cc race. Trying hard to close an almost insurmountable gap to race leader Duffus, he overdid it at the Waterworks, leaving Duffus to take his second successive victory in the class.

Nevertheless, with Hislop having exited the TT the path was clear for McCallen to take over, in the big bike races at least. He duly delivered too, and in 1996 he made history with four wins in a week, the first man to achieve the feat.

His cause was helped by the reintroduction of the Production race. Technology had improved considerably since the last race took place seven years before, particularly the game-changing Honda Fireblade, which was released in 1992. The bikes were still fast, but the chassis had improved, the tyres were better and the rules now allowed minor modifications to be made.

Honda was desperate to prove the Fireblade was the best road bike in the world, and they weren't going to let anyone else win, so they spared no effort in recruiting the best riders. The Production race was held over three laps, and McCallen edged out Duffus, setting a new lap record of 118.93mph, and although Nigel Davies finished third on a Yamaha Thunderace, seven of the top ten were on Fireblades.

The Senior race took place later the same day and, having already won the Formula One and Junior races, McCallen found himself on the edge of history. Moodie, on an ex-factory World Superbike Kawasaki, challenged him in the early stages before retiring on the fifth lap, and McCallen duly took his fourth win of the week.

Dunlop continued to extend his record as the most successful TT rider ever with wins in the Lightweight 250cc and Ultra-Lightweight 125cc races, taking him to 21 in total. A holed exhaust meant McCallen could only finish fourth in the 250cc race, while Dunlop used his extensive course knowledge to navigate banks of mist over the mountain and overhaul Gavin Lee in the 125cc encounter.

Moodie had better luck in the Singles race, taking his fifth TT win, and after a three-year wait local hero Molyneux was back on the top step of the podium in the two Sidecar races. Not only that, he and passenger Peter Hill set the first ever 110mph laps by a sidecar, raising the outright lap record to 111.02mph to give themselves a permanent place in the record books.

Away from the victors, 1996 was significant as three young riders made their debuts: David Jefferies, John McGuinness and an unknown New Zealander, Bruce Anstey. All three impressed, with Jefferies winning the Newcomers trophy after finishing tenth in the Production race.

After the mixed weather of 1996, the following year was the opposite, with race week bathed in glorious sunshine throughout. Although he couldn't repeat his four-timer, McCallen's status as the current king was clear as another hat-trick moved him up to 11 TT wins, matching Hislop's total, and putting him behind only Dunlop and Hailwood.

The Senior victory was particularly impressive as just two days earlier McCallen had come to grief in the four-lap Lightweight race at more than 120mph. Two seconds behind Dunlop at the fuel stop, McCallen opted to change his rear tyre, losing time but hoping to claw back the deficit with fresh rubber. Pushing too hard, McCallen, known for his hard-charging style, overdid it at Quarry Bends and was fortunate to escape injury when he slid down the middle of the road. Dunlop took a comfortable win over Lougher, with McGuinness not only finishing third in just his second year at the TT but also setting the fastest lap of the race at 116.83mph.

> ...after a three-year wait local hero Molyneux was back on the top step of the podium in the two Sidecar races

Lougher took a narrow win over Denis McCullough in the 125cc race, but the biggest cheers were saved for the man in third place: Robert Dunlop. It had been a long road back from his big crash in 1994, with countless operations and recuperation followed by medical objections to his return to racing. He was left with a shortened leg and tendon damage restricting movement in his wrist, so Dunlop's third place was a phenomenal effort.

In the Junior race, Ian Simpson, who along with Moodie and Michael Rutter was one of the few British Championship riders competing at the TT, denied McCallen victory. The 1994 British Superbike champion narrowly missed out on the first ever 120mph lap by a 600cc machine, but the win saw him follow in the footsteps of his dad Bill and become a TT winner, just the second father-and-son combination to do so.

Another popular victory came in the first Sidecar race. Favourite Rob Fisher retired early, and the next race leader Ian Bell soon fell by the wayside too. Greg Lambert's Honda engine then expired, meaning it was Roy Hanks/Phillip Biggs who emerged victorious, 2.2s ahead of Vince Biggs/Graham Biggs. The family

McCallen's Fabulous Four
1996

Not many riders can claim to have won an Isle of Man TT, but even fewer can boast of winning multiple races in a week. In 1996, Phillip McCallen etched his name in the Isle of Man history books by taking that even further — he became the first rider to win four in a week.

Born in Portadown in 1963, McCallen had made a name for himself on the roads long before 1996, having been signed by Honda Britain in 1990. He took his first TT win in 1992 and built a reputation as a fast and fearless competitor; by the time race week rolled around in 1996, the stars were aligned for a memorable TT.

McCallen's incredible run began in the Formula One TT on the dominant Honda Britain RC45. Despite facing stiff competition from Iain Duffus, Michael Rutter and Nick Jefferies, McCallen led from start to finish to claim his first win of the week.

Wet weather may have delayed proceedings for the Junior race, but it didn't slow McCallen down as he claimed his second win, finishing nearly 18s ahead of Duffus. The Production TT, which was making its return to the event for the first time since 1989, proved a closer affair later that same evening, with McCallen having to dig deep. He won by just 6.1s to claim his hat-trick.

McCallen had his crowning moment in the Senior TT, the week's showpiece event. With the pressure mounting, he delivered one of his finest performances and remained in command from the start, crossing the line to take his fourth win of the week — a first in the TT's (then) 89-year history.

While that week cemented McCallen's legend, he returned in 1997 to take another hat-trick in his final wins around the Mountain Course. His achievements in 1996 would remain unbeaten for 14 years, until a certain Ian Hutchinson did what many thought impossible.

◀ Starting at number one, victory in the Senior race was McCallen's history-making fourth win of the week.

▲ V&M Honda teammates Ian Simpson and Michael Rutter peel into Douglas Road Corner in Kirk Michael during an evening practice session in 1997.

affair was complete with Tom Hanks taking third, and for Roy it was a dream fulfilled, with the victory coming some 30 years after his debut.

Meanwhile, the poorly supported Singles class was rapidly becoming a lacklustre affair. Just 23 riders started, with 16 still running at the end, but class specialist Dave Morris gave BMW their first solo TT win since Georg Meier's Senior victory in 1939.

1998 was a big year for Honda. While interest from other manufacturers remained low, Honda was putting everything into the TT, as 1998 marked Honda Motor Company's fiftieth birthday. World champions of the past and present were flown over, including Freddie Spencer, Jim Redman and Luigi Taveri, with a vast array of machinery to complement them.

No stone was left unturned to ensure they won every race, with two full-factory RC45s flown over for the Formula One and Senior races, bristling with the latest technology and costing £100,000 each just to lease them.

However, Honda's plans were almost scuppered when McCallen damaged three vertebrae in a short circuit crash at Thruxton, and Joey Dunlop broke his left hand and collarbone and cracked his pelvis at the Tandragee 100. McCallen was ruled out, and Dunlop pronounced he was too sore to ride anything bigger than a 250.

To add to the mix, there was unrelenting rain throughout the fortnight. The RC45s went to Simpson and Michael Rutter, son of seven-time winner Tony, and they immediately took a 1–2 in the shortened Formula One race. Despite the damp conditions, Simpson lapped at 123.28mph, only 2.9s outside the lap record, as he beat his teammate by 2.2s.

The opening Sidecar race fell victim to the weather, and if truth be told, the Lightweight 250cc race should have gone the same way. To say conditions were horrendous would be an understatement. The race was cut from four laps to three and the rain was torrential, but through the gloom one man stood out – Joey Dunlop. Retirements came thick and fast, with many riders pitting at the end of lap one, but Joey pressed on, confident that the race wouldn't go the full three laps.

Sure enough, the race was reduced to two laps and Joey won by more than 40s from Bob Jackson, another veteran who followed the same strategy, and

▼ Honda's Ian Simpson leads the similar RC45 machine of James Courtney through Kirk Michael in the 1998 Formula One race.

Yamaha
1961–present
131 wins

Yamaha's story is one of innovation, resilience and landmark achievements. Another manufacturer that forged its name at the Isle of Man TT, Yamaha made its debut at the event in 1961 as part of its first season on the global stage. They claimed a podium just two years later with Japanese rider Fumio Ito, while Phil Read – one of their star riders – took the marque's maiden victory in the 1965 125cc race and set the first 100mph lap by a 250cc machine.

Yamaha's presence at the TT continued through the 1960s and into the 1970s, but it truly came into its own in the late 1970s and early 1980s, particularly with the iconic TZ 250cc and 350cc machines. During this period Tom Herron, Chas Mortimer, Joey Dunlop, Charlie Williams, Barry Smith, Tony Rutter, Phil Mellor and Steve Hislop all added their names to the victors list.

As the 1980s turned into the 1990s, Yamaha experienced a somewhat lean time as Honda dominated. After success with their 400cc and 600cc Supersport machines – with Brian Reid, Jim Moodie, Dave Leach and Iain Duffus among the winners – David 'DJ' Jefferies turned the TT on its head in 1999, with the all-new YZF-R1 and a hat-trick of victories in the Senior, Production and Formula One TTs.

Three more victories came the following year at the hands of DJ, kick-starting a decade of success, with Moodie, Bruce Anstey, John McGuinness and Steve Plater all tasting the victor's champagne.

More recently, Yamaha has enjoyed unprecedented success in the Supersport class once more, with Ian Hutchinson, Lee Johnston and Michael Dunlop. In 2023 Dunlop became the first rider to break the 130mph lap barrier on a 600cc machine. Peter Hickman is the most recent rider to add his name to Yamaha's impressive victory tally, with a memorable win in the second Supertwin TT in 2023.

With over 60 years of success around the Mountain Course, from two-strokes to cutting-edge superbikes, Yamaha's TT history is a testament to their passion for road racing.

▶ Phil Read won five of his eight TT races when riding Yamaha machinery.

McGuinness took third. The fastest lap of the race, just 100.50mph, highlighted how bad the conditions were when compared to the lap record of 117.80mph.

Driving in Honda Britain colours, Molyneux returned after a year's absence to win the only Sidecar race to be run, this time with Doug Jewell in the chair. Robert Dunlop's victory in the 125cc race was the stuff of fairytales, especially as, on top of his debilitating injuries from 1994, a broken fibula sustained at the North West 200 just two weeks before the TT looked to have ruled him out.

Undeterred, round-the-clock treatment got him out on the track, even if he did have to hobble to the grid on crutches. The decision to opt for slick tyres on a drying track worked out perfectly and his win was undoubtedly the most popular of the week, his guts and determination at new heights.

Rutter claimed his first TT win in the Junior race, which saw worsening weather across the three laps, and there was more joy for Honda when Moodie won the Production race, not only giving the Japanese giant their hundredth TT win but also setting the first ever 120mph lap on a Production machine.

The Fireblade had again seen off all competition, particularly Yamaha's all-new R1, but David Jefferies' fourth place gave a glimpse of what was to come.

> Robert Dunlop's victory in the 125cc race was the stuff of fairytales

Meanwhile, Dave Morris won the Singles race for the second successive time, the BMW rider denying Honda a clean sweep as Moodie took second.

Simpson wrapped up proceedings with victory in the Senior. His teammate Rutter set the initial pace only to suffer a front wheel puncture, leaving a battle royal between Simpson and Jackson, who, in scenes reminiscent of Dunlop's famous 1980 Classic race victory, had fitted a huge 32-litre tank to his McAdoo Kawasaki for a one-stop race.

With a lead of more than 30s, everything was going to plan for Jackson until the filler cap jammed in the pits. He lost 52s and it looked like it was all over, but Jackson dug deep and was only 3.7s adrift at the chequered flag. Jefferies was again fourth.

Aged just 28, Simpson now had three TT wins and was the third-fastest rider around the Mountain Course. With a Honda contract in his pocket, everything was in place for him to become the latest TT great, but short circuit injuries in both 1999 and 2000 resulted in badly broken legs, and he'd never contest a TT race again.

McCallen returned in 1999 with Yamaha, but he wasn't the same rider, and as the 1990s neared an end the racing world started to change. The Formula One class had long disappeared (the final World Championship took place in 1990), and it now only existed at the TT and in Japan.

Subsequently, the TT Formula One race increased its capacity limit to 1000cc, thus making the Honda Fireblade and Yamaha R1 eligible. That saw the entry swell considerably, and although the Honda RC45 line-up of Dunlop and Moodie was still seen as the ones to beat, the Fireblade and R1 were now the choice of the privateer.

V&M's Jack Valentine and Steve Mellor took full advantage of the new rules, with Jefferies and Duffus taking first and third on their yellow and red R1s. It

was Jefferies' first TT win as he beat Dunlop, back to his best on the big bike, by 15.8s, and the 6'2" Yorkshire rider also won both the Production and Senior races to establish himself as the new 'number one' when it came to the TT.

Jefferies finished second in the Junior race, which Moodie won, and the latter made history in the Senior with an opening lap of 124.45mph that broke Fogarty's seven-year-old outright lap record. The rapid pace proved too much, though, and he retired on lap two with a destroyed rear tyre.

As well as Jefferies, another new TT winner was crowned in the shape of his good friend McGuinness. He dominated the Lightweight 250cc race, helped to a near-34s victory by a lap of 118.29mph that broke Lougher's class lap record of 1990. New Zealand's Paul Williams won the concurrently run Lightweight 400cc race and Morris made it three consecutive Singles victories, while Molyneux/Craig Hallam and Fisher/Rick Long shared the two Sidecar races.

Jefferies, Moodie and Dunlop all returned in 2000, with Jefferies joined by Rutter at V&M, Dunlop now on a V-Twin VTR1000 SP1 and Moodie campaigning Honda's flagship Fireblade. However, veteran Dunlop, now in his nineteenth successive year with Honda, expressed his dissatisfaction with his machine at the North West 200, which prompted Honda to fly over a full-factory World Superbike motor for the Formula One TT.

With the former Honda president Kiyoshi Kawashima looking on, there was little to choose between Dunlop and Jefferies for the first four laps of the Formula One race. Jefferies was just half a second clear at two-thirds race distance when his Yamaha's clutch basket exploded at Ballig on lap five, and Dunlop duly brought the Honda home for his seventh and most popular Formula One victory. One of his final hours around his beloved Mountain Course was undoubtedly one of his finest.

Dunlop shared the podium with Rutter and McGuinness, both 20 years younger, but at 48 Joey was riding as well as ever, which he demonstrated later that week when he won both the 250cc and 125cc races. This took his total to a staggering 26 wins, 12 more than the second-highest tally of Mike Hailwood.

McGuinness and Jason Griffiths gave Chrysalis Racing an emotional 1–2 in the Singles race, the team competing in memory of founders Dave and Alison Morris, who had both sadly passed away soon after the 1999 meeting. There was another New Zealand success in the 400cc race, from Brett Richmond, and Fisher/Long took two more Sidecar wins.

After winning the very wet Production race, Jefferies wrapped up TT 2000 with victory in the Senior and a new outright lap record of 125.69mph, while Rutter and Dunlop took second and third. Dunlop posted his best lap of the Mountain Course, 123.87mph, on what would prove to be his final lap.

Tragically, the man everyone thought was invincible died less than a month later in a road race meeting in Tallinn, Estonia. The racing world was stunned, and the TT was about to encounter one of its most challenging periods.

◀ Joey Dunlop (125cc Honda) passes Guthrie's Memorial en route to his third win of the 2000 event. It would prove to his final TT victory.

The 12-month Organisational Cycle

Speaking with the Clerk of the Course, it's surprising how many think he and the ACU Events Ltd team – the Race Organisers – arrive a couple of days before the start of the TT, manage the racing aspect of the event and then disappear, to return a day or two before the start of the Manx GP/Classic TT in August.

Many will ask, 'What do you do for the rest of the year?', but many will appreciate the organisation of the Isle of Man TT Races on both sides of the fence, i.e. the Promoter and the Race Organiser is a full-time, 12-months-of-the-year role for all involved.

The Promoter by definition promotes, markets and financially supports the event in all its guises. The Race Organiser is appointed by the Promoter to organise and deliver the racing aspect of the TT Races, for and on behalf of the Promoter. So, what does a 12-month cycle look like for the Race Organiser? Below gives an idea of the work involved on a month-by-month basis.

June — Post-event, debrief meetings are held with the various agencies to take forward lessons learnt to continuously improve the TT in all aspects.

July — Budget submissions prepared and sent for next year's event.

August	Manx GP/Classic TT event runs parallel to the process starting on reviewing/amending the TT Supplementary Regulations.
September	Post-Manx GP/Classic TT debriefs, which may benefit the TT. Revision of other documentation, such as Event Safety Plan, Course Equipment Manual, Prohibited/Restricted Area Manual.
Oct–Nov	TT Course Sector Review with all Chief Sector Marshals, Clerk of the Course, and the two Deputy Clerks of the Course. This kick-starts the formal Risk Assessment process. Submit final version of TT Supplementary Regulations to ACU Ltd for the issue of an ACU Permit.
November	Finalise budget figures (income v expenditure) and submit final budget figures for events held during the year. Review/issue contracts for service providers.
December	Publish TT Supplementary Regulations and open entries for the next year's TT. Submit final versions of the Risk Assessment and Event Safety Plan to the Department of Infrastructure (DOI) and the Department of Home Affairs (DHA) for review. Once review is complete, DOI will issue the Race Authorisation. There are two legal documents required for the TT and the Manx GP/Classic TT to be held: the ACU Permit, which gives formal approval that the Regulations are in accordance with the ACU National Sporting Code and the ACU Road Races Standing Regulations; and the Race Authorisation issued by the DOI that allows the Clerk of the Course to legally close the roads in accordance with the published schedule.
January	TT entries close. The Race Management Team meets to accept or decline entries to all classes.
February	Competitors are informed if they are unfortunately not accepted. Tabletop Exercise: Race Control staff meet and several scenarios are worked through to test processes and procedures for the forthcoming events. Several scenarios are put together (without the knowledge of Race Control personnel) so that during the exercise they react as they would on event.
March–April	Review Rider/Officials Briefings. Continual review of documentation. Updates/amends sent to competitors/teams as appropriate. Course Contractor begins course build (putting in place Recticel, course protection, etc.).
May	Rider/Officials briefings commence online. First practice commences late May bank holiday.

◀ Fans watch on as Finland's Erno Kostamo prepares to start a race in 2024.

In addition, there is a constant review of the TT Course regarding the road surface, and John Barton (Deputy Clerk of the Course and Event Safety Officer) is in regular contact with the DOI to determine what areas need resurfacing and where work needs to be carried out in readiness for the next event.

Over and above what has been outlined, there is a continuous stream of emails on a daily basis. The Race Organiser is also responsible for the delivery of the spectator speed-controlled lap, formerly known as the Simon Andrews Legacy Lap and now known as the TT Legacy Lap. Risk Assessments need to be prepared for this.

It goes without saying that a huge amount of work goes on behind the scenes by dedicated staff who work on a full-time basis to deliver the oldest, most thrilling, and arguably the most famous motorcycle sport event in the world.

It is hard work for all concerned, with its ups and downs, and it can be as frustrating as it can be fulfilling, but that's the TT! Everyone who is involved is engaged and invested in making the TT the best event it can possibly be.

It's a similar story on the Isle of Man. In terms of the organisational hierarchy and structure, the Isle of Man government has a National Motorsport Committee, which is its overarching strategic group, made up of those departments who collectively deliver the TT, acting on behalf of the Isle of Man government's Council of Ministers. This group is made up of departmental CEOs from the member departments as well as selected other key individuals. The departments represented are:

Department for Enterprise (DFE) – lead department in terms of delivery, the Promoter and commercial rights owner of the TT Races, owner of the brand IP and responsible for the operational budget, facilities, infrastructure, marketing, broadcast, sales, customer services, licensing, ticketing, etc. The DFE appoints a Race Organiser (ACUE Events Ltd) to run the races on its behalf and holds the rights to stage the TT through a long-term licensing agreement with the Auto Cycle Union, first put in place in 2004.

Department for Home Affairs (DHA) – policing, fire and public safety.

Department of Infrastructure (DOI) – provision of the road closure order, preparation of the course and provision of key infrastructure and personnel, as well as non-race responsibilities for public transport, ferry ports, etc.

Manx Care (the NHS) – provision of medical services for visitors and residents alike. It is also worth noting here that the event has its own world-leading medical service provider (MRMS) which is contracted by the Race Organiser to provide the medical services to the event itself. MRMS works with Manx Care in terms of accessing their facilities (i.e. the hospital, helipad, UK trauma care network, etc.).

As the primary department in delivering the TT, the DFE has its own in-house delivery team, known as the Motorsport Team, led by Paul Phillips.

The team is responsible for setting the strategy for the event, the current version of which was brought forward in 2021 and is designed to ensure the long-term sustainability of the event. It is measured primarily in terms of its economic impact, by attracting visitors to the island, and its support of the wider visitor economy.

The Motorsport Team is based at the TT Grandstand and oversees the delivery of the event year-round, working alongside a wide range of contractors. It is unique in terms of sports promotion, being an internal government agency rather than a private company or arm's-length organisation. The team manages hundreds of contractual relationships that support the delivery of the event, including logistics, utilities, regulatory, commercial, marketing, legal and customer services.

Delivering potentially the most complex mass-attendance event of any kind in the British Isles, affecting an entire (small) country, the Motorsport Team is split into several areas:

Sales – raising millions of pounds' worth of direct income through sponsorship, broadcast sales, licensing, ticketing, concessions and a range of other smaller income streams. This income is used to offset the cost of delivering the event.

Marketing and Communications – the in-house marketing team is responsible for creating and delivering the year-round marketing approach, supported by a wide range of external service providers. The team is responsible for the design and execution of all content, supported by a range of videographers, photographers, writers and other digital businesses. The team is also responsible for internal and external communications, media relations and the provision of a year-round press office.

Customer Services – managing the operational delivery and administrative elements of the Motorsport Team's work, including areas such as ticketing, sponsorship account management, live events and experiences, invoicing, complaints, corporate governance, IP protection, etc.

Facilities – year-round management of assets and infrastructure, with responsibility for the construction, operation and dismantling of the 30-acre site, leading a team of over 30 contractors and other staff.

Sport – developing the sporting product in line with the strategic aims; working closely with the Race Organiser and their contractors, teams and competitors; managing the team appearance fee payments, prize funds, travel payments, etc. The delivery of the broadcast content also sits in this area of the Motorsport Team for both TV and radio.

Paul Phillips, as the strategic lead for the team, ensures that it works efficiently and strategically to deliver the event successfully, and increases the benefit to the economy. It delivers on an annual basis both through increasing the number of visitors it attracts and increasing the direct income it generates. Phillips also holds the overall budgetary accountability for the event as well as responsibility for human resources.

As you can see, and probably expect, staging the TT Races is a massive undertaking, but between them the Race Organiser and Race Promoter don't do a bad job at all!

CHAPTER FIVE

2000–2025

At the end of the 2000 season the Isle of Man TT was still reeling from the death of Joey Dunlop, the event's most celebrated and decorated hero, and it soon faced another blow when the 2001 event was cancelled.

There was an outbreak of foot-and-mouth disease in the UK, and while the Isle of Man was unaffected, the Manx government was eager for it to remain that way. Disinfecting 40,000 visitors to ensure the disease was kept off the island would have proven near impossible and so the borders remained closed.

Outside of the two wars it was the first time the event had been cancelled, which was a huge disappointment for all concerned. But the TT returned in 2002 with a largely unchanged programme – the only difference was the Singles race was scrapped and a race for 600cc Production machines was added. The teams and riders were also largely the same, although the depth of field was noticeably changing and the speed differential between the fastest and slowest rider was substantial.

Safety was becoming even more of an issue than it already was. The leading riders were able to contend with the dangers of the course itself and the trackside furniture, but now they were being faced, certainly in practice, with the scary prospect of riders on the racing line travelling some 50–60mph slower than them. The ACU was accepting entries from largely unknown overseas riders to justify the tag of an international event and it wasn't a great look; an accident was waiting to happen.

The man of the moment David Jefferies had switched teams, moving from V&M Yamaha to TAS Suzuki, the team spearheaded by Northern Ireland businessman Hector Neill. He'd taken Norman Brown to victory in the 1982 Senior TT and was keen to repeat that success.

> The man of the moment David Jefferies had switched teams, moving from V&M Yamaha to TAS Suzuki

Jefferies opened his account for the week with a record-breaking start-to-finish victory in the Formula One race, increasing his own outright lap record to 126.68mph and coming home 36s clear of Honda's John McGuinness. The only issue Jefferies encountered was on the final lap, when the bike was stuck in third gear from Ramsey onwards.

Win number two for Jefferies came in the three-lap Production 1000cc race, this time defeating teammate Ian Lougher. New Zealander Bruce Anstey completed the podium as the all-new GSXR1000 Suzuki filled six of the top eight positions.

Jefferies was out of luck in the Junior 600cc race, as Jim Moodie took his eighth TT win on the V&M Yamaha with Lougher again in second. Lougher claimed the top spot in the Production 600cc race and was joined by Anstey and Moodie on the podium.

▲▲ Aviating the front wheel of his Honda through St Ninian's crossroads, John McGuinness claimed his sixth Senior TT win in 2013.
▶ The 2002 Senior race saw David Jefferies take his third successive TT hat-trick.

David Jefferies

▲ David Jefferies and V&M Yamaha were a formidable combination.

From	Baildon, England
Years Active	1996–2003
Wins	9
Podiums	10
Fastest Lap	127.29mph
Manufacturers	Yamaha, Suzuki, Honda

One of the most formidable figures in TT history, David 'DJ' Jefferies stood out with his six-foot-two frame. Yet, despite his stature and fierce riding style, the gentle giant was rarely seen off the bike without a smile.

Coming from a family with a rich TT heritage – his father Tony and uncle Nick were both winners – Jefferies made his TT debut in 1996 and immediately impressed by taking the Newcomers Trophy. An injury sidelined him in 1997, but he returned in 1998 to take two fourth-place finishes in the Senior and Production races aboard the new Yamaha R1.

DJ stamped his authority on the 1999 TT, taking the V&M R1 Yamaha to victory in the Formula One and Senior races and placing second in the Junior. He also won the Production race, earning his first hat-trick.

The new millennium saw him take another hat-trick with wins in the Junior, Production and Senior races, setting an outright lap record in the process and becoming the first rider to lap at over 125mph.

After a year's lay-off due to foot-and-mouth disease, the TT returned in 2002 with a new chapter for DJ. Now riding for TAS Suzuki, he achieved a third consecutive hat-trick with Formula One, Production and Senior wins and increased the lap record again to 127.69mph.

With more dominance expected over the subsequent years, Jefferies' career was tragically cut short during practice for the 2003 TT, in a fatal 160mph crash at Crosby. The accident sparked reform in the way the TT was run and, with his nine victories and frequent lap records, DJ's legacy endures today.

When it came to the Senior, though, no one was stopping Jefferies, and it was another record-breaking performance from the big Yorkshireman. He pulled clear of Lougher with a new outright lap record of 127.29mph and eventually won by 22.1s. McGuinness was again on the podium in third.

Elsewhere, Richard 'Milky' Quayle won the Lightweight 400cc race to become just the third Manxman to win a solo TT and the first since Neil Kelly in 1967. Lougher and Anstey won the 125cc and 250cc races respectively, both of which were poorly supported, and Rob Fisher/Rick Long won both Sidecar races, moving the Cumbrian driver on to ten TT wins.

The 250cc race was discarded for 2003, although the quarter-litre machines were still allowed to enter the Junior race, with the first rider home being awarded a class win as opposed to an outright one. But TT 2003 will always be remembered for the events of Thursday 29 May.

Jefferies wasn't quite his usual self in practice week as issues with his machinery were holding him back. He set the fastest lap of the week on the opening lap of Thursday afternoon's practice session, but four miles into his second lap the nine-time winner and outright lap record holder crashed at 160mph at Crosby and was killed instantly.

The crash brought down a telegraph pole and Moodie was lucky to escape serious injury when the wires got tangled round his neck and pulled him off the back of his bike. Riders complained about a lack of flags to warn them of the danger and it later emerged oil had been laid down on the track by an earlier machine, which caused Jefferies' tragic crash.

▼ V&M Yamaha's Jim Moodie celebrates victory in the 2002 Junior with team owner Jack Valentine.

The Anatomy of a Modern TT Bike

While motorcycles still have an engine, two wheels and brakes, the modern TT Superbikes of Peter Hickman, Michael Dunlop and Dean Harrison look vastly different to those that once dominated 'between the hedges'. With modern bikes regularly nudging 200mph, every aspect of the machine is being pushed to its maximum as riders eke out every last tenth around the course.

While the outlines of these Superbikes closely resemble their counterparts in the World or British Superbike Championships, these bikes are exclusively built to contend with the unique nature of the Isle of Man.

The Modern Classes

The modern Isle of Man TT is broken down into several classes, notably the Superbike/Senior, Superstock, Supersport and Supertwin. The Superbikes are the pinnacle of the event, and consist of production-derived 1000cc machines. Delivering well over 200bhp, these bikes can be heavily modified to include full race suspension, lightweight wheels, aftermarket electronics and race-spec engines.

The Superstock class features the same 1000cc machines, but they must remain much closer to the production model that customers can buy from their local dealer. Despite being a lower-specification machine compared to a Superbike, many riders prefer to use their stock bike, and the outright lap record is currently held by Peter Hickman on his stock BMW.

Traditionally home to 600cc four-cylinder bikes, the Supersport class has expanded in recent years to include triples and twin-cylinder machines up to 955cc. Engine tuning is permitted within certain limits, while aftermarket suspension, brakes and bodywork are also allowed.

The final solo class is the Supertwins, in which bikes are based on modified middleweight twin-cylinder production models.

▶ Peter Hickman and the Smiths Racing BMW S1000RR.

1 Engine

The engine is the beating heart of the machine and is tuned to deliver maximum performance and reliability to ensure it can withstand the immense challenges of the TT course. Across every category, riders require relentless torque, sharp acceleration and consistent high speeds, which means engines need to withstand prolonged high-rpm running, elevation changes and nearly two hours of racing.

2 Frame and Chassis

Just like the engine, the frame and chassis have to withstand incredible forces during the course of a TT race. They need to provide high-speed stability, nimble handling and maximum feedback to ensure riders can have the confidence to attack the course.

3 Suspension

Unlike race circuits, which are usually billiard-table smooth, the Isle of Man TT course is full of bumps, jumps, uneven surfaces, manhole covers and leaves, which means the suspension is working in overdrive. To combat this, many riders will run slightly softer setups than they would in short-circuit racing, to allow the bike to absorb the bumps more easily and remain more stable.

4 Brakes

While the first TT bikes featured drum brakes, modern machines feature the latest in brake technology, with calipers and oversized discs as standard to quickly reduce speed into sections like Braddan Bridge or Parliament Square. While carbon brakes are the norm in MotoGP, the TT machines will usually feature steel options to ensure durability and performance throughout the race.

5 Tyres

TT tyres are built for endurance, not just grip. The front tyres will need to last the full six-lap race, while the rears will need to last for up to four, all while maintaining performance. Unlike short circuit racing, where riders spend more time leaning over, the TT sees sustained high speeds, which means the centre of the tyre needs to be made of a harder compound.

6 Aerodynamics and Bodywork

Fairings must resemble their road-going counterparts but are often made from lighter materials. At the Isle of Man, aerodynamic stability is critical at high speeds – especially over the mountain, where crosswinds can unseat a rider. In more recent years, winglets have started to appear, which help to increase downforce and overall front-end stability.

7 Electronics

Modern TT bikes use advanced ECU systems to manage power delivery, traction control and engine braking. However, electronics are often simplified compared to those used in MotoGP or World Superbikes, as consistency and reliability take priority. In fact, many of the current TT riders prefer more minimal intervention to help them maintain a natural connection with the bike.

8 Fuel Tank

In modern TT races riders and bikes do two full laps of the course before pitting to refuel, which means fuel tanks need to cover over 75 miles of high-speed racing. To combat this, bikes feature a larger tank than the stock bike, but it must not exceed 24 litres.

9 Dashboard and Switchgear

Digital displays show critical data to riders, such as gear position, rpm and warning lights. Switches are mounted within easy thumb reach to toggle mapping, activate the pit lane speed limiter or even engage the rear brake.

▲ Kiwi Shaun Harris won both the 600cc and 1000cc Production races in 2003, 12 years after making his TT debut.

As days and weeks passed, more came to light as to just how poorly equipped the marshals and race organisers were to deal with such an incident. The TT was arguably at its lowest ebb, but if any good came out of DJ's crash it was that the TT was given a major overhaul immediately afterwards, with a substantial increase in professionalism and standards both on and off the track.

The tragedy overshadowed the 2003 event, but the racing continued and, with the blessing of the Jefferies family, TAS Racing and Adrian Archibald took their place on the grid. In a perfect tribute, Archibald won both the Formula One and Senior TTs, with McGuinness and Lougher joining him on the podium in each.

McGuinness beat two more Northern Irishmen, Richard Britton and Ryan Farquhar, in the Lightweight 400cc race, and 1998 British Champion Chris Palmer claimed the honours in the concurrently run 125cc race.

Both Production races went the way of New Zealand's Shaun Harris, who had made his TT debut back in 1991, with the 600cc race stopped after two of the scheduled three laps due to mist descending on the mountain. Meanwhile, the Sidecar races were shared between Ian Bell/Neil Carpenter and Dave Molyneux/Craig Hallam.

The most popular win of 2003, though, was that of Anstey in the Junior race. With V&M having disbanded, Jack Valentine set up the Triumph ValMoto team with Anstey, Moodie and McGuinness as the riders. Anstey was, arguably, the number three rider but he saw off the challenge of Lougher and Archibald to give Triumph their first TT victory since 1975.

McGuinness switched to Yamaha in 2004, the last year the Lightweight 400cc, 125cc and Formula One races would be held on the Mountain Course, and he opened race week with victory in the latter where he set a new outright lap record of 127.68mph. Archibald and new TAS Suzuki teammate Anstey took second and third.

McGuinness added further race wins in the Lightweight 400cc and Junior 600cc races to claim his first hat-trick, setting another lap record in the Junior, but he was second best to Anstey in the Production 1000cc encounter, where Jason Griffiths took third.

As well as McGuinness, Anstey was the rider of the week as he took five podiums from five starts, with second-place finishes in the Production 600cc race, where Ryan Farquhar secured his maiden TT victory, Kawasaki's first since 1984, and the Senior. The Senior was a 1–2 for TAS Suzuki, with Archibald repeating his 2003 win after early leader McGuinness retired with clutch trouble on lap two.

Local hero Gary Carswell finished third in the Senior race, the first Manxman on a Senior TT podium since Tom Sheard won in 1923. There was further joy for the island's population as Molyneux/Dan Sayle dominated the Sidecar races, Molyneux moving up to 11 wins and overhauling the previous record tally of ten by Rob Fisher. The final 125cc race went the way of Palmer to make it two wins in two years for the Castletown-based rider.

▼ Former 125cc British Champion Chris Palmer claimed his first TT victory in the 2003 125cc race.

▲ Ian Lougher exits Signpost Corner on his way to victory in the first Junior race of 2005.

Changes were evident in 2005, with the Formula One and Production 1000cc races replaced by the Superbike and Superstock, thus bringing them in line with championships across the world. A slimmer seven-race schedule was announced, with the Lightweight 400cc, 125cc and Production 600cc races scrapped but a second Junior race added.

There was hard work going on behind the scenes as the British Superbike Championship teams returned, impressed by the new regime now running the event and new, exciting and high-calibre newcomers being attracted. Talented youngster Guy Martin had lapped at 122mph in 2004, and in 2005 riders including Australian Cameron Donald made their TT bow.

AIM Yamaha, TAS Suzuki, Stobart Honda, MSS Kawasaki and Vitrans Honda were just some of the British Championship teams taking part, with McGuinness riding for AIM Yamaha. Having lost his good friend David Jefferies, it would have been easy for McGuinness to walk away from the TT, especially as he was the first on the scene of the devastating crash, but instead he stepped up to fill the gap left by DJ.

Having won his first 'big bike' race the year before, McGuinness and Yamaha left no stone unturned in 2005. With a tactic of being fast out the blocks, the Morecambe rider was able to fully transfer his short circuit skills to the Mountain Course, building up a lead on the opening laps and then managing it from there. He did that in both the Superbike and Senior to win each by more than half a minute.

Regular sparring partner Lougher won the first Junior race and McGuinness took second, but they both retired from the second race with Farquhar, single-

Bruce Anstey

▲ Always laid-back, Bruce Anstey relaxes between races.

From	Wellington, New Zealand
Years Active	1996–2019
Wins	12
Podiums	37
Fastest Lap	132.398mph
Manufacturers	Suzuki, Honda, Yamaha, Mugen

Another rapid New Zealander, laid-back Bruce Anstey firmly established himself as one of the most popular, and successful, road racers of the 2000s. Known for his smooth style and remarkable consistency, he made a relatively low-key TT debut in 1996, finishing twenty-ninth in the Lightweight race.

After missing the 1997 meeting due to illness, Anstey returned in 1998, placing twentieth in the Senior TT on his 250cc Yamaha. Despite the modest result, he turned heads by setting the fifth-fastest lap in practice for the Lightweight class.

His first podium came in 2000 with second in the Lightweight 250cc race behind Joey Dunlop, followed by his maiden TT victory in the same class in 2002. That year he also scored podiums in both the Production 600 and 1000 races.

In 2003, Anstey stunned many by winning the Junior TT on a Triumph, the marque's first TT win in 27 years. In subsequent years, when riding for TAS Suzuki and Padgetts Honda, he continued to collect podiums and wins, ultimately achieving 12 TT victories and 37 podiums across every major class. He earned particular success in the Supersport and Superstock categories, the latter earning him the nickname 'Mr Superstock'.

One of Anstey's finest moments was in the 2015 Superbike TT, where he claimed victory with a new race record and the fastest lap. In 2017 he became the first (and only) rider to lap the Mountain Course at over 120mph on a 250cc machine, winning the Lightweight Classic TT.

In 2018 Anstey was diagnosed with cancer, forcing a racing hiatus, but he made a powerful and emotional comeback the following year, winning the Lightweight 250cc Classic TT in dominant fashion.

handedly flying the flag for Kawasaki, coming out on top from Griffiths, who was third in race one, and Ireland's Raymond Porter.

Anstey won the Superstock race, but only after teammate Archibald retired at the Bungalow on the final lap. Team boss Hector Neill had failed to put enough fuel into the big Suzuki at the solitary pit stop and Archibald's tank ran dry, gifting the victory to Anstey ahead of Lougher (Honda) and Farquhar (Kawasaki), making it three different makes in the top three.

The two Sidecar races were shared between Manxmen Molyneux/Sayle and Nick Crowe/Darren Hope, with Molyneux/Sayle posting the first sub-20-minute lap and raising the three-wheel lap record to 116.04mph. Race week again concluded with the Senior, where McGuinness had a trouble-free ride to win ahead of Lougher with Martin taking a sensational third place in only his second year at the TT.

Further changes came in 2006 with just four solo races held – Superbike, Junior, Superstock and Senior – to accompany the two Sidecar races. Safety and rider welfare was becoming more prevalent, an example being that newcomers were now given an escorted lap behind an experienced rider liaison officer or travelling marshal before the opening practice session.

McGuinness had made the headlines during the winter months by switching from Yamaha to HM Plant Honda, but it was business as usual as he took his second hat-trick, beginning with another start-to-finish victory in the Superbike race. Increasing his outright lap record to 127.933mph, he came home 39s ahead of Lougher (Honda), with new challenger Ian Hutchinson third for Kawasaki.

◀ John McGuinness approaches Whitegates on the AIM Yamaha in 2005. McGuinness won both the Superbike and Senior races that year.
▼ Irishman Martin Finnegan was one of the most popular riders in the early 2000s, and certainly one of the most spectacular!

Bridging the Gap Between the Tower and the Track

As one of the largest motorsport events of the year, the Isle of Man TT has evolved into a global spectacle of high-octane, adrenaline-fuelled action. It takes a team of dedicated individuals to ensure everything runs smoothly, and it's down to Rider Liaison Officers John Barton and Richard 'Milky' Quayle to act as the crucial link between the riders on the track and the Clerk of the Course, Gary Thompson, in the tower.

Both Barton and Quayle are former Isle of Man TT racers themselves; Milky is a proud Manxman and race winner in 2002, and John is a long-time island resident (albeit with his native Essex twang, still) with two podiums and almost 70 TT race starts to his name.

It's this racing pedigree and understanding of the unique challenges of the TT that make them the ideal pairing. Whether it's weather updates, delays, changes to scheduling or addressing rider concerns, the duo operate as conduits for the fast and accurate flow of information between competitors and those in charge. Barton explains:

'That connection between the tower and the ground is vital for a number of reasons. We've got to make sure the riders are 100 per cent focused on the job, so we're on hand and ready to quickly resolve any niggles or problems that might come up.'

In an environment as unforgiving as the TT, those niggles can be anything from track condition queries – as seen in the sighting lap ahead of the 2025 Senior TT – to last-minute technical issues. Barton and Quayle, having 'been there and done it', know instinctively what's likely to be going through a rider's mind.

'I think what works so well for Milky and me is that we've been there, we've done it. We know what is going through the riders' minds and what might be bothering them, so we're on it straightaway. I'd like to think that most times we're able to pick up on things before they actually become a problem.'

However, their remit extends far beyond managing the logistics and rider wellbeing during race week. One of their most significant contributions lies in the mentoring of TT newcomers. For those riders who are new to the TT, the challenge that lies ahead of them is nothing short of immense.

The Mountain Course is 37.73 miles of relentless concentration, with over 200 corners, countless jumps and a vast array of reference points to learn, including kerbs, trees, lamp posts and manhole covers, all of which serve as visual cues for apexes, braking markers and hazards.

Unlike short circuits, where visibility is largely clear and corners are repeated lap after lap, the TT is a high-speed memory test on public roads, with the consequences for error often severe. The Mountain Course is like nowhere else in the world, which means preparation needs to begin long before riders head off down Glencrutchery Road.

Typically, riders will arrive at the TT having come via one of two routes. Some (such as Jamie Coward, Dominic Herbertson and Nathan Harrison) choose to build experience at the Manx Grand Prix first, while others (such as Peter Hickman, Josh Brookes and Glenn Irwin) arrive with top-tier short circuit credentials. However, no matter their background,

▲ Prince William enjoys a tour of the control tower with current Clerk of the Course Gary Thompson.

they all turn up as newcomers and are treated the same way.

'The first thing I will ask people is, "How do you normally learn a new circuit?" Because everybody's different, and what works for one person might not work with another.'

Barton continues:

'However, you also have to be careful because there is so much to learn, and you don't want to overwhelm or overload a newcomer with information.
   'You can see when their minds are blown, and you need to avoid that because it will only set them back, so you need to learn, go away, process it all and then come back to it. That's the same for if you're watching onboards, driving laps or even playing the computer game.'

Only once Barton and Quayle are satisfied with a rider's mental preparation and course knowledge is their TT entry formally accepted. Their first closed-road lap will then be completed behind either Barton or Quayle, who closely monitor the progress of each newcomer throughout their debut event and the years to come.
   So while the role of Rider Liaison Officer might not make the headlines, and the only time spectators trackside or following along at home might hear either John or Milky is when they're interviewed on the TV or radio, without them the TT would lose one of its most vital support systems. Their job is equal parts fixer, teacher, advocate, and occasionally therapist, and they are the steadying voices when nerves and tension are at their highest.

John McGuinness

The most famous name in twenty-first-century road racing, John McGuinness is a true TT legend. With an incredible 23 wins and 47 podiums, he sits third on the all-time winners list and is one of only four riders to have made over 100 TT starts.

From	Morecambe, England
Years Active	1996–present
Wins	23
Podiums	47
Fastest Lap	132.701mph
Manufacturers	Honda, Yamaha, Aprilia, Mugen, Norton, AMDM/BMW, Ducati

Affectionately dubbed the 'Morecambe Missile', McGuinness began his TT career in 1996, finishing fifteenth in the Lightweight TT. His first podium came the following year with third in the same race along with the fastest lap, a feat he repeated in 1998 before taking victory in 1999.

Further podiums and wins came over the following years, with his first 'big bike' success coming on the R1 Yamaha in the 2004 Formula One race. Further wins in the Junior and Lightweight 400cc races gave him his first hat-trick.

McGuinness had victories in the F1 and Senior in 2005, before switching to Honda in 2006, where he claimed another hat-trick, this time in the Superbike, Junior and Senior races. In 2007 he won both the Superbike and Senior races again and became the first rider to break the 130mph lap barrier.

McGuinness continued winning aboard the factory Honda, with multiple Superbike and Senior victories, but arguably his most iconic win came in the 2015 Senior. Many had written him off at the age of 43, but he dominated from start to finish, setting a new outright lap record of 132.701mph and taking his twenty-third and, to date, final TT win.

With an enduring passion for the island and the sport, John's impact both on and off the track has made him a genuine TT legend, and he continues to inspire the next generation of road racers.

▲ John McGuinness celebrates victory in the 2007 Senior, the race which saw him set the first ever 130mph lap.

It was a similar outcome for McGuinness in the Junior race. Hutchinson was his closest rival but was disqualified from second for a technical infringement, which promoted Anstey to second with the consistent Griffiths in third.

Suzuki's Anstey chalked up another win in the Superstock race, Hutchinson and Griffiths alongside him on the podium – the Honda Fireblade was not as competitive in Superstock trim. Anstey was the man to beat in the class and had rightly earned himself the nickname 'Mr Superstock'.

There was no stopping McGuinness in the Senior, though, where he again led all six laps and again improved the outright lap record, this time to 129.451mph, which now meant a 130mph lap was within touching distance. Donald, in just his second year of competition around the Mountain Course, finished in a superb second place with Anstey third.

There was drama during practice in the Sidecar class, when Molyneux/Hallam escaped serious injury when their Honda outfit flipped over on the 140mph jump at Rhencullen. The sidecar was destroyed and they were out of the races, leaving fellow Manxmen Crowe/Hope to win both.

In 2007 the TT celebrated its centenary and all the stops were pulled out to make it an event to remember. The first race of 1907 was re-enacted on the original St John's Course, and a parade of former winners, including Giacomo Agostini, Phil Read, Jim Redman, John Surtees and Carl Fogarty, was arguably the best seen.

▼ With the spectacular Isle of Man coastline behind him, Guy Martin passes through Guthrie's on his AIM Yamaha.

High-calibre newcomers like British Champion Steve Plater, Gary Johnson and Keith Amor were on the entry, with double podium finisher John Barton joining Richard Quayle as a rider liaison officer, a role that was proving both pivotal and crucial for course debutantes.

McGuinness was joined at HM Plant Honda by Hutchinson, with Martin riding for the highly professional Hydrex Honda team. Suzuki still had Anstey and Archibald, and the list of high-level privateers also included the likes of Lougher, Farquhar, Martin Finnegan and local stars Nigel Beattie and 21-year-old Conor Cummins, who'd made his debut the year before.

McGuinness was on a roll and seemed untouchable in the 'big bike' races, seeing off the early and considerable challenge of Martin to win the Superbike race, which had been delayed by two days, by 26s. Hutchinson took third, but he got his revenge in the Supersport race, when he claimed his maiden TT victory from McGuinness by just 2.84s, with Martin in third.

Anstey took his now customary Superstock victory, setting a new lap record of 128.400mph on his way to defeating Honda teammates McGuinness and Hutchinson. Both Sidecar races went to HM Plant Honda's Molyneux and new passenger Rick Long.

That just left the Senior, and McGuinness's second lap of 130.354mph put him in the record books once more, with the first 130mph lap of the Mountain Course. He went on to win by more than half a minute, taking his thirteenth TT victory, and in a repeat of the Superbike race Martin and Hutchinson again took second and third place. Steve Plater finished seventh and became the fastest ever newcomer with a lap of 125.808mph.

But the event was marred by tragedy, when a crash at Joey's on the fifth lap of the Senior not only claimed the life of newcomer Marc Ramsbotham, but also those of spectators Dean Jacob and Gregory Kenzig. Race marshals Hilary Musson and Janice Phillips were also injured in another dark hour in the history of the TT.

> McGuinness's second lap of 130.354mph put him in the record books once more

In 2008, a second Supersport race was added to the schedule, and in a radical and controversial move organisers once more included races for the 125cc and 250cc classes. As in the 1950s, they weren't to be held on the Mountain Course and instead were to take place on the 4.25-mile Billown Course, used annually for July's Southern 100 meeting.

There was no official Honda team, instead the manufacturer supported several privateer teams, such as Padgetts and Hydrex, with McGuinness and Martin, respectively, lining up for them. However, both retired from the opening Superbike race, Martin on lap four while holding a 10s lead, which allowed new TAS Suzuki signing Donald to take his first TT win from teammate Anstey. Former team member Adrian Archibald finished third.

Donald was the first Australian victor since Graeme McGregor in 1984, and he didn't have to wait long for win number two, as victory came in the Superstock race despite some tricky conditions early on. McGuinness and Martin got their week up and running in second and third.

McGuinness Forms the 130 Club
2007

Nowadays, the 130 Club is a burgeoning group that every TT rider aims to join. The likes of Michael Dunlop and Peter Hickman have now attained those speeds on their Supersport bikes. However, back at the start of the 2007 TT, the 130mph lap was still an elusive achievement.

With 2007 marking the Isle of Man TT's hundredth year, the island was buzzing more than usual, and all eyes were on race favourite John McGuinness — who had already won the Superbike and Junior races earlier in the week — to see if he could become the first rider to lap the Mountain Course in under 17min 24.827s. With bad weather affecting the opening half of race week, it looked like the milestone would go untouched once more… until the week's final race.

With near-perfect conditions all around the island, McGuinness and his HM Plant Honda Fireblade were in imperious form from the very start. Storming away down Glencrutchery Road, he steadily pulled clear of the pursuing riders; an opening lap of 129.883mph gave him a lead of almost ten seconds as he flashed over the line to start what would be a historic second lap.

As the timing screens showed him under the lap record and on course for the 130, the fans trackside came alive, cheering him all the way around from the hedges and grass bankings. Despite needing to slow down to make his first pit stop, John's lap speed was 130.354mph, cementing his status as the inaugural member of the racing world's most exclusive club.

As if the record wasn't enough, John went on to win the race comfortably for his then-thirteenth TT victory. However, it was that 130mph lap that defined the day, and arguably his career, and marked the dawning of a new era in TT racing that would see the pursuit of speed continue to accelerate.

◀ John McGuinness passes through Union Mills on his way to making history in the 2007 Senior race.

Anstey then won the opening Supersport race – or, at least, he thought he had. The New Zealander had dominated proceedings to win by over 20s, but he was removed from the results when the exhaust cam was found to be illegal to what was homologated. That promoted Plater to first with McGuinness and Amor completing the podium.

With the issue corrected, Anstey served up a repeat performance in the second race and officially took his seventh TT win. Challenged early on by Hutchinson, now riding for Yamaha, Anstey pulled clear to win by more than 34s as Farquhar took third for his first podium finish since 2005.

Crowe, with new passenger Mark Cox, won both Sidecar races, where newcomer Tim Reeves, a world champion on the short circuits, proved to be the sensation, with third- and sixth-place finishes alongside passenger Patrick Farrance. The last time a Sidecar newcomer had finished on the podium was Jock Taylor in 1978. The 125cc and 250cc races, not universally popular with the fans, saw wins by wily veterans Palmer and Lougher at Billown.

After a mixed week, luck finally smiled on McGuinness in the Senior where he battled with Donald for five of the six laps. The duo were never more than a few seconds apart, but an oil leak, sustained after an extra hard hit to the bike at the bottom of Barregarrow, caused Donald to slow on the final lap. McGuinness won by 51.95s to equal Mike Hailwood's tally of 14 TT victories, as Hutchinson ended his 2008 campaign in third.

▼ Australian Cameron Donald claimed victory in the 2008 Superbike race ahead of fellow Suzuki riders Bruce Anstey (left) and Adrian Archibald (right).

▲ The garage forecourt is a good vantage point at Parliament Square as double race winners Nick Crowe/Mark Cox lead Dave Molyneux/Dan Sayle in 2008.

Donald was in the headlines again in 2009 when he unofficially smashed the outright lap record in practice, with a lap of 131.457mph. But a missed gear at Keppel Gate during the following evening's practice session saw him crash out with a dislocated shoulder, and his TT was over.

More headlines came with the organisers' decision to run a one-lap race for electric motorcycles, titled TTXGP. Split into two classes, the machines varied greatly in quality and made practically zero sound. With fewer than 20 entries it was far from a spectacle, although it was hoped interest would grow in subsequent years. The controversial 125cc/250cc races on the Billown Course remained.

The opening Superbike race was delayed 48 hours due to bad weather and McGuinness grabbed the lead from the off. The HM Plant Honda rider was never headed and came home 18s clear of new teammate Plater, with Martin (Hydrex Honda) rounding out the podium.

Hutchinson was fourth in the Superbike race; now riding for Padgetts Honda he made the next two races his own, with victories in both the Superstock and opening Supersport races. On each occasion he saw off the close challenge of Martin, and another Honda rider, Amor (Wilson Craig Racing), took third in both races.

Course assessment

ACU Events Ltd have been responsible for the organisation of the Isle of Man TT Races since 2008. Since then, the TT has experienced significant development and growth across almost every area of the event.

Racing speeds, visitor numbers and audience growth have all reached new heights in this period, but with that has come increased complexity and new pressures to the events delivery. One aspect that has remained relatively unchanged in that time is the structure and human resource of the Race Organiser.

Over the last few years, John Barton has been working his way through the levels of Clerk of the Course certification and, in addition to his work as Rider Liaison Officer at the TT, he's also Deputy Clerk of the Course under Gary Thompson, alongside the experienced Lizzie Kinvig, bringing increased resilience and bandwidth to the team in Race Control.

However, it's John's recent appointment to the role of Head of Infrastructure that arguably brings the biggest benefits to the Race Organiser. Essentially, he's responsible for the course build, preparing 37.73 miles of public highway for use as a race course where speeds of 200mph are reached.

The Job at Hand

For the TT Course to be used as a race course, it must be certified each year by the ACU – the governing body for motorcycle racing in Great Britain (not Northern Ireland) and the Isle of Man. A Course Equipment Manual details everything that needs to be done: the location and number of Recticel barriers, the position of signage detailing restricted and prohibited areas, scaffolding platforms for marshal points, the distribution of firefighting equipment, even the location of Portaloos for the army of marshals dotted around the TT course. A place for everything and everything in its place.

The course build starts ten weeks before the first bike heads off down Bray Hill, and while there are teams of contractors doing the work, it's Barton's responsibility to make sure those people are in place and that it's all delivered on time and to the specification set by the ACU. But nothing stays still in racing, and there are always things to improve, which, in turn, means more work for John:

> *'We're constantly increasing the amount of Recticel we have to put around the course, as well as upgrading the existing stock of equipment we already have. More equipment means more planning and more time to put it all into place.'*

Understandably, the Course Equipment Manual is a highly detailed and sizeable document, but there are certain things it can't account for. The kind of things that happen when a race course is used by tens of thousands of cars, buses and HGVs every day for 365 days of the year and is lined by trees, bushes, lamp posts, telegraph poles and walls.

This means that year-round John has monthly inspections of the course to identify issues and grade them in order to prioritise any works that are required. He then works closely with the Isle of Man government's Department of Infrastructure (DOI) and Department of Environment, Food and Agriculture (DEFA) to make it all happen.

▲ Michael Rutter flies high on the Bathams Racing BMW through St Ninian's crossroads.

'I'm lucky enough to be working with a great group of people across the DOI and DEFA. Making the various organisations work together in the best possible way is a big part of my job. There's a lot of planning that has to be done before the work even starts, especially when we need road closures to get stuff done.

'The TT's the biggest thing in the world for me, but the other departments obviously have their own priorities and local residents also want to live their lives with as little disruption as possible, so we make sure we get everyone working together on this.

'There's a number of improvements to the road surface each year – recent years have seen this take place at Greeba Castle, Sulby Straight, the Waterworks and then Casey's, the thirty-second milestone, Windy Corner and Brandywell up on the mountain, but one of the most noticeable things has been through Glen Helen and Kerrowmoar.

'We've got about 1,000 trees around the course that are diseased and dead, so they need to come down before they fall down onto the course. The last thing we need is Michael Dunlop coming round the corner to some great big elm tree in the road! For that reason, we took down a large number through Glen Helen, and it's remarkable how different it looks as you go through there now.'

But it's not all about trees, roadworks and barriers for John. Far from it.

Evolution

A new Safety Management System introduced during the Covid-enforced break set the Race Organiser the task of doing absolutely everything in their power to minimise risk in every area they possibly could. That's not about speed limiters or engine limits; the spectacle of the TT isn't going anywhere. It's about a systematic approach to the risks associated with the TT that is driven by data and feedback, and for the benefit of everyone concerned.

As Head of Infrastructure, John is responsible for pushing things forward and striving to improve safety standards on and around the Snaefell Mountain Course.

2022 saw the introduction of a new digital red flag system at 28 positions around the course, which received unanimous praise from throughout the paddock. As a result, John deployed a further seven units for 2023, and expanded their scope to also 'black flag' any faulty machines.

'It doesn't happen too often, but there are times where Race Control will be informed about a bike going round with a mechanical issue. In those situations time is of the essence, and we have to act quickly for both that rider and all the others out on the course.

'At the moment, Race Control will get a report in from the marshals about a bike with an issue, we'll confirm the details and then we'll radio ahead to the next sector to get that bike pulled in and checked. It doesn't take long for that process to happen, but the guys are covering distances so fast these days.

'For instance, if we get reports of a bike at Crosby with an issue, we'll look to pull them in at Ballacraine, about three miles further down the road. But they'll cover that distance in less than a minute and so we might not get the message through in time to flag them down, or the riders might even miss the signal. It might be a couple more miles down the road at Glen Helen when we can next intervene safely.

'It's a little over two minutes, but that's potentially five miles of road that's contaminated. So we also use the digital flag system to issue black flags. Our marshals are still out there as the frontline, reporting the issues and flagging riders down, but the technology supplements their work.'

Revolution

While it's an evolutionary step for the digital flag system, there's also been a revolutionary change overseen by John, with the introduction of GPS tracking for competitors in 2023.

GPS technology is nothing new but – as with many things – the TT Course throws up its own set of challenges. High speeds, lean angles, bumps, tree cover and coverage black spots thanks to the lay of the Manx land are just some of the challenges the GPS tracking faces. But after a rigorous testing programme over the past few years, the system is now mandatory for all machines taking to the TT Mountain Course, and it's John's job to oversee its implementation and delivery.

'Don't get me wrong, I'd be lying if I said I knew everything about the technology inside the boxes! But I do understand how much of a difference it's going to make in running an event safely and managing any incidents that might occur, and so I'm very proud to have taken it on and worked with the riders to ensure there's been a successful implementation.'

His new roles and responsibilities may have put an end to John's racing career at the TT, but don't feel too sorry for him just yet. He'll still get his TT fix when he leads the newcomers around for their first ever taste of the Mountain Course, as well as going out for inspection laps ahead of practice sessions and races to ensure the course he's helped put together is in the best possible shape, and as safe as possible, for those speeds of 200mph and more to be attained.

◄ Davey Todd about to enter Hillberry where spectators get extremely close to the action.

The second Supersport race started in damp conditions, which played into the hands of 20-year-old Michael Dunlop. He'd made his TT debut two years earlier after winning the 2006 Newcomers Manx Grand Prix, but although he was quickest in practice, he'd retired in the opening three races. However, he set a scorching pace in the damp and eventually won by more than half a minute from Anstey and Cummins.

Victory saw Michael emulate the feats of his father, Robert, who'd tragically been killed at the North West 200 the year before. His maiden TT victory was the start of an amazing career on the Mountain Course.

The opening Sidecar race went the way of Molyneux/Sayle but the second was only half a lap old when it was stopped due to a serious crash at Ballacobb involving 2008 victors Crowe/Cox. The duo crashed after hitting a hare and both were badly injured as debris was strewn across the road. Neither competed again.

> TTXGP honours went the way of Rob Barber and Chris Heath, Barber setting the fastest lap at 87.434mph

TTXGP honours went the way of Rob Barber and Chris Heath, Barber setting the fastest lap at 87.434mph. McGuinness then set the early pace in the Senior, raising his outright lap record to 131.578mph on lap two. On lap four, his race was over as the chain snapped exiting Parliament Square, and teammate Plater took over to win by almost 20s from Cummins and Gary Johnson.

Ian Lougher won the last 125cc and 250cc races at Billown before they were dropped from the 2010 race schedule.

In what would prove to be a historic week, the 2010 TT was also the subject of a new documentary called *TT3D: Closer to the Edge*, which would propel the TT to new heights.

Plater was absent after sustaining injuries at the preceding North West 200 meeting, and it was Cummins who made a blistering start to the Superbike race, lapping at 131.511mph from a standing start. McGuinness retired at Sulby with a faulty crank sensor and Cummins extended his lead until the second pit stop, when the McAdoo Kawasaki refused to fire.

Just a few miles later, Cummins was out at Laurel Bank with clutch trouble and, able to ease off in the closing stages, Hutchinson won from Dunlop by 34s with Donald fighting back from thirteenth to third after overshooting the Nook on the opening lap.

Fourth in the Superbike race after being hit with a 30s penalty for speeding in the pit lane, a fired-up Martin led the opening Supersport race in the early stages, but Hutchinson led at half-race distance. It remained close, though, and at the chequered flag Hutchinson's margin of victory was just 3.03s, with Dunlop finishing a disappointed third.

In the following Superstock race, Hutchinson was embroiled in an even closer battle, this time with Farquhar (KMR Kawasaki), who led for the first three

◀ Jumping Ballaugh Bridge, Steve Plater won the 2009 Senior on the 1000cc HM Plant Honda.

▲ 2010 was an unforgettable year for Ian Hutchinson and his Padgetts Honda team.

laps. However, with a stunning new lap record of 130.741mph, the first 130mph lap in the class, Hutchinson got the verdict by a slender 1.32s, with a third for Cummins going some way to making up for his Superbike disappointment.

Hutchinson's superb week continued when victory in the second Supersport race saw him equal Phillip McCallen's 1996 record of four wins in a week. Both he and Dunlop broke Amor's two-day-old lap record, and although Dunlop was quicker at 127.836mph, Hutchinson got the win by 1.45s.

Hutchinson was on course to make history, and after two laps of the Senior only 6s covered race leader McGuinness, Hutchinson, Martin and Cummins. Shortly afterwards the race was red-flagged, when Martin crashed heavily at 160mph at Ballagarey, but he miraculously escaped with non-serious injuries.

The race was restarted over four laps, and Hutchinson led McGuinness by 0.6s after the first lap. Another faulty crank sensor put McGuinness out again, then Cummins crashed at the Verandah and viciously cartwheeled down the mountainside. Hutchinson now had a comfortable lead, and he made history with his fifth win of the week, Farquhar and Anstey taking second and third.

The Sidecar races were also close. Austrian Klaus Klaffenbock and local man Dan Sayle defeated Molyneux/Farrance by 2.63s in the first race, and John Holden/Andrew Winkle by just 1.12s in the second. Having made his debut in 2004, former world champion Klaffenbock became the second Austrian to win a TT race after Rupert Hollaus in the 1954 Ultra-Lightweight race.

Hutchy's Fantastic Five
2010

Few riders have been through, and overcome, as many challenges as Ian 'Hutchy' Hutchinson. Over the years, the softly spoken Yorkshireman has established himself as a firm fan favourite, but it's his feats in 2010 that will see him immortalised in TT history.

Already a multiple TT winner by 2010, Hutchy was one of the favourites coming into race week, but nothing could have prepared the road racing world for the record-breaking dominance he would show. Kicking things off with a dominant display in the Superbike TT, the Padgetts Honda rider claimed his first win of the week by almost 34s over Michael Dunlop.

Things were much closer in Monday's two races. The four-lap Supersport TT saw Hutchy cross the finish line just three seconds ahead of Guy Martin, while in the afternoon's four-lap Superstock race things were even closer, with just 1.32s between Hutchinson and Ryan Farquhar.

Having already joined an exclusive club of riders to claim three wins in a week, Hutchy remained ice-cool, claiming victory in the second Supersport outing to become the first rider since Phillip McCallen in 1996 to win four in the same event.

This was already a momentous achievement, but by the time the final solo race of the week arrived – the blue riband Senior – the entire island was questioning whether Hutchinson could take five. Initially planned for six laps, the race was red-flagged on lap three following Martin's now-infamous fireball crash at the high-speed Ballagarey, which he thankfully walked away from with minor fractures.

The race was re-run over four laps and Hutchinson was able to lead from lap one, but he had John McGuinness, Conor Cummins and Bruce Anstey in very close contention. Continuing to stretch out his lead over the remaining three laps, he eventually crossed the line to take an unprecedented fifth win by over 37s, with Farquhar once more taking second place.

To win every solo race in a week was a feat of endurance, skill and supreme mental strength – something that may never be matched! Just three months later, though, Hutchinson crashed in a British Championship race at Silverstone, and a badly broken leg resulted in more than 30 operations and almost three years lost from his career.

▲ Ian Hutchinson made history with victory in the 2010 Senior giving him his fifth win of the week.

Event Safety Plan

To complement the TT course risk assessment, the Event Safety Plan is drafted by the Race Organiser to ensure that in accordance with the safety management system, an effective documented set of procedures exist to ensure the health, safety and welfare of spectators, officials and competitors while at the Isle of Man TT Races.

Safety Policy

ACU Events Ltd (ACUE) are focused on safety throughout the planning and delivery of the TT Races, and their core objective is to plan and run a safe TT event where the risk to the public, spectators, competitors and officials is minimised. The Race Organiser puts in place an effective method to close the roads in readiness for practice, qualifying and racing to take place.

The TT course is 37.73 miles long and, generally speaking, from the time the roads close to the first competitive bike setting off down Bray Hill, there is a 30-minute gap; not bad, considering at the height of the TT the public road is really congested as thousands of spectators make their way to their selected viewing points.

As part of the planning process, ACUE also ensure that the marshals and medical and air med cover are deployed appropriately around the TT course. The two air med helicopters (Air Red and Air Blue) are deployed to two sections of the course, Alpine Cottage and Keppel Gate, in readiness for the race action to begin.

As well as being available for racing incidents, the comprehensive medical cover around the TT course is also on hand to deal with any spectator injuries that might occur, irrespective of whether those injuries are race related or not. Residential medical emergencies inside the course can also be managed.

As well as recognising the hazards to spectators, officials and competitors, the Race Organiser must also consider any hazards to the environment and as such needs to mitigate against the risk of pollution or any other threat or hazard to the environment.

What goes into an Event Safety Plan?

Gary Thompson, the TT Clerk of the Course, drafts the Event Safety Plan. If he was taken out of the picture, someone with the appropriately graded Clerk of the Course licence and with a degree of previous experience of the TT course would be able to pick up the Event Safety Plan document and, with the risk assessment, be able to organise the racing aspect of the TT Races. The document is very comprehensive and should be used very much as a tool, a guidance to the race organisation. As an indication of the breadth of the document, it includes such items as:

- A general health and safety statement
- Race organisation structure
- Road closure periods
- Race control processes and procedures
- Incident management, which includes red flag protocols, red flag positions, black flag positions, digital flag positions

- TT Snaefell Mountain Course radio communications and locations of tetra radio handsets
- Locations of medical support
- Job descriptions for key officials
- Marshalling on the Mountain Course
- Travelling marshal and course car driver procedures
- Serious incident plan
- Press and media accreditation access to the TT Races
- Newcomer training
- The practice, qualifying and race day schedules.

▼ Course marshals continue to be vital in the safe and successful running of the Isle of Man TT Races.

While comprehensive, the list gives an overview of what is contained in the TT Event Safety Plan, but the actual content goes much deeper into processes and procedures.

Red Flag Protocols

Given the speeds achieved nowadays by TT competitors, it is imperative that an effective procedure is in place to be able to stop a practice, qualifying session or race as safely and as quickly as possible to potentially save lives. A comprehensive red flag procedure is in place and is well known by the whole race organisation. This stops the session so that assistance can be given to the marshals to ensure the best possible care can be afforded to the injured competitor.

At any time during practice, qualifying or a race, the Clerk of the Course may, if he deems a situation necessary, authorise the use of red flags or digital red flags. The Clerk of the Course (or his deputy) is the only person with the authority to do this. Once authority has been given for red flags to be deployed, the whole of the Mountain Course will be affected and a full course red flag procedure will be put in place.

This means all competitors must come to an immediate, controlled and safe stop and follow the instructions of the marshals. The Clerk of the Course will stop any bikes waiting on the start line or on the south ramp to start practice, qualifying or a race, from leaving the start line or accessing the TT course.

The nearest travelling marshal to the location of the incident will be deployed to assist at the incident. If required, air med will be dispatched and/or emergency vehicles authorised (by the Clerk of the Course) to enter the TT course and be escorted to the incident by travelling marshals and give assistance where necessary.

The incident is then dealt with, and only when the incident is clear and the road is deemed fit for racing to continue will the Clerk of the Course consider a race restart, once he has contacted Noble's Hospital to ascertain whether the hospital is in a position for racing to continue.

A lot to think about? Just a bit.

▲▲ Austrian Klaus Klaffenbock and Manx passenger Dan Sayle won both Sidecar races in 2010.
▲ American Mark Miller (MotoCzysz) leaves the line at the start of the 2010 TT Zero race.

▲ It's not all about the racing: the stunning Douglas Bay.

The electric race, now called TT Zero, was won by American Mark Miller on the beautifully engineered MotoCzysz at a speed of 96.820mph, while Jenny Tinmouth cemented herself in the history books with a final lap of 119.945mph in the Senior, making her the fastest ever female solo competitor around the Mountain Course.

TT3D: Closer to the Edge captured all the dramatic moments of TT 2010 and received critical acclaim, grossing $2 million. A commercial boom followed, with more high-profile sponsors queuing up to be involved and spectator numbers increasing year on year as a result.

2011 was the 100th anniversary of the Mountain Course, and it was celebrated in style with the 'Milestones of the Mountain Course' parade lap, which commemorated and featured former heroes with expert commentary provided by the inimitable Murray Walker.

The HM Plant livery had disappeared from the factory Hondas, which now competed under the Honda TT Legends banner with McGuinness and Amor. Anstey and Donald had left TAS Suzuki to move to Padgetts and Wilson Craig Racing respectively, both fielding Honda machinery, and Martin replaced them on the black Suzukis.

Dunlop was now Kawasaki-mounted for the 1000cc races, as was Cummins, although he was still recovering from the extensive injuries of the previous year. But Hutchinson was absent. He was due to ride for Swan Yamaha, but serious left leg injuries sustained in a short circuit crash at Silverstone, which saw him face amputation, ruled him out.

The continuity of staying with the same team and manufacturer played into the hands of McGuinness, and he got back to winning ways in the Superbike race. He swapped the lead with Anstey initially, but after retaking the lead on lap three he was never headed again. Anstey retired at Quarry Bends and Martin coasted to a halt at Hillberry, so McGuinness won by almost a minute from Donald and Johnson.

Anstey had better fortune in the first Supersport race, where Dunlop, fastest in practice, was an early retirement. Donald led until his engine blew at Kirk Michael on the final lap, and Anstey won by 8s from Amor and Martin. Dunlop made amends in the Superstock race later in the day, though, giving Kawasaki a rare TT win ahead of McGuinness and Martin.

▼ The TV helicopter follows John McGuinness as he races towards victory in the 2011 Superbike race.

▲ Gary Johnson takes the chequered flag and victory in the second Supersport race of 2011 for his maiden TT success.

McGuinness and Martin were second and third once more in the second Supersport race, which was restarted after the first attempt had begun on damp roads before heavy rain intervened. Victory in the restart went to Johnson and his privateer East Coast Racing Honda, the first win for the Lincolnshire rider four years after he made his debut.

The two MotoCzysz machines of Michael Rutter and Miller dominated the TT Zero race, raising their top speed to 150mph along the Sulby Straight, and Rutter took his second TT victory. The Sidecar races were shared between Klaffenbock/Sayle and Holden/Winkle, the latter winning for the first time in a TT career that had started back in 1988.

The Senior was delayed by four hours, and although Martin led McGuinness in the early stages, the Honda man slowly got into his stride. McGuiness took the lead on the third lap and controlled the race from there, eventually winning by 7.2s from Martin and Anstey. Meanwhile, a young Dean Harrison appeared for the first time.

Changes off-track in 2012 saw Gary Thompson take over Clerk of the Course duties from Eddie Nelson. Monster Energy continued as event title sponsor, and Dainese, Royal London 360 and Pokerstars were among the race sponsors. A new three-lap Lightweight race for Supertwin machines was added to the schedule.

There was no change in the Superbike race, though, and McGuinness was again victorious for his eighteenth TT success. Familiar adversaries Donald and Anstey joined him on the podium. Martin just missed out in fourth as Hutchinson,

▲ Ryan Farquhar (KMR Kawasaki) exits Ballaugh on his way to third place in the 2012 Superstock TT.

still far from fit, made his return to TT competition in eighth. McGuinness also won the Superstock race for the first time, this time on the Padgetts Honda, with Dunlop second for Kawasaki and Farquhar in third on another ZX-10R.

Anstey, the previous master of the Superstock division, finished fourth but took his almost obligatory victory earlier in the day when he defeated Donald by just 0.77s in the opening Supersport race. It was the second-closest margin of victory in an interval start race after the 0.6s difference between Mark Baldwin and Mick Lofthouse in the 1995 125cc race.

Long-time leader Johnson ran out of fuel on the final lap and early pacesetter Dunlop retired at Ballig with a blown engine. Dunlop won the second race, though, with Donald again in second and Farquhar in another third place.

Rutter and MotoCzysz again won the TT Zero race, with the lap record moving up to 104.056mph. Although there were fewer than ten starters, there was added intrigue with the addition of the all-new Mugen Shinden from Japan. McGuinness took second ahead of Miller on a second MotoCzysz.

Farquhar had practically invented the Supertwin class, so it was fitting he won the highly competitive Lightweight race on his KMR Kawasaki; Rutter, his teammate for the race, finished third as rising star James Hillier split them in second. With over 60 entries, it was a popular addition to the race programme.

Almost 30 years since he made his debut, Dave Molyneux was still winning races, and with passenger Patrick Farrance he took a resounding double in the Sidecar races, this time using Kawasaki engines, to follow on from the wins he'd had with Yamaha, Honda and Suzuki.

The meeting ended on a low note with the cancellation of the Senior due to poor weather. It was the first time the blue riband race hadn't taken place and the first race cancelled since 1987, but it marked a change in TT race procedure. Safety was becoming more important, and with Superbikes hitting speeds of 200mph, never again would they compete on wet or even damp roads.

One of the biggest stories in 2013 was Dunlop following in the footsteps of his Uncle Joey to ride for the official Honda UK team, where he lined up alongside McGuinness and Rutter. Equally as big a story was British Superbike Championship runner-up Josh Brookes making his TT debut, while Norton also made a low-key return.

To mark the thirtieth anniversary of Joey's first TT win for Honda, McGuinness lined up in tribute livery, but his chances of victory disappeared when he was hit with a one-minute time penalty for speeding in the pit lane.

Dunlop was already leading from Johnson and Martin, and he duly won by more than 40s for his first Superbike victory. Donald came through for second, and McGuinness set a new outright lap record of 131.671mph on the final lap to snatch third from Martin. Brookes finished tenth and lapped at 127.726mph to become the fastest newcomer in TT history.

The opening Sidecar race had started proceedings after an extra practice session was run for the solos due to mixed weather earlier in the week, but a new winner was crowned in the shape of Tim Reeves who, with Sayle in the chair, defeated Conrad Harrison/Mike Aylott and Molyneux/Farrance.

Dunlop was on a roll in the two-wheel classes and won both Supersport races and the Superstock to make it four wins in a week. New lap records were set in both – 128.667mph in the Supersport category and a superb 131.220mph on his stock Honda – which allowed him to overhaul race leader Johnson.

▼ Dave Molyneux/Patrick Farrance have a gentle jump over Ballaugh Bridge, the duo winning both Sidecar races in 2012.

The Anatomy of a Sidecar

The Sidecar class brings an entirely different kind of spectacle to the TT, and it puts both rider and machine to the ultimate test. Over the years, it has seen a number of iterations, but the challenge of taking two people around the 37.73-mile course as fast as possible on three wheels remains the same.

The Sidecar Class

The Sidecar class has become something of a mainstay of the modern TT despite an inauspicious start in the 1920s. And although technology has evolved significantly since the first race in 1923 the concept remains relatively unchanged, with riders still racing over three laps.

The class was dropped in 1926 due to a lack of support (only 18 entered in 1925), but it returned on the Clypse Course in 1954 as part of the World Championship and has remained a staple of the TT fortnight ever since. Outfits were initially not allowed to exceed 500cc capacity and the race continued on the Clypse Course until 1960 when they returned to the Snaefell Mountain Course.

In 1968 capacity was increased to 750cc engines and two races were included on the schedule, and there was a further increase in 1975 to 1000cc. However, in 1990 TT organisers adopted the new FIM Formula 2 Class rules that allowed two-stroke engines not exceeding 350cc or four-stroke engines not exceeding 600cc.

The latter soon took over, and nowadays the modern era sidecars are powered by 600cc four-cylinder, 675cc three-cylinder, and 900cc parallel-twin engines. The 600cc engine remains the most popular.

1. Engine

Sidecar TT regulations require powerplants to be relatively close to production spec. Most teams use 600cc four-cylinder engines from Supersport bikes, such as the Yamaha R6 or Honda CBR600RR, although some now opt for 900cc parallel-twin engines for more torque.

The engine must be positioned behind the steering head and in front of the driver, with drive transmitted through the rear wheel.

2. Frame and Chassis

The main frame must consist of a steering head, a frame to accommodate the engine and a main spar to the sidecar wheel. The tubing used to construct the frame can be of circular or non-circular sections and all components must be permanently fixed via welding or brazing.

The layout typically places the driver in a low-slung seat on the right, with the sidecar platform for the passenger mounted to the left. Overseas competitors in the 1950s and 1960s typically ran the outfit in the opposite configuration, with the passenger on the right. A third wheel – the sidecar wheel – sits independently and is not powered.

The choice of chassis, largely built by specialists as opposed to manufacturers or mass produced, is wide-ranging, and over the years they have been built by companies such as Busch, Windle, LCR, Ireson and DMR, the latter the brainchild of 17-time winner Dave Molyneux.

3. Suspension

Suspension has limited travel but is highly bespoke and adjusted to suit the asymmetric loads caused by having a sidecar. All three wheels require careful setup to provide both stability in fast sections and enough compliance to absorb bumps and uneven surfaces.

4. Brakes

Braking is managed by the driver. All three wheels need to have brakes and only use ferrous brake discs. Given the combined weight of the outfit and its occupants, stopping distances are longer compared to solo bikes, and brake cooling and fade management are critical over a full race distance.

5. Wheels and Tyres

All three wheels run on wide, low-profile slick racing tyres, designed for high-speed stability and durability. The sidecar tyre must withstand lateral loads in right-hand bends, while the front and rear tyres manage more typical braking and traction duties.

6. Aerodynamics and Bodywork

Sidecars are designed with aerodynamic efficiency in mind, but they also have to accommodate the movement of the passenger. Sleek, low-profile fairings are used to reduce drag, particularly down fast sections like Sulby Straight. However, the bodywork must be open enough to allow the passenger to shift their bodyweight quickly and safely.

7. Passenger Platform

The sidecar passenger's role is critical. Their platform, extremely small and compact, is constructed with strategic handholds, footrests and cutaways, enabling them to move their body from one side of the machine to the other. In right-handers, riders will lie flat over the bike, while in left-handers they will hang out to counteract lift.

8. Controls and Dashboard

The driver's controls include a low-slung set of handlebars, foot controls and a thumb brake or linked braking system. Displays are typically minimalist, often just a basic rev counter or shift light.

9. Fuel Tank

Sidecar outfits require enough fuel to complete the full three-lap race without stopping. Tanks are shaped to fit low within the chassis to aid the centre of gravity.

◀ Ryan and Callum Crowe and their LCR Honda get airborne at Rhencullen 2.

Yet again Rutter and MotoCzysz won the TT Zero race with an increased lap speed of 109.675mph, but it was closer this time as McGuinness and the Mugen were only 1.672s adrift. The second Sidecar race saw more first-time winners in Ben and Tom Birchall, who, like Reeves, were former world champions, and it was a similar story in the Lightweight race, where Hillier lapped at 119.130mph to win from another rising star, Dean Harrison.

Dunlop was on course to match Hutchinson's five wins in a week, and he led the Senior after the first lap, but McGuinness was in determined mood. He grabbed the lead on lap two and crept clear, although the gap between the two riders at the end of the six laps was only 10s. Anstey edged out Hillier for third by a single second.

By now the TT had reinvented itself as an international spectacle, aided by North One's superb television coverage, which perfectly showcased the extremities and difficulties of the Mountain Course and the extraordinary feats of the riders. Beamed into UK homes every evening on ITV4, the TT was also being seen on TV around the world, and with an estimated 30 million viewers its fanbase was increasing rapidly.

The breathtaking on-track entertainment, where safety was increasing all the time with slick, professional marshalling and the use of air fencing, and riders remaining highly accessible and authentic, played a huge part.

2014 continued the trend. McGuinness was struggling as he recovered from a badly broken wrist from an enduro bike accident and Dunlop had moved to BMW to ride their latest-spec S1000RR. It was a full-factory effort as BMW looked to celebrate the seventy-fifth anniversary of Georg Meier's win in the 1939 Senior.

> ...the TT was also being seen on TV around the world, and with an estimated 30 million viewers its fanbase was increasing rapidly

Never one to shy away from controversy, Dunlop switched from Pirelli tyres to Dunlop mid-week and ultimately delivered the goods once more, opening his account for the week with victory over Martin and Cummins, who'd replaced Dunlop at Honda, in the Superbike race. Fourteenth at the end of the first lap, Anstey posted a final lap of 132.298mph to move up to fourth and wrench the outright lap record away from McGuinness.

Dunlop repeated the performance in the Senior, but this time Cummins got the better of Martin for second as McGuinness followed up his seventh in the Superbike race with sixth. Another rider grabbing the headlines was BSB race winner and newcomer Peter Hickman who lapped at 129.104mph to oust Brookes as the fastest newcomer ever.

Sandwiched in between were victories for Dunlop in the Superstock and second Supersport races, although he could only manage third in the opening 600cc encounter. Victory there went to a flying Johnson, who took his second

▶ A traffic jam at Ballaugh Bridge as Ben Wylie leads Ivan Lintin and Simon Andrews in the 2013 Supersport race.

TT win in superb fashion and gave Triumph their first TT success since Anstey's win in the same race 11 years earlier.

With no MotoCzysz in the field, the two Mugens of McGuinness and Anstey dominated another poorly supported TT Zero race, although a new lap record of 117.366mph proved the technical progress being made by the battery-powered machines.

Harrison/Aylott and Molyneux/Farrance shared the Sidecar wins, and there was further joy in the Harrison household when Conrad's son Dean also claimed his first TT win in the Lightweight race. Ex-Moto3 Grand Prix rider Danny Webb impressed on his debut, with Hickman's fellow BSB rider Martin Jessopp doing similarly in his races.

In 2015, Dunlop moved teams again, this time to Milwaukee Yamaha, while McGuinness and Cummins remained with Honda TT Legends. Anstey remained at Padgetts, as did Martin and William Dunlop at TAS Racing, although they switched from Suzuki to BMW. Hutchinson's fitness was improving all the time, and he lined up for PBM Kawasaki in the 1000cc races.

After a disappointing North West 200, Dunlop experienced problems with the R1 Yamaha in the opening practice sessions and sensationally quit the Milwaukee team mid-week. His old Hawk Racing team hastily sent over a BMW for him to ride, but it was Anstey who came out on top in the Superbike race. Hutchinson and Hillier completed the podium, but Dunlop crashed out at the Nook on the final lap after hitting the already crashed bike of Scott Wilson.

▼ After all his injuries, victory in the 2015 Superstock race was Ian Hutchinson's first TT success since 2010.

Triumph
1907–present
17 wins

As one of Britain's most iconic motorcycle manufacturers, Triumph's story at the Isle of Man TT began in 1907, at the very beginning. Securing podiums in their first year with Jack Marshall and Frank Hulbert, the brand climbed the top step for the first time a year later, when Marshall won the Single Cylinder race. A century of success has followed, something no other manufacturer can claim.

Following Marshall's win, Triumph machines regularly appeared on the podium, but it wasn't until the post-war era that they began to have a greater impact on the event. A win by Ernie Lyons in the 1946 Manx Grand Prix showed the brand's competitiveness, while the following year Bill McVeigh powered his Triumph to victory in the 1947 Clubman Lightweight TT.

The arrival of the iconic Bonneville Thruxton and Trident in the 1960s marked a turning point for the brand, as both privateers and supported riders demonstrated their prowess, particularly when the Production TT and Formula 750 races were introduced.

During the late 1960s and early 1970s, John Hartle, Ray Knight, Malcolm Uphill, Ray Pickrell, Tony Jefferies, Mick Grant and Alex George all claimed victories, with the famous 'Slippery Sam' machine dominating the Production race in the early 1970s.

The 1980s and 1990s would prove to be leaner years for the British manufacturer as the Japanese brands dominated, but at the turn of the millennium Triumph was back and setting its sights on victory.

New Zealander Bruce Anstey picked up the mantle, taking a memorable win in the 2003 Supersport race, and 11 years later Gary Johnson added his name to Triumph's TT victors list, while Peter Hickman joined him in 2019. To this day Triumph remains a competitive force in the Supersport class around the 37.73-mile Mountain Course, and it has maintained its presence in the entirety of TT history.

▲ Bruce Anstey's victory for Triumph in the 2003 Junior was the first for the British manufacturer since 1975.

Ben Birchall

▲ With brother Tom, Nottinghamshire's Ben Birchall won 14 TT races between 2013 and 2023.

From	Mansfield, Nottinghamshire
Years Active	2009–present
Wins	14
Podiums	19
Fastest Lap	120.645mph
Manufacturers	LCR Honda

Mansfield's Ben Birchall redefined the world of three-wheeling at the Isle of Man TT, as he and brother Tom established themselves as sidecar greats. Making his debut in 2009, the same year he was crowned Sidecar World Champion for the first time, his first podiums came in 2012, with second- and third-place finishes.

The following year, Ben and Tom claimed their maiden Isle of Man TT win; however, a nasty crash in the opening race of the 2014 event left Ben with a badly damaged right hand and put his whole career in jeopardy. Fighting back in style with an emotional double victory the following year, the duo went on an 11-race winning spree between the second race of 2016 and the second encounter in 2023.

Ben has continued to push the limits of sidecar racing, repeatedly breaking the lap record, and in 2023 he and his brother became the first outfit to lap the Mountain Course at over 120mph. That year also marked their final TT together, with Tom announcing his retirement following their fourteenth TT victory.

Still hungry for success, Ben returned in 2024 with relative newcomer Kevin Rousseau as passenger. Although a practice crash ruled the duo out of race one, they bounced back in race two with a strong second-place finish.

It was all change again in 2025, with Ben teaming up with Patrick Rosney. The pairing proved an instant success, with a brace of second-place finishes. With the hunger and desire as strong as ever, Ben has clearly set his sights on a return to the top step of the podium in 2026.

▲ Ben and Tom Birchall lift a wheel as they approach the Gooseneck during the second Sidecar race of 2015.

Hutchinson was back to his best, winning the Superstock race ahead of Dunlop and Lee Johnston, and both Supersport races, this time riding the Team Traction Control Yamaha owned by Keith Flint, front man of rock group The Prodigy. Anstey finished second in both 600cc races, Johnson and Martin sharing the third-place positions.

The Birchall brothers were firmly getting into their stride now and won both Sidecar races, the second after a close battle with 17-time winner Molyneux and new passenger Ben Binns, who set a new lap record of 116.785mph. A new race winner was crowned in the Lightweight, when Ivan Lintin held off Hillier's challenge, the latter lapping at 120.848mph on his final lap.

McGuinness won the TT Zero race from Mugen teammate Anstey once more, the lap record now an impressive 119.279mph, and the Morecambe rider was more fired-up than ever for the Senior after seeing his odds at a local bookmaker were 18–1.

The race was restarted over four laps after Jamie Hamilton crashed heavily at the end of the Cronk-y-Voddy straight and McGuinness led Hutchinson by 1.2s after the opening lap. The gap was just 0.6s at Ramsey second time around, but after Hutchinson overshot Signpost Corner McGuinness was in control, and with a new outright lap record of 132.701mph he swept to his twenty-third TT victory ahead of a flying Hillier and Hutchinson. Little did we know this would be John's last TT win.

McGuinness and Cummins remained at Honda in 2016, but there was change elsewhere as Hutchinson moved to TAS Racing and BMW. Also contesting the British Superstock Championship, he arrived on the island with the confidence only track time and victories bring.

Dunlop sensibly chose to stay with Hawk Racing BMW, and while Anstey did similar at Padgetts, they parked their reliable Honda Fireblade to run the Moto-GP-derived Honda RC213V-S instead. At £138,000 it sounded superb, but a crash in practice at Keppel Gate affected Anstey's campaign.

After sustaining substantial injuries at the previous year's Ulster Grand Prix, Martin was a notable absentee, and given his fledgling TV career one had to wonder if he'd return. But Hillier, Rutter and Johnson were all back, and Hickman and Harrison were now very much in the ascendancy.

Practice week saw the intensity between Dunlop and Hutchinson build throughout, each desperate to get the upper hand on the other. Dunlop drew first blood with a dominant victory in the Superbike race, where he posted the first ever sub-17-minute lap of the Mountain Course. Raising the outright lap record to 133.393mph, Dunlop finished 21s ahead of Hutchinson as McGuinness and Hickman claimed third and fourth respectively.

Hutchinson responded with his own dominant performance in the four-lap Superstock race, where he set an almost unbelievable lap record of 133.098mph. Dunlop retired at the end of the first lap with a broken gear lever, and it was Kawasaki young guns Harrison and Hillier who completed the podium.

Hutchinson won both Supersport races on the Team Traction Control Yamaha to take his number of TT wins to 14. Harrison and Hillier were again on the podium in race one with Dunlop disqualified for an illegal engine. Dunlop finished second in race two, with Harrison taking third on this occasion, and the bitter rivalry between him and Hutchinson continued to increase on and off the track.

The Senior was the final opportunity for both riders, but Dunlop wasn't to be denied and pushed the lap record up even further, to 133.962mph. Hutchinson was more than half a minute adrift in second and suggested Dunlop had been provided with a higher-speed engine; the post-race press conference only served to highlight just how much the two riders disliked each other.

McGuinness placed third again, but he missed the podium completely in the TT Zero race after accidentally hitting the kill switch at Ballacrye, and Anstey won the race. Lintin and RC Express Racing repeated their Lightweight victory of 2015, and Hillier and Jessopp joined him on the podium.

In a TT blessed with superb weather, Holden/Winkle and the Birchall brothers shared the Sidecar victories, although the second race was marred by the death of 2003 winner Ian Bell in a crash at Ballaspur.

The big news for 2017 was the return of Guy Martin. He joined McGuinness at Honda but the dream team rapidly turned into a nightmare. After issues pre-season with the electronics and throttle on the new Honda Fireblade, McGuinness was thrown off at high speed at the North West 200 and serious injuries ruled him out for the season.

◀ Ian Hutchinson (Tyco BMW) sweeps through Tower Bends as he heads towards victory in the 2016 Superstock race.

▲ Michael Dunlop powers towards Bishopscourt to give Suzuki a rare victory in the 2017 Senior.

Practice week on the island, where weather conditions were far from ideal, was no better for Martin. A lowly twenty-seventh quickest, he lapped at 124mph compared to Hutchinson's 132mph. Martin only got as far as Doran's Bend on the first lap of the Superbike race when the bike jumped out of gear and saw him crash out. Uninjured, he understandably withdrew from the Senior.

Dunlop and Hutchinson remained with the same teams, but Hawk Racing had switched to Suzuki, and some questioned the competitiveness of the GSXR1000 at the TT. Nevertheless, Dunlop led in the early stages of the Superbike race only to retire on lap two, and after a close battle first with Harrison and then Hickman, Hutchinson got the better of the latter by 5s. Harrison snatched third from the consistent Hillier.

With a first race retirement, and having lost out to Hutchinson in the last four Supersport races, Dunlop was fired-up for the first 600cc race. Damp patches remained from the overnight rain – ideal conditions for Dunlop. Challenged early on by Hillier, he pulled away to come home 13.2s ahead of the Kawasaki rider with Hickman in third.

Further weather issues meant the second Supersport race was cancelled, but before that Hutchinson was again victorious in the Superstock category. He finished 22.2s ahead of fellow BMW rider Hickman, and local rider Dan Kneen, who'd been a regular top ten finisher in recent years, secured his first podium in third ahead of Rutter.

At 45, Rutter was the same age as McGuinness, but he had his moment of glory riding a Paton in the Lightweight race, when he got the better of Jessopp

Michael Dunlop

▲ Michael Dunlop in the number one position has been a recurring theme for more than a decade.

From	Ballymoney, Northern Ireland
Years Active	2007–present
Wins	33
Podiums	51
Fastest Lap	135.970mph
Manufacturers	Honda, Yamaha, Suzuki, Kawasaki, BMW, Paton, Ducati

Born in Ballymoney, Northern Ireland, in 1989, Michael Dunlop is widely regarded as the greatest Isle of Man TT rider in history. He made his debut in 2007, aged 18, and went on to claim his first victory in the second Supersport TT just two years later, kick-starting an incredible career.

As a member of the legendary Dunlop racing dynasty – son of Robert Dunlop, brother of William Dunlop, and nephew of Joey Dunlop – Michael has had big shoes to fill and plenty of heartache to overcome. But after his maiden TT appearance, the subsequent years have seen him amass a current record 33 TT victories and 51 podium finishes, surpassing Joey's tally of 26 wins, previously thought unbeatable, in 2024.

His dominance spans every class, with multiple victories in Superbike, Supersport, Superstock and Supertwin categories, and he has also achieved the extraordinary feat of winning four races in a week on five separate occasions (2013, 2014, 2023, 2024 and 2025). His win in 2025 for Ducati was the seventh different manufacturer he'd won with, following on from Yamaha, Kawasaki, Honda, BMW, Suzuki and Paton.

In 2016 he became the first rider to break the 17-minute lap barrier, and in 2023 he was the first Supersport rider to set a 130mph lap. Dunlop also holds several class lap records (as of 2025), including the Superbike, Supersport and Supertwin races.

With an aggressive riding style earning him the nickname 'The Bull', Dunlop is very much his own man and controversy is never too far away, but he's showing no signs of slowing down. It remains to be seen just how many more wins he can achieve. In 2025, Dunlop became the latest in a long line of TT racers to have their achievements recognised by being appointed a Member of the Order of the British Empire (MBE) for services to motorcycling in the King's Birthday Honours.

by just under 9s. Hickman, this time riding a KMR Kawasaki, finished third ahead of former double winner Lintin.

Anstey and Martin – in his last TT race – took a 1–2 for Mugen in the TT Zero race, which was now on borrowed time due to the lack of support, with the Birchalls claiming a Sidecar double. The Nottinghamshire brothers were now the team to beat, as seen by their new lap record of 117.119mph.

The Senior saw good conditions and there was little to choose between Hutchinson and Hickman in the first half of lap one. But Hutchinson crashed heavily at the twenty-seventh milestone, fracturing the same leg and ankle he'd almost lost to amputation in 2010.

Dunlop made use of the stoppage to change the Suzuki's rear shock and the move paid dividends, as he was never headed in the shortened four-lap race. Hickman and Harrison's superb weeks concluded with second and third. Norton enjoyed a strong campaign, with the Australian duo of Brookes and David Johnson taking sixth and seventh, each lapping at more than 130mph.

Dunlop was back on a BMW in 2018, this time for Tyco/TAS Racing, where he was joined by Kneen. Hutchinson, still recovering from his injuries, moved to Honda, while Hickman (Smiths Racing BMW), Harrison (Silicone Engineering Kawasaki) and Hillier (Bournemouth Kawasaki) stayed where they were. Cummins spearheaded Padgetts' attack after Anstey was ruled out, having been diagnosed with cancer for a second time.

▼ With the famous Creg-ny-Baa in the background, Derek McGee (IEG/KMR Kawasaki) heads towards second place in the 2018 Lightweight race.

▲ Josh Brookes leaves Union Mills in the second Supersport race of 2018.

McGuinness was also absent. His recovery had initially gone well, and he penned a deal with Norton, but he broke his leg again on a family holiday in March, and with only a few weeks to go before the TT he wisely sat the event out.

Dan Kneen had got his big breakthrough with TAS Racing, and Tuesday evening's practice session saw him lap at 132.258mph, comfortably his quickest ever, but the following evening he crashed at Churchtown and sadly died from his injuries.

Shortly after Kneen's crash, riders were allowed to return to the Grandstand along the course but in the opposite direction. A course car had been sent to the site of Kneen's crash and an incident at Ballacrye saw the car collide with Steve Mercer, leaving the popular Kent rider with life-changing injuries.

Race week started in a sombre fashion, but in scenes similar to 2003, when Adrian Archibald won for TAS Racing after the loss of David Jefferies, Dunlop did the same in the Superbike race. Harrison set a new outright lap record of 134.432mph from a standing start and led by 16s but clutch trouble put him out on lap four.

Dunlop inherited the lead and won from Cummins and Hillier with Hickman another high-profile retirement. Hickman bounced back in the Superstock race, though; despite overshooting Braddan Bridge on lap one, he claimed his first TT victory and set a new lap record of 134.403mph as he defeated Dunlop by 4.5s, with Harrison taking third.

Peter Hickman

▲ Fourteen-time TT winner Peter Hickman has also held the outright lap record since 2018.

From	Burton-upon-Trent, England
Years Active	2014–present
Wins	14
Podiums	31
Fastest Lap	136.358mph
Manufacturers	BMW, Triumph, Yamaha, Kawasaki, MV Agusta, Paton

Few riders have made an impact on the Isle of Man TT in recent years in the way Peter Hickman has. In a little over a decade, 'Hicky' has gone from the fastest-ever newcomer to the outright lap record holder, pushing the limit to an astonishing 136.358mph.

Making his debut in 2014, Hickman set the tone for his TT career immediately by lapping at over 129mph by the end of the event. His first podiums were in 2017, with the fan favourite taking rostrums in the Senior, Superbike, Supersport, Superstock and Supertwin races. The following year saw his first victories around the island; he went on to claim 14 of them by the end of the 2024 event, much of his success coming with BMW.

Alongside his consistent podium finishes, Hicky has rewritten the record books time and again as he pushes the outright lap record higher. Yet despite his fierce competitiveness, behind the visor and away from the circuit the six-foot-two rider is renowned for his calm, approachable and laid-back persona. He can often be found taking selfies and meeting fans in the paddock.

Hickman's incredible run at the TT saw a dramatic twist at the 2025 event, however, when he crashed at 140mph at Kerrowmoar. Although he suffered multiple broken bones, he was relatively unscathed and able to return to the paddock just two days later to support the team.

If history has shown us anything, it's that you can guarantee Hickman will be back for the 2026 Isle of Man TT stronger than ever and looking to further rewrite the Mountain Course history books.

▲ Keen motorcycling enthusiast Prince William enjoys watching the races on his visit to the TT in 2019.

The Supersport races were shared between Dunlop and Harrison, with Hickman on the podium in each, and Dunlop set a new lap record of 129.197mph on his MD Racing Honda. He completed his hat-trick with victory on a Paton in the Lightweight race and another lap record of 122.750mph.

The Birchalls' dominance of the Sidecar class continued as they took another double and upped their own lap record to a mighty 119.250mph. Rutter, riding for Team Mugen, won the TT Zero race and increased the lap record further to 121.824mph – the first 120mph lap on a battery-powered machine.

The 2018 Senior is widely regarded as one of the greatest TT races of all time. Harrison and Hickman were separated by mere seconds for the entire six laps, with Harrison consistently the quicker rider until Ramsey, then Hickman excelling over the mountain.

Going into the final lap, Harrison led by less than 2s, but he lost the lead for the first time in the final third of the last lap and Hickman, with a new outright lap record of 135.452mph, the first ever 135mph lap, got the verdict by just 1.9s. Cummins took another podium in third and Brookes lapped at 131.745mph on his way to fifth place for Norton.

The weather at the 2018 TT was exemplary, but the opposite rang true in 2019. Indeed, it was one of the worst TTs on record, with endless rain and cold temperatures; countless days were lost to the weather.

The first three practice sessions were all affected by rain and Wednesday, Thursday and Friday's sessions were washed out completely. This led to organisers moving the Superbike and Sidecar races to Sunday, but further bad weather on Saturday, when additional practice was due to take place, meant it was Monday before the first races took place.

With such little practice, the form guide was sketchy to say the least, but Harrison and Hickman on their familiar Kawasaki and BMW mounts were soon in the groove in the Superbike race. Harrison led by a second after the first lap, but Hickman overhauled him second time around. The race was stopped prematurely on lap three though when Daley Mathison sustained fatal injuries in a crash at Snugborough.

Hickman was awarded the win from Harrison and Cummins with Dunlop back in sixth. Still with Tyco BMW, Michael had sat out the second half of 2018 after the loss of his brother William at the Skerries 100, and he was also carrying a hand injury. McGuiness returned to TT competition but retired the Norton, who were now in financial difficulty, after the first lap.

▲ Lee Johnston was a popular winner of the opening Supersport race in 2019.

The Birchalls won the opening Sidecar race from Holden/Lee Cain, and Lee Johnston claimed a maiden TT victory in the opening Supersport race from Hillier and Hickman. The race was stopped after two of the scheduled four laps due to deteriorating weather.

Heavy rain meant both Tuesday and Wednesday were lost, and Clerk of the Course Gary Thompson was left with little option other than to cut race distances and try to fit in as many races as he could, when he could. That led to an ambitious five-race programme on Thursday, with the Superstock, second Supersport and Sidecar, Lightweight and TT Zero races all taking place.

Hickman was, for once, fast out of the blocks in the Superstock race and led from start to finish, eventually winning by 26s from Harrison and David Johnson (Honda Racing). He then made it two wins in a day when he again got the better of Harrison in the second Supersport race, this time by 3.3s. Hillier was again on the podium in third.

The Lightweight race went to Dunlop, his only win at TT 2019, from Jamie Coward and Johnston, and the Birchalls repeated their race one victory in the second Sidecar encounter for their tenth TT win. In the final TT Zero race, the class having never evolved as organisers hoped, Rutter won from McGuinness and raised the lap record to 121.909mph.

After two weeks of disruption, organisers were determined to end on a high with a full-length Senior, and Hickman and Harrison again went head to head, Hickman leading by 17s at two-thirds race distance.

However, a water pump issue caused him to lose power and Harrison came through to take his third TT victory by almost a minute. Cummins was again on

Kawasaki
1966–present
20 wins

The iconic green colours of Kawasaki machines have been racing between the hedges for almost 60 years, having made their debut at the Isle of Man TT in 1966. The Japanese brand got its first taste of success three years later when Dave Simmonds – who would go on to win the world title that year – claimed the 1969 Lightweight 125cc race, kicking off a successful tenure that has yielded some 20 victories around the Mountain Course.

▲ Seen here at Tower Bends, James Hillier has had 15 TT podiums, all coming with Kawasaki, including victory in the 2013 Lightweight.

One of Team Green's early milestones was achieved in 1975, when Mick Grant powered his Kawasaki KR500 to victory in the Senior TT and broke Mike Hailwood's longstanding outright lap record in the Classic race on the larger KR750. Grant's win marked the brand's first blue riband victory, and the Yorkshire rider and Kawasaki continued to make history, winning back-to-back Classic TTs in 1977 and 1978, setting new outright lap records in both races.

The 1980s and 1990s proved a lean period for the brand, although victory came at the hands of Geoff Johnson in the 1984 Production TT, while Howard Selby, Nigel Davies, Steve Ward and Bob Jackson added to the podium tally.

The wins started racking up again after the turn of the millennium, with Ryan Farquhar taking the 2004 Production 600 and 2005 Junior races, and Michael Dunlop claiming the 2011 Superstock win. 2012 saw the return of the Lightweight category (more recently known as the Supertwin class), which proved to be a class that Kawasaki initially dominated, with five straight wins from Farquhar, James Hillier, Dean Harrison and a double for Ivan Lintin.

In 2012 Dave Molyneux and Patrick Farrance also claimed victory in both Sidecar races – Kawasaki's first TT success on three wheels – with the duo taking a further win in 2014.

In 2015 Ian Hutchinson added his name to the marque's winners list, but it was Harrison who enjoyed the most successful modern partnership with the brand. With regular podium finishes in every category, the highlights of his tenure were undoubtedly his 2018 Supersport and 2019 Senior victories.

▲ Dean Harrison gets sideways on the 160mph drop down Bray Hill.

the podium in third with Dunlop in fourth, but McGuinness's Norton nightmare ended with a retirement on the opening lap.

The world was then rocked by the Covid-19 pandemic. Like so many other sports that were put on hold, the TT suffered a similar fate and the Isle of Man borders remained closed to overseas visitors not just in 2020 but also in 2021. Everyone had to wait until 2022 for the TT to return.

When it did, the riders all eased their way back into the rigours offered by the Mountain Course and speeds were generally down. For the first time ever, live coverage of the practice and races was available, key in growing the event further, with slick presentation befitting an event of such stature.

Hickman continued with BMW but was now in the FHO Racing team owned by Macau businesswoman Faye Ho, while Dunlop, who'd been set to ride a PBM Ducati in 2020, moved to Hawk Racing, albeit on a Suzuki, for the big bike races.

McGuinness, set to make his hundredth TT start, returned to Honda, while Harrison and Cummins stayed with Kawasaki and Padgetts, the latter also fielding Davey Todd, the best newcomer in 2018. After more than a decade with Kawasaki, Hillier was now Yamaha-mounted and Hutchinson, close to full fitness, reunited with TAS Racing. British Superbike Championship front-runner Glenn Irwin, a multiple winner at the North West 200, was the highest-profile newcomer.

On the track, continuity and experience were key. That was seen in the 1000cc races where Hickman dominated, winning the Superbike, Superstock and Senior races. Harrison was again the bridesmaid in the Superbike and Senior encounters. Dunlop, struggling for pace with the Suzuki, and Cummins took a third place each.

Irwin was sensational in the Superbike race, finishing eighth – only three places behind teammate McGuinness – and lapping at 129.849mph to become the fastest newcomer ever. However, it would prove to be his only finish of the week, and he wouldn't return to the event.

Hickman's closest race was the Superstock, where the Padgetts Honda of Cummins pushed him hard, the Manxman posting his first ever 133mph+ lap. Davey Todd finished third to confirm his TT potential.

Dunlop won two close Supersport races where Harrison and Hickman shared the second- and third-place positions, with Dunlop setting a new lap record of 129.475mph in race one. The three riders were now head and shoulders above the rest of the field and regularly locked out the podium, with only Todd looking like threatening them.

Hickman and Dunlop, both Paton-mounted, could barely be separated over the first two laps of the Supertwin race (the new name for the Lightweight), but Dunlop slowed and was then black-flagged on the final lap. Hickman took the win ahead of Johnston and Paul Jordan.

The Sidecars had been hit hard by the break in racing, with many of the stalwarts retiring, and there were fewer than 30 starters in each race. Although the Birchalls continued to impress, winning both races again, and young Manx pairing Ryan and Callum Crowe, sons of former winner Nick, were revelations in just their second year at the TT, the class was struggling.

It was also hit hard by fatal accidents at Ago's Leap in each race, involving French newcomers Cesar Chanel/Olivier Lavorel and father-and-son pairing Roger and Bradley Stockton. Mark Purslow and the popular Davy Morgan also lost their lives, making it the deadliest TT since 1970.

It was another TT that saw triumph and tragedy mixed in equal quantities, but thankfully 2023 saw a blistering fortnight both in terms of the weather and the racing. Having not won a big bike race since 2018, Dunlop switched to Honda for the 1000cc races. Double British Superbike champion Josh Brookes

▼ The fan park has become a popular attraction for spectators both during and after the races.

A Lap with Peter Hickman

Sector 1

I've never been a nervous person in my entire career – excited is probably the word I'd use lining up on the grid. The first thing you need to get right is to make sure you're in first gear! I know that sounds stupid, but it's an easy mistake to make and people have got it wrong before, even at MotoGP level. I'm concentrating on making sure my front wheel gets up to the line to the exact point and getting my revs correct to the point where the clutch is biting just where I want it, so when I get the tap on the shoulder and the little flag goes up I'll be absolutely on the mark straightaway.

We're at 9,000–10,000 revs off the line, and then once over St Ninian's I stay tight to the left-hand side of the road down Bray Hill, straightening the bike up for the compression at the bottom. It's top gear all the way and then once over Ago's Leap I'm looking for the house on the left as my braking marker for the drop down into Quarter Bridge.

You back down from sixth to fifth, let go of the brakes before the little jump and then it's all the way down to first for the corner itself. It's always quite slippery here, and on the first lap especially, you always have to be careful. That applies after each pit stop too, when you've a full tank of fuel.

The entry to Braddan Bridge is the first left-hander you encounter so you have to be careful through there on the first lap, as you do on the immediate right too, as the road drops away quite a bit.

It's a fast run to Union Mills and there's always a bit of dust on the road as you go past the trading estate at Snugborough, and then once through Union Mills it's hard on the

▲ Six miles into sector 1, Peter Hickman exits Greeba Bridge on his Swan Yamaha Supertwin.

power up the Ballahutchin, where the bike wants to wheelie a fair bit. You keep it pinned in top gear through the right kink by the camp site at Glen Vine before running through Ballagarey, or Ballascary as the riders call it! The kerb sticks out, which you have to be mindful of, especially during evening practice when the sun's getting low.

You tend to stay in the middle of the road once you're out of Ballagarey – and staying in the middle of the road is a good place to be on the TT Course when you're learning and still a bit unsure of where you're going. Sitting on the white line gives you the most amount of room either side.

DJ's corner is really fast, as is this whole stretch – you're at full throttle for a good few miles from Union Mills to Greeba. Past the Crosby pub and it's important to stay on the right-hand side of the road in readiness for the jump – there's less of a jump on the right-hand side compared to the left, so you can keep the throttle open that little bit more.

For Greeba Castle on a Superbike it's sixth gear down to fifth, probably 150mph, and then down another couple of gears to third for the left–right flick, being mindful of the bump in the road on the way in. You use a lot of the track on the exit, drifting out to the barriers.

You have little markers all the way round the course to help you. After Greeba Castle, for example, you go through Appledene and you need to be over to the left-hand side of the road. Once you've gone by the little gap in the hedge you tip into the right turn, which takes you up to Greeba Bridge. You're immediately looking for the kerb that sticks out a little on the right, as that's your braking marker for the bridge itself, and you use all the road on the exit.

There are always little markers you can use, whether it's a tree, a white line, a kerb – anything – and once you've learned them you just get used to them and it becomes second nature.

It's then a high-speed run to Ballacraine, including Gorse Lea which is mega fast and where you need to be committed. The run from the start to Ballacraine is quite straightforward – fast, yes, but relatively easy to learn.

After Ballacraine, the course gets very technical through Glen Helen. Laurel Bank is a corner that can catch a lot of people out, and if you don't tip in early it's easy to miss the apex and run wide; you want to get in early and let the bike run out naturally on the exit. On the run to the Black Dub there's a little jump, and once you're over that it's back down to third gear for the left and right and then drive hard on the way out, moving over to the right of the road for Glen Helen 1.

You tend to use all of the road where possible because it gives you the optimum lines everywhere, so you're moving from left to right and then back again almost all the time. Glen Helen 2 is tricky as it's off camber, and you need to be careful when you're going fast, because you can tuck the front really easily.

Sector 2

After Glen Helen, you drive up the hill and through Sarah's Cottage and Lambfell before the course opens up onto the Cronk-y-Voddy straight. It's fast through Lambfell and you can use all the throttle, pulling a big wheelie over the rise onto the straight, and once at the end it's a fast, top-gear corner, Moly's, where the road drops away heavily on the exit. Then you stay pinned through the next right before braking hard and down two gears for the eleventh milestone.

Handley's is another high-speed left-right flick, famous for the massive stone wall on the right, and then it's through McGuinness's, named after John a few years ago. The next bit – the top and bottom of Barregarrow – is one of the scariest parts of the course for me. You can see it coming every lap and you know what's coming, which makes it worse.

Accelerating through the bottom is key, and before you know it you're in Kirk Michael village, which is probably one of my favourite sections – getting to go through a village at 170mph is pretty cool!

It's tricky if you catch someone here as it's near impossible to overtake. Catching people in sections in general can be tricky, especially if it's a rider you're not familiar with – during practice for example – as you don't know which way they're going to go. If you catch them at the wrong time you have to be both cautious and patient. You can't rush or force a pass around the TT course as it'll bite you if you do. You've got to be careful and as safe as possible when overtaking, whoever the rider is.

Kirk Michael to Ballaugh is another really fast section: sixth gear all the way through Bishopscourt then down to fifth for Alpine Cottage. You're constantly moving from one side of the road to another and it's particularly tricky when the sun's shining through the trees, because you get a strobe-light effect that can make visibility tricky.

You use all the road on the exit of Alpine and then you're straight back up to sixth gear all the way to Ballaugh, where it's back down to second for the jump over the bridge. Seeing the big crowds gathered around the bridge every lap, and all around the course for that matter, is just awesome, and seeing and feeling the crowd definitely spurs you on.

▲ The spectacular Ballacrye jump is just before the halfway point of the lap.

Sector 3

Quarry Bends is an important section as you know the long Sulby Straight follows it. Getting the exit right can be the difference between 190mph and 200mph along the straight, which can mean gaining or losing a few seconds. Of course, that applies to most of the TT Course – being fast on the exit is key.

After Sulby Bridge it's Ginger Hall, where getting the right line can be a bit tricky, and then it's bumpy all the way to Ramsey, but still fast. There are so many trees along here, and their roots create all the bumps under the road surface; the K-Tree is one of the most famous, and popular, vantage points for spectators. The tree's painted with a large 'K' just to remind you where the kerb sticks out. You can't see the kerb as it's past where the road drops down, so that big letter on the tree is a huge help!

Milntown and the big jump is flat out in fifth gear and then you're pinned all the way to Schoolhouse Corner, where I look for the pink or orange wall on the right for my braking marker. You can use the bus stop on the exit if you need that extra bit of road, but most riders tend to avoid doing that – I think I've only used it once, and once was enough as it's dusty out there!

Parliament Square is slow, but there's always loads of spectators through here, and then it's the bumpy run up May Hill and through White Gates and Stella Maris, a lovely on-camber right-hander, before getting hard on the brakes for Ramsey Hairpin, where the mountain section gets underway.

Sector 4

You must be careful immediately after the hairpin, especially if there's been any overnight rain as damp patches can remain and catch you out – it normally stays damp under the trees here. The second Waterworks corner is also very tight and a lot slower than what you want, so you must be patient as you can't force the pace through here.

The right-left of Tower Bends is another bumpy sequence of corners and then it's another fast right kink followed by a left, before you tip into the Gooseneck. Many riders have a pit board exiting the corner on the left, as it's a prime opportunity to get a good view of it and find out what's going on in the race.

Sometimes I have one a bit further along, though, maybe at somewhere like the Bungalow, as that gives me the time from Ramsey. You're always behind on the times due to the speeds we're going but you obviously need to give the guys or girls doing the boards enough time to get the information on there.

It's very fast over the mountain, and after Joey's, you have Guthrie's, which is really important as the Mountain Mile follows, which, as the name suggests, is a mile long! You must carry the momentum immediately through the left- and right-hand corners after Guthrie's to carry as much speed as possible along the Mountain Mile.

You're pinned in fourth gear coming onto the Mountain Mile and then you quickly move through fifth and into sixth. You don't shut off at all and it's flat-out all the way until the bridge just before the Mountain Box, where you're back to fourth gear.

There are several apexes after the Mountain Box, so you miss the first, clip the second, miss the third one and then hit the fourth one, where you move back up to fifth gear. It's all about keeping the momentum going as you're climbing all the time.

There's a right-hander before Casey's where I always think I can go through quicker and then it's the Verandah, which is four right-handers that you take as one, making the apex at the last one and using all the track on the exit. The Graham Memorial leads into the Bungalow, where there's a marshal's box prior to entry, which tells me where I need to apex on the inside.

▲ The mountain climb begins in earnest after the Gooseneck.

Sector 5

It's back from fourth gear to second for the Bungalow before clicking third gear on the changeover in direction, over the famous tramlines. The natural line means you're pretty much upright over them, so they don't cause any dramas. I have another pit board on the exit here.

The course starts to drop down shortly afterwards, once you're through Hailwood's Heights – the highest part of the course – and it feels like the bike's suddenly got a turbo. It's been pulling all the way up the mountain climb, so as you drop down towards the thirty-third and then Kate's Cottage the bike suddenly feels much faster and starts revving loads more!

The thirty-second is an awesome corner, well, two to three corners taken in one, and then it's a straight line into Windy Corner, so named because it's always windy! I used a bit too much road here in the 2018 Senior and it was really dusty, which made the bike spin up a fair amount. It cost me a little bit of time and drive, but fortunately not too much.

You're then pinned in sixth before going back a couple of gears and letting the brakes off for the first part of the thirty-third milestone. You're quickly back on the throttle, letting the bike run over the white line to the right-hand side of the road and then it's up to fifth gear before the left-hander of Keppel Gate.

The road drops steeply down through Kate's Cottage before the straight and jump heading down to the Creg-ny-Baa, where I'm all the way out to the white line on the exit, especially in practice. The crowd are always hanging off the bank here with their phones, so it's a good opportunity to make them all jump!

The bike is accelerating really fast on the run to Brandish, which is probably one of the fastest parts of the course. Brandish itself used to be a 90-degree left-hander but it was re-profiled in early 2007, so it's now one big sweep in fourth gear. It's an awesome corner on a Superbike.

The following right at Hillberry is another fast corner and another place where the fans are hanging off the stone wall with their phones!

Sector 6

Hillberry's an important corner as you need to get good drive up the hill to Cronk-ny-Mona, where the final, and shortest, sector starts. From the Cronk to the start and finish it only takes 50-odd seconds, but every second counts, and while the sector may only be a couple of miles long, the race can be won and lost through here.

The first bits at Signpost and Bedstead are okay but it gets really tight at the Nook, and from there to the exit of Governor's Bridge is the only section of the course that doesn't get used for everyday traffic. It used to be just Governor's Dip, but a new access road was added a few years ago so now it's from the Nook onwards.

It's narrow and twisty down to Governor's Bridge, which is taken in first gear and is probably the slowest corner on the course; it's always greasy and dirty in the dip due to all the overhanging trees and the road never getting used.

You drive out of the dip and then it's up to sixth gear as soon as you can get there, to start another lap! And when it's the final lap, especially a six-lap Superbike or Senior race, taking the chequered flag is an unbelievable feeling and an unbelievable achievement, whoever you are.

TT Numbers

Where are the three fastest points on the course for a Superbike?

1	Sulby Straight	204mph (326kph)
2	Mountain Mile	199mph (318kph)
3	Creg-ny-Baa to Brandish	195mph (312kph)

Where are the three slowest points on the course?

1	Governor's Bridge	21mph (33kph)
2	Ramsey Hairpin	26mph (41kph)
3	Parliament Square	36mph (57kph)

What are the biggest deceleration points?

1	Sulby Bridge	203mph to 57mph	6th gear to 1st	9.8bar
2	Ballaugh Bridge	175mph to 49mph	6th gear to 1st	10bar
3	Quarter Bridge	169mph to 42mph	6th gear to 1st	10bar

Apex speeds for the following corners

	Entry speed	Apex speed	Gear
Ballagarey	183mph	145mph	5th
Crosby	190mph	116mph	5th
Gorse Lea	174mph	154mph	5th
Molyneux's	190mph	158mph	6th
Ballacrye Bend	180mph	140mph	5th

How many gear changes are made per lap?

Superbike:	186
Superstock:	186
Supersport:	181

What percentage of the lap is spent at 100% throttle?

Superbike:	44%
Superstock:	46%
Supersport:	69%

How much of the lap is spent over 120mph?

Superbike:	69%
Superstock:	69%
Supersport:	71%

How much fuel is consumed per lap?

Superbike:	11.5 litres
Superstock:	10.8 litres

Where are the three hardest impacts on the suspension (in terms of travel, force and speed)?

1	Bottom of Barragarrow
2	Ballaugh Bridge landing
3	Bottom of Bray Hill

What data is there to show how bumpy Ginger Hall to Ramsey is?

Suspension speeds increase to 300–500mm/s as an average, with peaks of 900–1,000mm/s over the entire stretch. As a comparison, Quarry Bends to Sulby Bridge averages 30–100mm/s. Different suspension settings change velocities and rider feeling, so it is important to get the suspension working to reduce rider effort and fatigue through this section in particular.

▲▲ Jamie Coward powers through the high-speed Gorse Lea, just before Ballacraine, a popular vantage point for spectators.
▲ Peter Hickman leaps the Glen Auldyn jump on the high-speed run into Ramsey, the BMW rider winning both Superstock races in 2023.

returned to the event for the first time since 2018, lining up alongside Hickman on BMW. Hutchinson's woes continued as a stroke ruled him out.

But the biggest news was the change to the schedule. Keen to maximise the spectator experience, organisers added an extra Superstock and Supertwin race to make eight solo races in total. The opening Supersport race replaced the Superbike as the traditional curtain raiser to race week, and the races were held in two-day batches: Saturday/Sunday, Tuesday/Wednesday and Friday/Saturday.

It was an ambitious schedule, but with the sun shining throughout it all ran smoothly. Dunlop threw down the gauntlet on the final afternoon of practice with a lap of 135.531mph, and the Ulsterman won immediately, taking victory from Hickman and Harrison in the opening Supersport race.

It was Superbike success Dunlop craved most, and fitter and leaner than ever, that's what he got. He led the six-lap Superbike race from start to finish to defeat Hickman, whose quick shifter failed on the first lap, and won by 8.2s. Harrison again completed the podium in third. Hickman set the fastest lap at 135.445mph.

Victory saw Dunlop match McGuinness's tally of 23 TT wins, but Hickman got his revenge straightaway with a comfortable victory over fellow TT phenoms Dunlop and Harrison in the first Superstock race. Dunlop's response was to take win number 24 in the opening Supertwin encounter, winning from Mike Browne and Coward, with Hickman back in fourth on his all-new R7 Yamaha.

> The lap record was smashed in the Sidecar class too, when the Birchalls set the first ever three-wheel 120mph lap

Dunlop took his fourth win of the week in the second Supersport race, where both he and Hickman became the first riders to lap the Mountain Course at more than 130mph on a 600cc machine. Harrison was again third and Hickman won the second Supertwin race from podium debutantes Pierre Yves Bian and Brookes after Dunlop retired on the opening lap.

Sandwiched in between those two races was the second Superstock race, where Hickman was simply sensational. Having struggled with the handling on the M1000RR Superbike, Hickman was more at ease on his Superstock mount and not only did he comfortably beat Dunlop and Harrison, he smashed his own outright lap record with a stunning final lap of 136.358mph.

The lap record was smashed in the Sidecar class too, when the Birchalls set the first ever three-wheel 120mph lap. Having won the first race from nearest challengers Pete Founds/Jevan Walmsley, they lapped at a jaw-dropping 120.645mph in the second race. Founds/Walmsley also broke the 120mph barrier. It was Ben and Tom's fourteenth TT win.

With Dunlop on four wins and Hickman three, the scene was set for a thrilling Senior. Having made setup changes to his Honda, Dunlop was unable to replicate his pace from the Superbike race earlier in the week, and Hickman stamped his authority on the race from the outset. With more 135mph+ laps, he came home 20s clear of Harrison with Dunlop in third.

The Birchalls Break the 120mph Barrier
2023

Brothers Ben and Tom Birchall are the Isle of Man TT's most successful sidecar partnership, with only the legendary Dave Molyneux securing more driver wins around the Mountain Course. However, of all their impressive feats, it is their last outing together at the 2023 event that will stand out as their best.

With 2023 marking 100 years of sidecars at the TT, much of the pre-event press questioned whether the three-wheel crews could emulate the solo centenary celebrations of 2007, when John McGuinness broke the 130mph barrier.

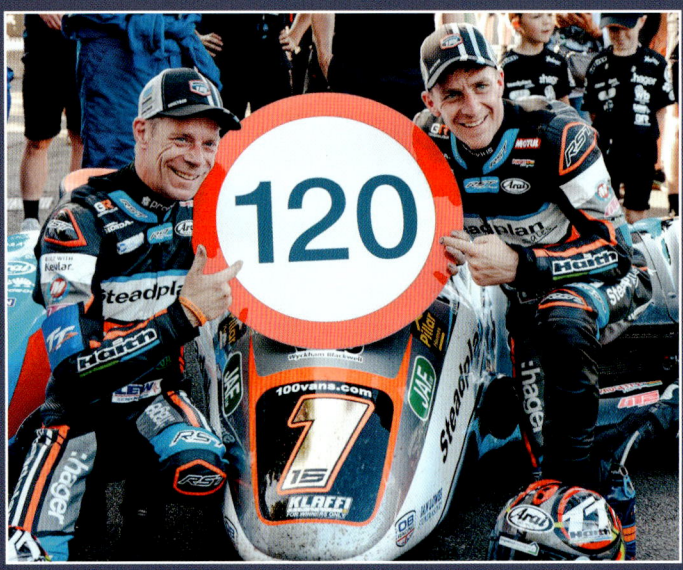

▲ After coming close between 2018 and 2022, the Birchalls finally cracked the 120mph barrier in 2023.

For the sidecars, that elusive lap speed was 120mph. Ben and Tom had held the lap record since 2016, with the mark standing at 119.250mph ahead of the 2023 event.

The duo were the pacesetters throughout practice week and wasted no time in making their mark in the opening race. Starting from first on the road, they already had a 3.9-second lead by Glen Helen and threatened a new lap record from a standing start, recording a 118.577mph lap.

Storming down Glencrutchery Road for lap two, the duo continued to pull away from second place, and as they progressed around the course it became clear they were on for a history-making lap. As they flashed over the line, they had done it – the first sidecar outfit to break the 120mph barrier with a 120.357mph lap! A 119mph third lap saw them take their thirteenth TT win.

The duo were not done there, though. In the week's second Sidecar race, they would better their record once again. That race saw them increase the outright sidecar lap record to 120.645mph on their way to a fourteenth win, drawing them level on wins with the late, great Mike Hailwood.

The 2023 Isle of Man TT was the last time the duo raced together, with Tom announcing his retirement later that year.

▲ Davey Todd celebrates after winning the 2024 Senior TT on his Milwaukee BMW.

The same schedule remained in 2024, with Dunlop and Hickman continuing with Hawk Racing Honda and FHO Racing BMW respectively. After a decade with Kawasaki, Harrison switched to Honda where McGuinness stayed, but Milwaukee TAS Racing BMW now fielded Todd.

Brookes was teammate to Hickman once more, with privateers Hillier and Coward both expected to feature. Hutchinson returned, again, and was reunited with his old Padgetts Honda team alongside Cummins. Elsewhere, the Birchall partnership came to an end in the Sidecar class after passenger Tom retired.

With 25 wins to his name, Dunlop was only one victory short of his Uncle Joey's record total of 26 and he immediately equalled the figure in the opening Supersport race. Untouchable in the 600cc class, Dunlop won from Todd, riding a Ducati in the class, and Harrison, with Hickman strangely out of sorts in ninth.

Dunlop was then on course for victory in the Superbike race when he led Todd by 25s after four of the six laps. However, a visor change at the second pit stop went wrong and he had to stop just after St Ninian's crossroads to remove his helmet and re-attach it. A final lap of 135.970mph pulled him up to fourth, but Hickman won his fourteenth TT by 5.8s from Todd.

Victory ahead of Hickman in the first Supertwin race saw Dunlop finally better Joey's tally of wins, and his record-breaking spree continued with further success in the second Supersport and Supertwin races moving him on to 29 wins in total. Dunlop's status as the most successful TT rider ever was categorically confirmed.

▲ At high speed through Kirk Michael, double Sidecar World Champions Todd Ellis and Emmanuelle Clement were TT newcomers in 2024.

In between, Todd delivered on the promise shown in previous years with a superb victory in the first Superstock race, 2.2s ahead of Hickman who set the fastest lap at 135.140mph. Dunlop, whose Honda Superstock was no match for the BMWs, finished third with Harrison fourth.

In the Sidecar class Ben Birchall recruited France's Kevin Rousseau, but a spill in practice meant they missed the first race and the Crowe brothers won their first TT. Birchall/Rousseau lined up for the second race but had to settle for second, with the Crowes again winning after lapping at 120.335mph.

Poor weather meant the second Superstock race was cancelled and the Senior was everyone's last chance for success. The race was cut to four laps and Hickman, who'd had, for him, a mixed TT, was on a mission from the start. An opening lap of 135.523mph gave him the lead over Todd by 2.7s. Dunlop retired at the Bungalow with a slipping clutch.

In lap two Hickman set some blistering sector times, and the outright lap record looked set to be smashed, but it all ended at Ginger Hall when he crashed out, fortunately without injury. That allowed Todd to have a trouble-free run to the flag, and he won by 39s from Brookes, who broke the 134mph barrier for the first time, and Harrison.

Dunlop wasn't about to rest on his laurels and 2025 further confirmed his status as the TT GOAT, but it was disaster for Hickman as he crashed out heavily at

▲▲ Manxman Michael Evans exits the top of Barregarrow on the back wheel.
▲ 2024 was the year when Michael Dunlop finally broke his uncle Joey's record tally of 26 wins.

Kerrowmoar during practice due to a component failure. He was lucky to escape with non-life-threatening injuries but was out of action for the next four months.

Hickman had set up his own BMW team, 8TEN Racing, with Todd, and Dunlop was back on a BMW for the big bike races, securing a full-factory spec M1000RR for the Superbike and Senior races. However, in a race shortened to four laps due to a weather-interrupted week, Todd prevailed in the Superbike race albeit just, his winning margin over Dunlop a slender 1.3s.

Dunlop was again imperious in the smaller classes. Switching to a 959cc Ducati Panigale V2 for the first time, he won both Supersport races, with Harrison finishing second on both occasions, to make it eight successive victories in the category. It was a similar story in the Supertwin races, where he chalked up two more comfortable wins on his Paton, raising his own lap record to 123.056mph.

But in the Superstock races Harrison dominated. His first year with Honda had been solid and, running full-time in the British Supersport Championship, the short circuit skills acquired were being put to good use on the Mountain Course. The first race, cut to two laps, saw him post a new personal best lap of 135.692mph as he defeated Todd by more than 11s, and it was a similar story in

▼ With less than a mile to go, Ryan and Callum Crowe round Bedstead Corner, as spectators watch on from their perch amongst the Isle of Man scenery .

▲ With his hometown of Ramsey behind him, Manxman Conor Cummins sweeps through Guthrie's Memorial.

the second race, when his eventual winning margin over Todd was 16s. Dunlop finished third in each race.

Both Sidecar races, where entries continued to hover around the 30 mark, were reduced from three laps to two, but it mattered little to the Crowes, who made it four wins in a row with their second successive double. They also broke the Birchalls' lap record with a speed of 121.021mph.

The weather had caused issues throughout the fortnight, made more frustrating by the heatwaves seen in the UK both before and after the event. Heavy overnight rain continually delayed the Senior on the final day of racing, but when the course had dried out sufficiently the riders were allowed to carry out an exploratory lap of the course.

However, by this time, the wind speed had increased substantially, and with strong gusts all around the course it was widely agreed it was unsafe for the race to start. For the first time since 2012, and for only the second time in its history, the blue riband Senior race was cancelled.

Recent Safety Measures

During the three-year hiatus of the Covid-19 pandemic, the Promoter of the Isle of Man TT Races worked closely with the race organisers, marshals, medics and police to instil a cultural change towards safety at the event.

As with all high-speed motorsports, there will always be inherent risk. The vital thing is to make sure that when there is an accident there is also a comprehensive investigation and analysis to mitigate the risk of that happening again, and to confirm that the rider was wearing the required kit, was in the best possible position health-wise, and that the rider and their bike were in a race-fit condition. This is why in 2022 the Isle of Man TT Races introduced a safety management system; this system wasn't one specific change and is a process of continuous improvement.

In addition to the comprehensive changes to accident investigation and reporting, the safety management system brings a raft of improvements to mitigate risk:

- Digital red flag system and GPS tracking to aid accident response
- Increased PPE standards for leathers, boots, gloves and body armour
- Reduction of starters in each race: 50 in 1000cc classes, 60 elsewhere
- More exclusive field to drive higher standards and professionalism
- Changed to single start (no longer pairs) for qualifying
- Longer afternoon session to open qualifying, easing pressure on teams
- Final qualifying moved to the afternoon, ensuring longer preparation and recovery time
- Course inspection lap on race days to give riders a feel for course conditions
- Increased medical and physical standards
- Access to trained occupational therapists
- Course simulation in addition to the continued newcomer mentor programme.

Race Control

In December 2020, Race Control was flooded by a defective water sprinkler system. The whole room had to be gutted – equipment, furniture, carpets, everything. This provided an excellent opportunity to redesign and put in place a Race Control to effectively manage and deliver the TT Races, and it was completed in time for TT 2022. The new Race Control gives the Clerk of the Course and his team far more visibility of the course through the enhanced technology now available.

Digital Flags

During the Covid-19 pandemic, work progressed on a digital flag system which, again, was in place for TT 2022. The TT course now boasts 41 digital flags placed to give maximum visibility to competitors. The digital flags are operated centrally from Race Control by the Clerk of the Course, and they are used mainly for red flag incidents and black-flagging riders who need to be stopped and checked, mainly because of possible technical or mechanical issues.

Once the race or an individual rider is stopped, technical checks are carried out by highly experienced travelling marshals, who are also qualified technical officials. It is important to note the digital flags are to enhance rather than replace marshalling, and it goes without saying that the TT course is still very much reliant on the volunteer orange army provided by the TTMA.

Enhanced PPE Standards

Standards for competitors' leathers, helmets, gloves and boots can be found in the ACU Standing Regulations for Road Racing. However, given the inherent risks of the Mountain Course, an increased set of PPE standards has been adopted to mitigate the risk of injury to TT competitors. As such, the Promoter and Race Organiser have worked closely with experts in the provision of PPE to ensure the highest standards are put in place.

Helmets must not be more than five years old from the date of manufacture, and any helmet produced that has the date stamp or date of manufacture removed cannot be used. Leathers must be CE (Conformité Européenne or European Conformity) approved and conform with European Standard EN17092. Leathers must be fitted with CE approved protection pads at the shoulder, elbow, knee and hip. The Race Organiser also highly recommends that leathers used should be certified to Class AAA or AA standard. Back protectors are compulsory and must be worn by all competitors, both Solo and Sidecar competitors.

Competitors must wear CE-marked gloves that conform to the European Standard EN13594 with a minimum level of 1-KP and boots must be CE marked to conform with European Standard EN13634:2017.

Increased Medical and Physical Standards

In 2024, ACU Events Ltd (ACUE) confirmed details of a new initiative to raise medical and physical standards for TT competitors that was introduced for the 2025 event.

The initiative's aim is to ensure competitors are in the best possible physical and mental state for the unique challenge of racing on the Mountain Course, and is part of the Race Organiser's continuous evaluation of risk management across the whole event. The project was done in collaboration with the Manx Road Racing Medical Services – the organisation providing doctors and paramedics for the TT and headed by the event's Chief Medical Officer, Dr Gareth Davies.

The project got underway at TT 2024 with a feasibility study, and several volunteer competitors from across the entry list underwent a range of physiological and biochemical assessments.

Index of Riders and Teams

8TEN Racing 248

Abbott, Ray 25
Abbott, Steve 138
Agostini, Giacomo 7, 73, 78, 99–102, 104–6, 109–11, 114, 122, 151, 195
AIM Yamaha 188
AJS 20, 27, 32, 34–8, 43–4, 46, 68–9, 71–2, 75, 83, 88–91, 97, 104, 106
Ambrosini, Dario 71, 72
AMDM/BMW 194
Amm, Ray 22, 72, 74–5, 79, 91
Amor, Keith 196, 198–9, 206, 211–12
Anderson, Bob 84
Anderson, Fergus 42, 72
Anderson, Hugh 85, 95, 97, 99, 139
Anstey, Bruce 139, 146, 166, 170, 180, 183, 186–7, 189, 191, 195–6, 198, 205–7, 211–14, 218, 220–1, 223, 225, 228
Applebee, Frank 24
Appledene 151, 237
Aprilia 194
Archangeli, Luigi 42, 43, 191
Archibald, Adrian 139, 186–7, 196, 229
Ariel 25, 48
Armstrong, Reg 22, 72, 75
Aro 111
Arthur, Kenny 123, 125, 128
Assen 68
Atkinson, Stewart 136
Auerbacher, Georg 110, 114, 115
Agusta, Count 73
Aylott, Mike 215, 220

Baldwin, Mark 164, 214
Ball, Brian 104
Barber, Rob 205
Barnett, Alan 110
Barrington, Manliffe 42, 67, 68
Barton, John 55, 176, 192–3, 196, 200–3
Barton Phoenix 142
Bartusch, Günter 109
Bashall, Harry 17, 24
BAT 17
Bateman, Frederick 25
Beattie, Nigel 196
Bell, Artie 68, 69, 70, 71
Bell, Geoff 157, 158
Bell, Ian 166, 186, 225
Benelli 60, 69, 71, 88, 106, 107, 124
Bennett, Alec 22, 32, 34–7, 41, 43–4, 48, 50, 52
Bentley, Walter 16–17
Beo 125
Bian, Pierre Yves 243
Bianchi 41
Biggs, Graham 166
Biggs, Phillip 166
Biggs, Vince 166
Biland, Rolf 115, 123, 125–6

Billown Course 196, 198, 199, 205
Bingham, Dennis 136, 138
Bingham, Julia 136, 138
Binns, Ben 223
Birch, Kenny 125
Birchall, Ben 146, 218, 222–3, 225, 228, 231–2, 235, 243–6, 249
Birchall, Tom 146, 218, 222–3, 225, 228, 231–2, 235, 243–5, 249
Birkin, Archie 43
Birks, Chas 126, 136, 138, 140, 142, 147–8, 156
Blackburne 32, 43, 46–7
BMW 60, 63, 75, 79, 83, 92, 95, 102–3, 110, 111, 114–15, 168, 171, 184, 218, 220, 225–8, 230, 232, 234, 243, 246, 248
Boddice, Bill 79
Boddice, Mick 126, 136, 138, 140, 142–3, 147–8, 156–8, 163
Bowen, Harry 17
Brandish, Walter 34, 35, 154
Brandish Corner 76, 122, 154, 240
Braun, Dieter 109
Bray Hill 4, 20, 27, 37, 74, 76, 125, 150–1, 200, 208, 236
Bremgarten 68
Brett, Jack 71, 72, 75, 79
Britton, Richard 186
Brookes, Josh 22, 152, 192, 215, 228, 231, 235–6, 243, 246
Brough 25
Brown, Bob 77, 80, 82, 83, 84
Brown, Duggie 32
Brown, Norman 135, 136, 139, 180
Browne, Mike 243
Bryans, Ralph 97, 101
BSA 70, 92, 107, 110
BSB 220
Bultaco 102, 106
Burgess, Trevor 107
Burkhardt, Horst 92
Burnett, Roger 142–4, 147
Burns, Mick 117, 123
Burton, Lowry 142–3, 147–8
Busch, Dieter 115
Butenuth, Hans-Otto 103

Cain, Lee 232
Cama 79
Camathias, Florian 89, 92, 95, 97
Campbell, Keith 80
Cann, Maurice 42, 67, 68, 71
Carpenter, Neil 186
Carroll, Arthur 22, 49
Carruthers, Kel 107, 109
Carswell, Gary 187
Casey's 201, 239
Castrol Honda 163
Chadwick, Dave 84
Chanel, Cesar 235

Chrysalis Racing 173
Clark, RO 32
Clermont Ferrand 118
Cochrane, James 157
Coleman, Rod 72, 75
Colleda 139; see also Suzuki
Collier, Charlie 11, 13, 14, 17, 23, 27
Collier, Harry 11, 14, 17, 27
Colombo, Roberto 79
Cooper, Vernon 122
Cornbill, Keith 158
Cotton 35, 48
Cotton/Rotax 145
Courtney, James 164
Coward, Jamie 192, 232, 243, 245
Cox, Mark 198, 205
Crabtree, Syd 44
Craig, Joe 22, 44, 49
Creyton, Billy 17
Cron, Fritz 75
Crosby, Graeme 79, 126, 129–31, 133–5, 136, 139, 143
Crowe, Callum 235, 246, 249
Crowe, Nick 191, 195, 198, 205, 235
Crowe, Ryan 235, 246, 249
Croxford, Dave 116
Cull, Steve 129, 136, 142, 147, 148, 157
Cummins, Conor 153, 196, 205–7, 211, 218, 220, 225, 229, 231–5, 245
Cushnahan, Pat 142, 143, 147–8

Dähne, Helmut 103
Dale, Dickie 42, 68, 80, 83
Dance, George 32
Daniell, Harold 22, 60, 67–9
Davenport, Leo 49
Davies, Gareth 251
Davies, Howard 27, 32, 38, 39, 41
Davies, Nigel 165, 233
Davison, Geoff 34
de la Hay, Tommy 32
Degner, Ernst 92, 95, 97, 139
DeRosier, Jake 21, 23, 59
Deubel, Max 92, 97, 99, 101, 103, 115
Dixon, Freddie 32, 34, 35, 37, 43
DKW 48, 56, 58, 59, 60, 72
Dodson, Charlie 44, 46, 50
Donald, Cameron 139, 188, 196, 198–9, 211–14
Doran, Bill 68, 71, 151
Drion, Jacques 75, 96
Drive, Alexander 39
Ducati 84, 85, 88, 123, 126, 131, 136, 194, 227, 245, 248
Duff, Mike 97, 99
Duffus, Iain 163, 165, 167, 170, 171
Duke, Geoff 7, 22, 69–72, 74–5, 79–80, 82, 84, 91, 95, 99
Dunlop, Joey 4, 7, 91, 123–4, 129–31, 133–6, 138, 140, 142–4, 146–9, 153, 157, 160–1, 163–6, 168–71, 173, 180, 189, 215, 227, 245
Dunlop, Michael 7, 103, 139, 146, 153, 161, 170, 184, 197, 201, 205–7, 212, 214–15, 218, 220, 223, 225–7, 229, 231–5, 243, 245–6, 248–9
Dunlop, Robert 156–7, 160, 163, 166, 205, 227
Dunlop, William 220, 227, 232

East Coast Racing Honda 213
Edge, Selwyn 76
Edmond, Freddy 32
Ehrlich, Dr Joe 136
Ekerold, Jon 131–3, 135
Ellison, Karl 161, 163
EMC 88, 136, 138, 140–2
Enders, Klaus 102, 103, 109, 114, 115, 117
Engelhardt, Ralf 102, 109, 114
Evans, Lee 16
Evans, Percy 21
Excelsior 44, 50, 59, 60

Farquhar, Ryan 186–91, 196, 198, 205–7, 214, 233
Farrance, Patrick 161, 198, 206, 214–15, 220, 233
Fath, Helmut 89
FHO Racing 234
FHO Racing BMW 245
Findlay, Jack 114, 139
Finnegan, Martin 73, 196
Fisher, Rob 163, 164, 166, 171, 173, 183, 187
Fittipaldi, Emerson 123
Flaxman, John 107
Flint, Keith 223
FN 46
Fogarty, Carl 144, 145, 147, 148, 156, 157, 160, 163, 195
Fogarty, George 7, 123
Foster, Bob 52, 58, 67, 68
Founds, Pete 243
Fowler, Rem 13, 14, 22
Frend, Ted 68
Frith, Freddie 48, 52, 56, 58, 60, 63, 67–8, 82

Gall, Karl 63
Garelli 41
George, Prince 49
George, Alex 116, 122, 126, 129, 133, 146, 221
Ghersi, Pietro 41–3, 42, 44, 59
Gibbard, John 140
Gilera 42, 71–2, 75, 79–83, 95, 104, 106
Gleaves, Syd 50
Godfrey, Oliver 23, 27
Godfrey, Tony 95
Gonzalez 79
Gould, Rod 109, 110
Graham, Les 68, 69, 72, 73, 74, 139
Graham, Stuart 102, 139

Grant, Mick 4, 7, 110, 114, 116–17, 119, 122–4, 126, 129–31, 133–6, 138–40, 146, 221, 233
Greasley, Dick 117, 123, 125–6, 136
Griffiths, Jason 173, 187, 191, 195
Grunwald, Manfred 75, 79, 83
Guthrie, Billy 116
Guthrie, Jimmie 7, 22, 35–6, 39, 44, 46–50, 53, 56–8, 60, 91, 145, 153
Guy, Chris 131
Guzzi, Carlo 42, 43

Haas, Werner 72, 75, 78
Hahn, Hermann 110, 114
Hailwood, Michelle 88
Hailwood, Mike 7, 73, 84, 88–92, 95, 97, 101–2, 105–6, 109, 111, 116, 119, 123–4, 126, 129, 138–9, 146, 148, 160, 166, 173, 198, 233
Hailwood, Stan 88
Haldemann, Hans 85
Hallam, Craig 161, 171, 186, 195
Hallam, Dave 140
Hamilton, Jamie 223
Handley, Wal 32, 34–5, 37–9, 41, 43–4, 46, 48–50, 53, 67, 91, 152
Hanks, Roy 166, 168
Hanks, Tom 168
Hardman, Colin 156, 161
Harris, HF 32
Harris, Pip 79
Harris, Shaun 186
Harrison, Conrad 215, 220
Harrison, Dean 146, 184, 213, 218, 220, 225–6, 228–9, 231–5, 245–6, 248–9
Harrison, Nathan 192
Hartle, John 73, 79–81, 84, 89, 95, 102, 104, 221
Haslam, Ron 124, 126, 129–31, 133, 135–6, 143, 146
Hawk Racing 220, 226, 234
Hawk Racing BMW 225
Hawk Racing Honda 245
Heath, Chris 205
Heckles, Keith 52
Hector Neill Racing Suzuki 136
Hennen, Pat 123–4
Henshaw, Steve 156
Herbertson, Dominic 192
Heron Suzuki 117, 119, 123–4, 134
Herrero, Santiago 107, 109
Herron, Tom 117, 122–3, 125, 139, 170
Herzig, Alfred 95
Hickman, Peter 73, 103, 170, 184, 192, 197, 218, 220–1, 225–6, 228–32, 234–41, 243, 245–8
Hicks, Freddie 44, 52
Hill, Peter 166
Hillebrand, Fritz 75, 79, 83
Hillier, James 214, 218, 220, 223, 225–6, 228–9, 232–3, 245
Hinton, Harry 71, 72

Hislop, Steve 'Hizzy' 7, 22, 143–5, 147–9, 156–8, 160, 163, 165–6, 170
HM Plant Honda 191, 196–7, 199, 211
Ho, Faye 234
Hobson, Mac 117, 123, 125
Hocking, Gary 73, 78, 89–94, 101
Holden, John 206, 213, 225
Holden, Rob 164
Holland, Cliff 117
Hollaus, Rupert 75, 76, 206
Honda 2, 85, 87–90, 92, 94–5, 97–9, 101–2, 104–6, 110, 114, 123–4, 126, 133, 136, 138, 142–5, 146, 148, 156–7, 160–1, 163–6, 168, 171, 173, 180, 182, 189, 191, 194–6, 199, 211, 213–14, 217–18, 225, 227–8, 232, 234–6, 243
Honda, Soichiro 87, 89
Honda Britain 122–3, 126, 129–30, 158, 167, 171
Honda TT Legends 211, 220
Honda UK 215
Hope, Darren 191, 195
Horner, Emil 92, 97, 99, 101
Horton, Clive 114
Horton, Len 37
Howles, Kenny 147–8, 156
HRD 38, 43
Huber, Josef 117
Hughes, Dave 117
Hulbert, Frank 10, 11, 221
Humber 16, 21
Hunt, Tim 46–7, 49–50, 91
Hurst, Roger 144
Husqvarna 48, 50
Hutchinson, Boyd 164
Hutchinson, Ian 103, 146, 170, 191, 195–6, 198–9, 205–7, 211–14, 220, 223, 225–6, 228, 233–4, 243, 245
Hydrex Honda 196, 199

Indian 16–17, 20–1, 23, 25, 27, 32
Ireland, Dennis 126, 135, 139
Ireson, Trevor 126, 129
Irwin, Glenn 192, 234–5
Ito, Fumio 89–90, 95, 170
Itoh, Mitsuo 95
Itom 96
Ivy, Bill 101, 104, 106, 107

Jackson, Alan 126
Jackson, Bob 169–71, 233
Jansson, Börje 109
JAP 34, 46–7
Jawa 95, 107
Jefferies, David 'DJ' 7, 166, 170–2, 180, 182–3, 186, 229
Jefferies, Nick 163, 167, 182
Jefferies, Tony 110, 114, 139, 147, 156, 182, 221
Jessopp, Martin 220, 225, 226–8
Jewell, Doug 171
Johansson, Benga 128–9, 133, 135–6

Johnson, David 228, 232
Johnson, Gary 196, 205, 212–15, 221, 225
Johnson, Geoff 138–40, 143–4, 147, 233
Johnston, Lee 170, 223, 232, 235
Johnston, Paddy 41–3
Jordan, Paul 235

Kaaden, Walter 84, 92
Kalauch, Wolfgang 109–11, 114–15, 117, 126
Katayama, Takazumi 117
Kavanagh, Ken 42, 72, 75–9
Kawasaki 109, 116–17, 122–3, 126, 144, 161, 165, 187, 191, 211–12, 214, 225–7, 230, 232–4, 245
Kawashima, Kiyoshi 173
Kelly, Neil 52, 102, 183
Kennedy, Frank 129
Kickham, Eddie 24
King, Alistair 84
Kinvig, Lizzie 55, 200
Klaffenbock, Klaus 206, 213
Kluge, Ewald 59, 60, 68
KMR Kawasaki 205–6, 214, 228
Kneen, Dan 226, 228, 229
Knight, Ray 107, 221
König 117, 115
Kreidler 85
KTM 161
KTT Velocette 52
Kuhn, Gus 52

Lambert, Greg 166
Langman, Harry 37
Lavorel, Olivier 235
Law, Con 135, 136
Laycock, Eddie 143–4, 148, 156
LCR Honda 222
Le Vack, Bert 34
Leach, Dave 144, 147, 148, 156–8, 170
Lee, Gavin 166
Leoni, Gianni 72
Levis 32
Lintin, Ivan 223, 225, 228, 233
Lockett, Johnny 69, 71, 72
Loctite Yamaha 157
Lofthouse, Mick 164, 214
Lomas, Bill 42, 73, 79
Long, Rick 161, 171, 173, 183, 196
Longman, Frank 41, 44
Lougher, Ian 156, 157, 166, 180, 183, 186–91, 196, 198, 205
Luthringhauser, Heinz 114
Lyons, Ernie 68, 221

Maico 109
Marshall, Jack 10, 11, 14, 221
Marshall, Roger 136, 138, 143
Martin, Guy 188, 196, 199, 205–7, 212–15, 218, 220, 223, 225–6, 228
Martin, Keith 114
Martini Yamaha 123
Masetti, Umberto 71, 72
Mason, Hugh 25

Matchless 11, 13, 14, 17, 20, 21, 23, 35, 36, 106
Mathison, Daley 232
McAdoo Kawasaki 171, 205
McCallen, Phillip 7, 157, 158, 163–8, 171, 206–7
McCandless, Cromie 69, 72
McCandless, Rex 69
McCullough, Denis 166
McDonnell, Gene 140–2
McElnea, Rob 136, 138–9, 143
McGregor, Graeme 126, 135–6, 138, 156, 196
McGuinness, John 7, 146, 161, 166, 170–1, 173, 180, 183, 186–91, 194–9, 205–7, 211–15, 218, 220, 223, 225–6, 229, 232, 234, 238, 243–4
McIntyre, Bob 7, 79–84, 89, 91–2
McVeigh, Bill 221
MD Racing Honda 231
Medd Honda 163
Meier, Georg 63, 103, 168, 218
Mellor, Phil 136, 138, 143, 156, 170, 241
Mellor, Steve 171
Mellors, Ted 60
Mercer, Steve 229
Millar Racing Yamaha 136
Miller, Mark 211, 213–14
Miller, Sammy 79, 83
Milwaukee Yamaha 220
Minter, Derek 89, 92, 95, 97
Molyneux, Dave 7, 139, 156, 161, 163, 166, 171, 186–7, 191, 195–6, 205–6, 214–15, 217, 220, 223, 233, 244
Mondial 42, 69, 72, 78, 83, 88, 104
Montesa 79
Moodie, Jim 163, 165–6, 170–1, 173, 180, 183, 186
Morgan, Davy 235
Morini 89, 105
Moriwaki Kawasaki 126, 134
Morris, Alison 173
Morris, Dave 103, 168, 171, 173
Morrison, Brian 144, 148
Mortimer, Chas 109–10, 114, 116–17, 126, 156–7, 170
Moto Guzzi 36, 41–2, 44, 48, 53, 56, 59–60, 67–9, 71–2, 75, 79–80, 83, 104
MotoCzysz 211, 213–14, 218, 220
MSS Kawasaki 188
Mugen Shinden 189, 194, 214, 218, 220, 223, 231
Müller, Hermann Paul 75, 79
MV Agusta 69, 72–5, 77–81, 83–5, 88–93, 95, 99–102, 104–7, 109–10, 112, 114, 230
MZ 84–5, 89, 92–3, 97, 109, 139

Nation, Trevor 138, 142–3, 157
Neill, Hector 180, 191
New Gerrard 35
New Hudson 36, 44
New Imperial 32, 34, 37, 48, 49, 58
Newsome, Billy 16, 25
Nicholls, Roger 122, 123

253

Nieto, Angel 78, 110
Noll, Willi 75
Norton 13, 22, 32, 36–7, 43–4, 46–50, 53, 56, 60, 63, 67–9, 71–2, 75, 79–81, 83–4, 88, 91–3, 98, 106, 110, 145, 147, 157–8, 160, 194, 215, 228–9, 231–2, 234
Norton, James 16–17
Nott, Ernie 46, 47, 50, 53
NSU 60, 72, 75, 79, 81, 83, 88
NUT 25
Nutt, Les 75, 76

O'Dell, George 123
OK-Supreme 36, 44, 47
Oliver, Eric 75, 76
Ossa 107
Oxley, Mat 140

Padgett, Gary 135, 142, 199
Padgetts 211, 220, 225, 228, 234
Padgetts Honda 189, 196, 207, 214, 235, 245
Pagani, Alberto 97, 110
Palmer, Chris 186, 187, 198
Parker, Len 41
Parkins, John 126
Parlotti, Gilberto 105, 110, 112
Parodi, Giorgio 42
Paton 88, 97, 226–8, 230–1, 235, 248
PBM Ducati 234
PBM Kawasaki 220
Penny, Bill 109
Perris, Frank 95, 107, 139
Peugeot 13, 14
Philip, Prince 68
Phillis, Tom 89–92, 98
Pickrell, Ray 107, 110, 221
Pike, Roland 68
Pirelli 218
Plater, Steve 170, 196, 198–9, 205
Pointer, Steve 147–8, 156
Pollington, Clive 126, 129
Porter, Jock 35, 37
Porter, Raymond 191
Potts, Joe 79
Povey, Fred 52
Prentice, Doug 32
Provini, Tarquinio 73, 76–8, 83–5, 89, 105
Pullin, Cyril 27
Purslow, Mark 235

Quayle, Richard 'Milky' 192–3, 196

Raleigh 46–7
Ramsbotham, Marc 196
Randle, Barry 104
Randle Armstrong 131
Ravelli, Giovanni 42
RC Express Racing 225
Rea, Johnny 156, 157
Rea, Jonathan 156

Rea Racing 130
Read, Phil 7, 85, 90–1, 95, 97–9, 102, 104, 106–7, 110, 112, 122–3, 126, 139, 146, 170, 195
Redman, Jim 7, 85, 89, 92, 94–5, 97–9, 101, 106, 146, 168, 195
Reed, Harry 14
Reeves, Tim 198, 215, 218
Reid, Brian 138, 140, 147, 157–8, 163, 170
Rex-Acme 38, 39, 43, 44, 46–7
Richards, Ian 117, 129, 134
Richmond, Brett 173
Robb, Tommy 92, 102, 114
Roberts, Eddie 116, 123, 140
Robinson, Dudley 110
Robinson, John 95, 101
Robinson, Mervyn 129
Roche, Nick 157
Rogers, Tony 109
Rollason, Nigel 142
Roper, Dave 136
Rosney, Patrick 222
Rossi, Valentino 4
Rothmans Honda 138, 142
Rousseau, Kevin 222, 246
Rover 25
Royal Enfield 27, 48
Royal London 360 213
Rudge 21, 25, 27, 44, 46–7, 49–50, 53, 68
Ruffo, Bruno 72
Rusk, Walter 50, 53
Russell, Gordon 125
Rutter, Michael 166–7, 169, 171, 173, 213–15, 218, 225–8, 231–2
Rutter, Tony 7, 110, 114, 117, 126, 131, 135, 136, 138–40, 169–70

Sandford, Cecil 72, 73, 75, 78, 79, 83
Saville, Dave 157
Sayle, Dan 139, 161, 187, 191, 205–6, 213, 215
Schauzu, Siegfried 102–3, 107, 109–11, 114, 117, 158
Scheidegger, Fritz 92, 95, 97, 101, 115
Schneider, Horst 102, 107, 109, 111
Schneider, Walter 77, 79, 84, 103
Scott 24, 25, 27, 48
Selby, Howard 233
Seward, Mike 156
Sharpe, Martin 114
Sheard, Tom 32, 34, 37, 102, 187
Sheene, Barry 106, 110, 117
Shepherd, Alan 97
Simmonds, Dave 109, 233
Simpson, Bill 117
Simpson, Ian 166, 169, 171
Simpson, Jimmy 7, 32, 35, 37, 39, 43–4, 46–50

Singleton, Dale 133
Skeels, Mick 123
Smith, Barry 107, 126, 129, 131, 170
Smith, Bill 102, 110, 114, 126
Smith, Shaun 138
Spencer, Freddie 168
Sports Motorcycles Ducati 122
Šťastný, František 95
Steinhausen, Rolf 114, 117, 123, 126
Stobart Honda 188
Stockton, Bradley 235
Stockton, Roger 235
Stoll, Inge 75, 96
Strauss, Hans 77, 79, 84
Sturmey-Archer 20
Sunbeam 27, 32, 34, 44, 46
Surridge, Victor 21
Surtees, Jack 81
Surtees, John 7, 73, 79–84, 89, 195
Suzuki 88, 89, 92, 95, 97, 99, 102, 104, 106–7, 109, 114, 117, 119, 123–4, 126, 129–31, 133–4, 136, 138–9, 142–4, 148, 156, 161, 180, 182, 189, 191, 195–6, 211, 214, 220, 226, 227–8, 234
Swain, Beryl 96
Swan Yamaha 211–12
Swann, Ray 156

TAS Racing 139, 186, 220, 225, 229, 234
TAS Suzuki 180, 182, 187–9, 196, 211
Taveri, Luigi 78–9, 84–5, 89, 91–2, 94, 97, 99, 101, 146, 168
Taylor, Fred
Taylor, Jock 125–6, 128–9, 133, 135–6, 156, 198
Team Green Kawasaki 233
Team Traction Control Yamaha 223, 225
Tenni, Omobono 42, 59, 68
Thomas, Ernie 60
Thornton, Joe 152
Thruxton 168
Tinmouth, Jenny 211
Todd, Davey 103, 234–5, 245–6, 248–9
Tonkin, Steve 131, 135
Trachsel, Ernst 125
Triumph 16, 17, 20, 25, 32, 34, 102, 110, 114, 187, 189, 220, 221, 230
'Slippery Sam' 116, 221
Triumph ValMoto 186
Trollope, Dennis 128
Tucker, George 37
Twemlow, Eddie 37, 41
Twemlow, Kenneth 37
Tyco BMW 232
Tyco/TAS Racing 228
Tyrell-Smith, HG 46–7, 49, 53, 60

Ubbiali, Carlo 7, 72–3, 75, 77–9, 84–5, 89, 93
Uphill, Malcolm 109, 221

V&M 171, 173, 186
V&M Yamaha 180, 182
Valentine, Jack 171, 186
van Dulmen, Boet 133
Velocette 32, 43–4, 46, 48, 50, 52–3, 56, 60, 67–8
Velocette Thruxton 52
Vincent, Chris 92
Vinicombe, Terry 107
Vitrans Honda 188

Waddon-Ehrlich 135
Walker, Graham 39, 44, 46, 47, 49, 50
Walker, Murray 39, 44, 211
Walmsley, Jevan 243
Ward, Steve 129, 163, 164, 233
Watson-Bourne, Jack 32
Webb, Danny 220
Wells, Billy 13
Wells, Dave 157, 158
West, Jock 63
White, 'Crasher' 53, 56, 60
Whiteway, Frank 109
Whitham, James 144, 156
Williams, Charlie 114, 116, 123, 126, 129, 138, 170
Williams, Cyril 27, 32
Williams, Donny 142, 143
Williams, Eric 27, 32
Williams, John 110, 114, 116–17, 119, 123, 126, 139
Williams, Kenny 125
Williams, Paul 173
Williams, Peter 102, 114
Willis, Harold 44
Wilson Craig Racing 199, 211
Wilson, Scott 220
Winkle, Andrew 206, 213, 225
Wohlgemuth, Alfred 89
Wood, S 'Ginger' 60
Wood, Tim 25, 27
Wood, Tommy 42, 72
Woodland, Barry 142, 143
Woods, Stanley 7, 22, 32, 34–6, 39, 42–4, 47–50, 52–3, 56, 58–60, 63, 67, 91, 102, 110–11
Wünsche, Siegfried 60, 72
Wynn, Michael 163

Yamaha 88–90, 92, 95, 97–9, 101–2, 104, 106–7, 109–10, 112, 114, 117, 123–4, 130–1, 143–5, 148, 156–8, 161, 163, 165, 170–1, 173, 182, 187–9, 191, 194, 198, 214, 217, 220, 227, 230, 234, 243
Yamaha, Mitsui 129
Yamsel 110

Zeller, Walter 103

Acknowledgements

The author would like to thank Mike Aylwin for all his assistance; Gary Thompson, John Barton, John Watterson, Paul Phillips, Peter Hickman and Peter Clifford for their valuable input; John McGuinness for agreeing to write the foreword; all the photographers for their excellent images; Matt Roberts for the initial recommendation; Sam Fitzgerald for his advice throughout the project; and Gerry Breslin for getting it all up and running.

Image credits

front cover iomttraces.com
back cover LAT Images/Stringer/Getty Images
p. 3 Dave Kneen Photography
p. 5 Stephen Davison/Pacemaker Press
p. 6 iomttraces.com
p. 8 Topical Press Agency/Stringer/Getty Images
p. 10 Manx National Heritage
p. 12 Topical Press Agency/Stringer/Getty Images
p. 13 Manx National Heritage
p. 14 Manx National Heritage
p. 16 Manx National Heritage
p. 18 Heritage Image Partnership/Alamy Stock Photo
p. 20 Manx National Heritage
p. 21 Topical Press Agency/Stringer/Getty Images
p. 22 ANL/Shutterstock
p. 23 Topical Press Agency/Stringer/Getty Images
p. 24 Manx National Heritage
p. 25 Manx National Heritage
p. 26 Manx National Heritage
p. 27 Topical Press Agency/Stringer/Getty Images
p. 28 Fox Photos/Stringer/Getty Images
p. 30 Manx National Heritage
p. 31 Manx National Heritage
p. 33 (top) Manx National Heritage; (bottom) Manx National Heritage
p. 34 Manx National Heritage
p. 35 Manx National Heritage
p. 36 Central Press/Stringer/Getty Images
p. 37 Manx National Heritage
p. 38 Heritage Image Partnership/Alamy Stock Photo
p. 39 ANL/Shutterstock
p. 40 (top) Manx National Heritage; (bottom) Manx National Heritage
p. 41 Motoring Picture Library/Alamy Stock Photo
p. 42 ANL/Shutterstock
p. 43 Fox Photos/Stringer/Getty Images
p. 44 Manx National Heritage
p. 45 Manx National Heritage
p. 46 Manx National Heritage
p. 47 (top) Manx National Heritage; (bottom) Manx National Heritage
p. 48 History and Art Collection/Alamy Stock Photo
p. 49 Manx National Heritage
p. 50 Heritage Image Partnership/Alamy Stock Photo
p. 51 (top) Manx National Heritage; (bottom) Motoring Picture Library/Alamy Stock Photo
p. 52 ANL/Shutterstock
p. 53 Manx National Heritage
p. 54 LAT Images/Stringer/Getty Images
p. 56 Manx National Heritage
p. 57 Manx National Heritage
p. 58 Manx National Heritage
p. 59 Brandstaetter Images/Getty Images
p. 61 Fox Photos/Stringer/Getty Images
p. 62 Manx National Heritage
p. 63 Hulton Archive/Stringer/Getty Images
p. 64 Keystone Press/Alamy Stock Photo
p. 66 Keystone/Stringer/Getty Images
p. 67 Smith Archive/Alamy Stock Photo
p. 69 Hulton Deutsch/Getty Images
p. 70 Picture Post/Stringer/Getty Images
p. 71 Hulton Deutsch/Getty Images
p. 73 Olycom Spa/Shutterstock
p. 74 Smith Archive/Alamy Stock Photo
p. 77 Heritage Image Partnership/Alamy Stock Photo
p. 78 ANL/Shutterstock
p. 80 Keystone Press/Alamy Stock Photo
p. 81 Heritage Image Partnership/Alamy Stock Photo
p. 82 Keystone/Stringer/Getty Images
p. 83 Popperfoto/Getty Images
p. 85 Smith Archive/Alamy Stock Photo
p. 86 Smith Archive/Alamy Stock Photo
p. 87 World Image Archive/Alamy Stock Photo
p. 88 Don Morley/Getty Images
p. 90 Heritage Image Partnership/Alamy Stock Photo
p. 91 Associated Press/Alamy Stock Photo
p. 93 Smith Archive/Alamy Stock Photo
p. 94 Associated Press/Alamy Stock Photo
p. 95 Phil Wain Family Archive
p. 96 Smith Archive/Alamy Stock Photo
p. 97 Phil Wain Family Archive
p. 98 ANL/Shutterstock
p. 99 Smith Archive/Alamy Stock Photo
p. 100 Smith Archive/Alamy Stock Photo
p. 103 iomttraces.com
p. 104 Bentley Archive/Popperfoto/Getty Images
p. 105 ANL/Shutterstock
p. 106 Smith Archive/Alamy Stock Photo

- p. 107 Phil Wain Family Archive
- p. 108 Mirrorpix/Getty Images
- p. 111 Mirrorpix/Getty Images
- p. 112 Trinity Mirror/Mirrorpix/Alamy Stock Photo
- p. 113 ZUMA Press/Alamy Stock Photo
- p. 115 Peter Pittilla/ANL/Shutterstock
- p. 116 Phil Wain Family Archive
- p. 118 Bob Thomas/Getty Images
- p. 119 Don Morley/Getty Images
- p. 120 LAT Images/Stringer/Getty Images
- p. 124 The Archive/Alamy Stock Photo
- p. 125 John Watterson
- p. 127 Don Morley/Getty Images
- p. 128 John Watterson
- p. 130 Phil Wain Family Archive
- p. 131 Phil Wain Family Archive
- p. 132 (top) Phil Wain Family Archive; (bottom) Phil Wain Family Archive
- p. 133 Getty Images
- p. 134 John Watterson
- p. 135 The Archive/Alamy Stock Photo
- p. 137 (top) John Watterson; (bottom) Phil Wain Family Archive
- p. 139 Stephen Davison/Pacemaker Press
- p. 140 The Archive/Alamy Stock Photo
- p. 141 LAT Images/Stringer/Getty Images
- p. 142 The Archive/Alamy Stock Photo
- p. 143 Phil Wain Family Archive
- p. 144 Phil Wain Family Archive
- p. 145 John Watterson
- p. 146 iomttraces.com
- p. 147 Phil Wain Family Archive
- p. 148 Phil Wain Family Archive
- p. 149 LAT Images/Stringer/Getty Images
- p. 150 Richard Sowersby/Alamy Stock Photo
- p. 151 iomttraces.com
- p. 152 The Archive/Alamy Stock Photo
- p. 153 Ed Rhodes/Alamy Stock Photo
- p. 154 Independent/Alamy Stock Photo
- p. 155 Isle of Man/Alamy Stock Photo
- p. 158 John Watterson
- p. 159 LAT Images/Stringer/Getty Images
- p. 160 John Watterson
- p. 161 iomttraces.com
- p. 162 LAT Images/Stringer/Getty Images
- p. 164 Phil Wain Family Archive
- p. 165 Phil Wain Family Archive
- p. 167 PA Images/Alamy Stock Photo
- p. 168 LAT Images/Stringer/Getty Images
- p. 169 Phil Wain Family Archive
- p. 170 Associated Press/Alamy Stock Photo
- p. 172 Ian Walton/Getty Images
- p. 174 iomttraces.com
- p. 178 iomttraces.com
- p. 181 LAT Images/Stringer/Getty Images
- p. 182 Stephen Davison/Pacemaker Press
- p. 183 Stephen Davison/Pacemaker Press
- p. 184 iomttraces.com
- p. 186 LAT Images/Stringer/Getty Images
- p. 187 Stephen Davison/Pacemaker Press
- p. 188 Stephen Davison/Pacemaker Press
- p. 189 Linden Adams Photography/Getty Images
- p. 190 Robin Sanders/Alamy Stock Photo
- p. 191 Stephen Davison/Pacemaker Press
- p. 193 iomttraces.com
- p. 194 iomttraces.com
- p. 195 Stephen Davison/Pacemaker Press
- p. 197 iomttraces.com
- p. 198 iomttraces.com
- p. 199 iomttraces.com
- p. 201 iomttraces.com
- p. 202 Michael Steele/Getty Images
- p. 204 iomttraces.com
- p. 206 iomttraces.com
- p. 207 iomttraces.com
- p. 209 Gordon Hulmes Sport/Alamy Stock Photo
- p. 210 (top) iomttraces.com; (bottom) iomttraces.com
- p. 211 iomttraces.com
- p. 212 iomttraces.com
- p. 213 iomttraces.com
- p. 214 iomttraces.com
- p. 215 Action Plus Sports Images/Alamy Stock Photo
- p. 216 PRiMe Media Images/Alamy Stock Photo
- p. 219 Action Plus Sports Images/Alamy Stock Photo
- p. 220 iomttraces.com
- p. 221 Stephen Davison/Pacemaker Press
- p. 222 iomttraces.com
- p. 223 Action Plus Sports Images/Alamy Stock Photo
- p. 224 Adrian Gell/Alamy Stock Photo
- p. 226 iomttraces.com
- p. 227 iomttraces.com
- p. 228 iomttraces.com
- p. 229 Tim Keeton/Impact Images Photography
- p. 230 iomttraces.com
- p. 231 iomttraces.com
- p. 232 iomttraces.com
- p. 233 iomttraces.com
- p. 234 iomttraces.com
- p. 235 iomttraces.com
- p. 236 iomttraces.com
- p. 238 iomttraces.com
- p. 239 iomttraces.com
- p. 242 iomttraces.com
- p. 242 iomttraces.com
- p. 244 iomttraces.com
- p. 245 iomttraces.com
- p. 246 iomttraces.com
- p. 247 iomttraces.com
- p. 247 iomttraces.com
- p. 248 iomttraces.com
- p. 249 iomttraces.com
- p. 250 iomttraces.com